Community College Finance

Christopher M. Mullin,
David S. Baime,
and David S. Honeyman

Community College Finance

A Guide for Institutional Leaders

JB JOSSEY-BASS™

A Wiley Brand

Published by Jossey-Bass
A Wiley Brand
One Montgomery Street, Suite 1000, San Francisco, CA
94104-4594—www.josseybass.com/highereducation

Jossey-Bass books and products are available through most bookstores. To contact Jossey-Bass directly call our Customer Care Department within the U.S. at 800-956-7739, outside the U.S. at 317-572-3986, or fax 317-572-4002.

Wiley publishes in a variety of print and electronic formats and by print-on-demand. Some material included with standard print versions of this book may not be included in e-books or in print-on-demand. If this book refers to media such as a CD or DVD that is not included in the version you purchased, you may download this material at **http://booksupport.wiley.com**. For more information about Wiley products, visit **www.wiley.com**.

Library of Congress Cataloging-in-Publication Data is on file.

978-1-118-95491-1 (hbk.)
978-1-118-95495-9 (ebk.)
978-1-118-95493-5 (ebk.)

Printed in the United States of America

FIRST EDITION

HB Printing 10 9 8 7 6 5 4 3 2 1

To the loves of my life:

My parents, siblings, children, and wife

For my family and friends—in whom I have been most blessed

Contents

Leadership Resources

List of Figures and Tables

Figures

Tables

Acknowledgments

We would like to acknowledge the numerous community college chancellors, presidents, administrators, faculty, and staff we have had the pleasure to work with during our professional tenure. Their input and frank conversations regarding approaches to higher education signify all that is right with the educational enterprise.

We would also like to express our appreciation for the editorial staff at Jossey-Bass. We are particularly grateful to both David Brightman, who served as the catalyst for the book, and Erin Null, who served as the steward of its development. Additionally, Shauna Robinson promptly and politely answered the various questions we had during the production process, making the experience ever more enjoyable.

In 1992 David Pierce hired David Baime to work at the American Association of Community Colleges, and the result has been a tremendously satisfying journey. Dave was as kind as the day is long, and that was accompanied by a marvelous self-deprecating humor, dogged intelligence, and complete honesty. He is missed.

Christopher M. Mullin. I would like to acknowledge the support of my family as I worked on this book. Of particular importance is the support of my wife, Candide, who kept the family going during the missed dinners, soccer practices, and weekends. I would not have been able to embark on this project without her support and that of my kids, Mila and Luke. Finally, I would like to acknowledge the contributions of my coauthors, David Baime and David Honeyman, who have served as both mentor and boss. From David Baime I have learned the importance of integrity, credibility, and responsiveness in one's professional life. I have also learned a great deal about the community college sector and the higher educational landscape through the opportunities Baime allowed me to partake in, along with the conversations we had while colleagues at the American Association of Community Colleges. David Honeyman introduced me to the world of community college finance—how caring for students was integral to the study of educational finance and how to maintain one's sense of self in a world dominated by ego—but most important, he facilitated my growth rather than directing it.

Preface

The last book that directly addressed financial leadership in the American community college was John Lombardi's *Managing Finances in Community Colleges* (1973). Since that time much has changed. The number of students attending community colleges has grown from 2.5 million to over 8 million, the number of community colleges from just over 900 to over 1,000, the Pell Grant program was implemented and now supports 3.5 million community college students, the importance of the role of tuition and fee revenues has increased substantially, and the support for infrastructure and facilities has evolved.

A multitude of books have focused directly on community colleges, but few have focused on finances in community colleges. And even these contributions to the literature were focused on financing trends facing community colleges or their economics (Breneman & Nelson, 1981; Garms, 1977); only an occasional case study or chapter has focused on the practical aspects of community college finance.

This void may be due to the less-prominent role community colleges have played in the overall dialogue about higher education or the intense focus on tuition and fees and related student financial aid at four-year colleges that is evident in much of the higher education finance literature. It may also be the result of a generation of leaders who joined the community college movement as young professionals and have grown with it, shaping it along the way, and have been focused primarily on practice.

While all reasons (and others not mentioned here) are important, it is for this last reason that this book may be of the greatest importance. The ongoing change in leadership (Campbell, 2002; Phillippe & Tekle, 2013a) requires the education of new leaders, who arguably are more challenged than those from previous generations. At the same time, an increased focus on the community college in the twenty-first century necessitates a resource for noncommunity college scholars to better understand institutional finances. Too often the authors have been asked to explain community college finance to scholars who are making substantial policy recommendations, because there were no resource documents to address their questions.

Purpose and Structure

The goal of this book is to aid in the sound fiscal management of the community college, as well as to provide an analysis that helps those working outside of a college environment. We hope to achieve this goal by informing practitioners and scholars of both fundamental and advanced aspects of community college finance, by presenting an examination of community college finance in three distinct yet interrelated parts.

Part One: Community College Revenues

Part One focuses on where the money comes from. It begins with a chapter that discusses the foundational factors influencing revenues in the community college sector. The next chapter illustrates, in three different states, how revenue sources have changed over time and actions that may be implemented to stabilize funding.

Chapter Three details the categories of revenues for community colleges as well as their relative importance. Chapter Four focuses on tuition and fees and the total cost of education, including a discussion of tuition and fee philosophies that have been a hallmark of community college funding. Chapter Five examines the increasingly important role of student financial aid.

While postsecondary education evolves to provide more opportunities via asynchronous technologies that remove the barrier of place, community colleges remain as anchor institutions within their communities, for both the students and the community stakeholders with whom they engage. Addressing this, Chapter Six examines infrastructure funding, which is a critical and challenging component of community college finance. It covers public-private partnerships, replacement costs, and bonding.

Part Two: Expending Fiscal Resources

Part Two focuses on expenditures. Chapter Seven begins with a description of expenditure categories and continues with an overview of budgeting approaches. This discussion of expenditures is advanced in Chapter Eight, with a focus on the metrics being used to shape the community college mission in the current student success– and performance-based culture.

Chapter Nine discusses the use of cost studies in institutional management and introduces some of the related guiding perspectives of costs and productivity and efficiency. Chapter Ten examines the implications, at the campus level, of whether education is treated as an investment or a cost. Differences between sectors of higher education are presented, along with a discussion of practices to help ensure that institutional actions are economically and educationally justifiable.

Part Three: Leadership Resources

Part Three provides practical information to guide the management of fiscal policy by institutional leadership. Chapter Eleven presents foundational information related to enrollment- and performance-based funding models. Chapter Twelve clarifies the entities responsible for setting tuition and fees at community colleges and details some approaches that may be used in determining them. The next chapter provides practical answers to managing a fiscal crisis—unfortunately an all-too-common phenomenon—by drawing from previous experience. It suggests that planning for a fiscal downturn is the responsibility of community college leaders *before* one materializes.

Prior to the prospective discussion of community college finance provided in Chapter Fifteen, the authors discuss the role of advocacy in generating support for community colleges. Chapter Fourteen emphasizes the role of advocacy for college officials responsible for the financing of a department, unit, program, or college.

Audience

Nearly 90 percent of institutional chief financial officers are accountants or have a master's degree in business administration. While financial officers should find this book informative, it is written for all members of the college leadership team, from presidents to trustees to executive leadership staff. Effectively executing these positions requires knowledge of general concepts related to financial matters as well as a familiarity with various practices to best guide decision making. We also think this book, with its discussion of the philosophies and practices that drive fiscal policy for this key sector of higher education, should appeal to scholars with an interest in community college finance, academic researchers, policy analysts, legislative affairs staff, consultants, and graduate students.

Each chapter of the book stands on its own and may be used independently. However, the interlocking nature of all aspects of community college funding suggests this book is best used as a whole rather than in parts. The book is appropriate for use in institutional "grow your own" programs and graduate programs with a focus on higher education administration and/or community college leadership, by state agency staff and leadership, and by the larger policy and foundation community eager to better understand why college leaders make the decisions they do.

This book is ideal for a graduate higher education finance course, especially the more than 60 degree-granting programs with a community college focus. Often these courses cover the policy aspects of fiscal leadership, and though there are many research articles and books to be read, those treating the practical side are, surprisingly, less abundant. We hope that with the addition of this book to the literature, more will follow.

About the Authors

Christopher M. Mullin is assistant vice chancellor for policy and research at the State University System of Florida, Board of Governors. He is the co-author of *Higher Education Finance Research: Policy, Politics, and Practice* and coeditor of *Data Use in the Community College: New Directions for Institutional Research.*

David S. Baime has served as the chief architect of federal policy and strategy from the community college perspective for nearly 20 years as senior vice president of government relations and policy analysis at the American Association of Community Colleges in Washington, DC.

David S. Honeyman is emeritus professor at the School of Human Development and Organizational Studies in Education at University of Florida, Gainesville. He is the author of *A Struggle to Survive: Funding Higher Education in the Next Century.*

Part One

Sources of Revenue

Chapter One

Factors Influencing Community College Finance

America's social experiment with broad access to postsecondary education was initiated with the Morrill Act of 1862 (P.L. 37–108), which expanded publicly controlled and supported institutions of higher learning to those who either were destined for college or had the courage to attend (Morrill, 1887). This latter element—paying attention to the courage of people to attend college—embodies the open access philosophy of much of higher education.

In 1901, the first community college was established in Joliet, Illinois. The ensuing years witnessed the establishment of many more community colleges under both public and private control, often under the initiative of local efforts supported by state leaders.

In the middle of the twentieth century, states began making commitments to continue the legacy of the land-grant colleges by extending postsecondary educational opportunity to the masses, beginning the modern community college movement. The starting point for the development of community colleges in each state varied (Yarrington, 1966), but it was supported in part by the development of coordinated state systems of public higher education and in the establishment of some state community college systems (Tollefson, Garrett, Ingram, & Associates, 1999).

For many years, community colleges were not exclusively public colleges; in 1950 the balance between public and private institutions was nearly equal, with 297 public community colleges and 227 privately controlled community colleges. The public community college movement took root between 1960 and 1980, with the number of public institutions increasing from 328 to 945, while over the same time period the number of private community colleges decreased by 72, to 182 (Figure 1.1). By 2010 public

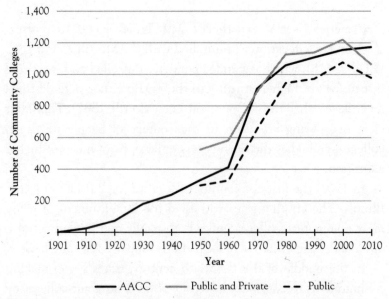

Figure 1.1 The Number of Community Colleges, by Type and Source: 1901 to 2010

Note: Three trends are provided for the number of community colleges. The American Association of Community Colleges (AACC) provides a count of member-eligible institutions that meet certain criteria and includes both public and private institutions. One reason the AACC trend line does not drop off as the others do in 2010 is that the criteria allow for the awarding of bachelor's degrees, whereas the other two data sources do not count an institution as a community college if it offers just one bachelor's degree.

Sources: Adapted from American Association of Community Colleges (2010), Phillippe and González Sullivan (2005), Snyder and Dillow (2013).

community colleges greatly outnumbered private community colleges, at 978 and 87, respectively.

Over time, higher education structures and governing arrangements developed by states have changed in the way in which they have provided educational opportunity. For example, states like Kentucky, Louisiana, Connecticut, Minnesota, Maine, Hawaii, and Alaska have, in the past 20 years, completely restructured their post-secondary education systems, while other states such as California and Illinois have stood firm in their vision. However, irrespective of the overarching state system, the innovation of the community college has expanded educational opportunity to the masses. Within these institutions, millions of economically and socially marginalized people have found their footing. Through the lens of time this chapter examines the factors shaping community college finance, including enrollments, employment, and competitors for resources.

The Public Community College Movement

Traditionally and primarily, though not exclusively, community colleges have been funded on the basis of enrollments, either by the governmental appropriations that are derived from enrollments or through tuition and fee revenue. This differs from those of their public higher education counterparts that receive substantial revenue from research activities, endowments, or other auxiliary services such as hospitals. These non-enrollment resources are enormous: total revenues for public four-year institutions are nearly five times as much as total revenues for community colleges, at $261.2 and $56.2 billion, respectively, in the 2011–2012 school year (Snyder & Dillow, 2014). Given the disproportionate reliance on enrollment-based revenue, the community college "movement" was fueled in large part by being able to identify new markets of students underserved by "traditional" institutions of higher education, while also enrolling students interested in transferring to a senior college.

Setting aside the financial dimension of enrollments, what is less emphasized in today's outcome-oriented climate is the central significance of access in the community college. Of particular importance at the community college is participation by nontraditional populations: those students who are not aged 18 to 24, do not live on campus, and do not have parental resources to help cover the costs of attendance. In 2015, the challenge for many community colleges is to ensure that nontraditional students are served well, given their intrinsic role in the nation's long-term prosperity. The community college leaders of the country recognize that enrollment in college is in and of itself an achievement, albeit not a sufficient one in most cases. So while some policymakers bemoan the fact that colleges are funded simply through people's being in seats—and therefore, they would assert, lacking accountability—the policymakers also show both a misunderstanding and an appreciation of the efforts of national and local leaders to remove barriers to opportunity and mobility that is accomplished through their local community college. We now briefly discuss a few factors that have contributed to the growth of the community college movement and, as a result, its funding.

Enrollment Trends

The GI Bill awakened the nation's awareness of the value of postsecondary education, as millions of returning servicemen who had not previously had postsecondary education ambitions attended college. Yet while community college enrollment doubled during the 1950s, the years following the end of the Second World War were not "boom" years for the community college sector to the extent commonly believed. In 1947 just over 163,000 students were enrolled at a public community college. By 1957 enrollment had increased to 315,990, a 94% increase. The period of greatest growth for the community college movement would occur in the next decade.

During the 1960s, growth in the community college sector was massive, increasing nearly fivefold, from approximately 400,000 to

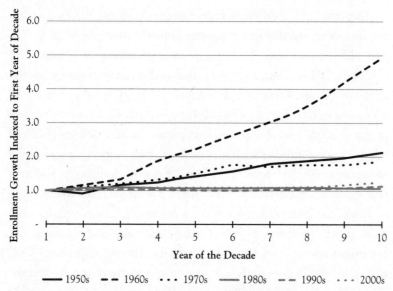

Figure 1.2   Enrollment Growth in Public Community Colleges Indexed to the First Year of the Decade: 1950s to 2000s

Note: Year "1" reflects the first year of the decade. For example, for the 1950s, year 1 represents 1950, year 2 represents 1951, and so on.

Source: Adapted from Snyder and Dillow (2014).

2,000,000 (Figure 1.2). Enrollment growth in the community college sector continued in the 1970s when 1.86 million additional students were enrolled.

Enrollment and Age

Since 1968, increased participation in higher education has been the trend across all age groups. Between 1968 and 2012 the percentage of each age group increased as follows (U.S. Census, 2014):

For ages 18 and 19, from 35.9% to 47.3%

For ages 20 and 21, from 31.2% to 51.4%

For ages 22 through 24, from 12.7% to 29.8%

For ages 25 through 29, from 6.0% to 13.6%

For ages 30 through 34, from 3.4% to 7.4%

Data for 2012 indicate that community colleges enrolled a large number of nontraditional students: both younger, those under 18, and older, those over 24 (American Association of Community Colleges, 2014). Between 1993 and 2009, the percentage of the national community college student body under the age of 18 increased from 1.6% to 7.0% (Mullin, 2012d). These are, of course, primarily dual enrollment students; that is, high school students who are also taking community college courses in one of a variety of settings. At the same time, 71% of the student body was over the age of 22. So although the median age was 22, the average age of the community college student body in 2012 was 28, due to a large older student population mathematically pulling the mean (average) age to 28 (American Association of Community Colleges, 2014). These enrollment patterns outside of the traditional 18-to-24-year-old undergraduate student body had much to do with the growth of community colleges, as these nontraditional students have traditionally been less represented in other sectors of higher education (though, as will be discussed, this has changed somewhat with the growth of corporate for-profit colleges).

Enrollment and Gender

Women students became a majority of community college enroll-ments in the late 1970s, a trend that continues to the time of this writing (Figure 1.3). Between 1960 and 2010, the gender balance of community colleges shifted from 1.8 men for every woman on campus to 0.8 man for every woman.

The shift to a greater number of women enrolling in college is not unique to the community college sector. However, a greater percentage of both the men and women enrolling are enrolling in community colleges. Data from the National Center for Education Statistics indicate that in 1970, 26% of all male students enrolled in college were attending community college (Snyder & Dillow, 2013); by 2010, 34% of male college students attended community college. In 1970, 25% of female college students were enrolled at community colleges; by 2010, that figure was 34%.

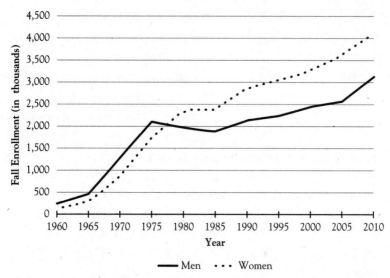

Figure 1.3   Fall Enrollment at Public Community Colleges, by Gender: 1960 to 2010

Source: Adapted from Grant and Lind (1973), Snyder and Hoffman (1995), and Snyder and Dillow (2013).

Access for Students of Color

Community colleges serve as a primary entry point to college for nonwhite populations. In 1964, a decade after *Brown v. Board of Education* (347 U.S. 483, 1954) and the year before enactment of the *Higher Education Act of 1965* (Pub. L. 89–329, 1965), just 6% of the student body in higher education was nonwhite (Mullin, 2012d). By 1976, the first year that comparable data were available, 20.6% of the community college student body was nonwhite, compared to 17.8% of the rest of higher education (Table 1.1). Thirty-five years later, in 2011, 40% of black students, 50% of Hispanic students, and 45% of Native American Alaskan Native students were enrolled at a community college.

The growth in the number of students attending community colleges underscores the role community colleges play in providing access to higher education. Historical trends—along with the current economic forces, the selectivity and cost patterns at

Table 1.1. Fall Term Enrollment at Community Colleges, by Race/Ethnicity: Select Years

Year (Fall)	Total	Race/Ethnicity				
		White	Black	Hispanic	Asian/ Pacific Islander	American Indian/ Alaska Native
Public Community College (in thousands)						
1976	3,748	2,974	410	208	78	39
1986	4,414	3,379	430	326	183	47
1996	5,315	3,613	597	631	318	67
2006	6,225	3,820	843	964	431	76
2011	7,063	3,907	1,081	1,330	427	76
Within Year Distribution						
1976	100.0%	79.4%	10.9%	5.5%	2.1%	1.0%
1986	100.0%	76.6%	11.2%	11.9%	6.0%	1.3%
1996	100.0%	68.0%	11.2%	11.9%	6.0%	1.3%
2006	100.0%	61.4%	13.5%	15.5%	6.9%	1.2%
2011	100.0%	55.3%	15.3%	18.8%	6.0%	1.1%
All Undergraduate (*not* including community college students; in thousands)						
1976	5,671	4,767	800	533	145	91
1986	6,384	5,179	1,050	566	237	210
1996	7,012	5,156	1,670	761	448	400
2006	8,959	6,065	2,664	1,164	846	567
2011	11,001	6,704	3,967	1,618	1,355	658
Within Year Distribution						
1976	100.0%	84.1%	14.1%	9.4%	2.6%	1.6%
1986	100.0%	81.1%	16.4%	8.9%	3.7%	3.3%
1996	100.0%	73.5%	23.8%	10.9%	6.4%	5.7%
2006	100.0%	67.7%	29.7%	13.0%	9.4%	6.3%
2011	100.0%	60.9%	36.1%	14.7%	12.3%	6.0%

Notes: Race/ethnicity may not sum to total due to rounding and the exclusion of other categories.

Sources: Snyder (1992), Snyder and Hoffman (2000), Snyder and Dillow (2010, 2012).

four-year institutions, and U.S. demographic trends—all suggest that enrollment at community colleges will keep growing, as long as they continue to serve the populations they have traditionally enrolled. Indeed, the recognition that college attendance is necessary for individual economic success is spreading broadly throughout the population.

Community Colleges and Unemployment

Whether funded through inputs or outcomes, enrollment is the driving factor in community college revenues. For public institutions, the reliance on public coffers to fund their activities means that the state's economy is integral to their financial well-being. A strong economy generally means lower enrollments with more funding per student, whereas a weak state economy generally results in more students with less funding.

Figure 1.4 illustrates the impact of the economy, as measured by unemployment rates, on community college enrollments. Over the

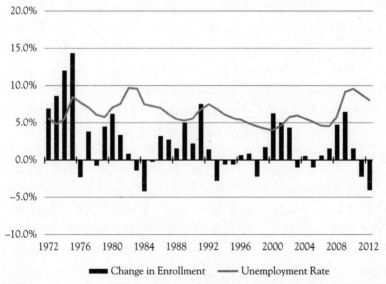

Figure 1.4   Annual Percent Change in Community College Enrollment and the National Unemployment Rate: 1972 to 2012

Sources: Adapted from Snyder and Dillow (2009, 2013) and U.S. Department of Labor (2014).

five periods shown in the figure, the same pattern appears: as unemployment increases, so does the yearly increase in enrollments. As the economy improves and unemployment drops, enrollments at community colleges tend to decrease as well. This trend held prior to the time show in the figure; from 1930 to 1935, enrollment at community colleges increased in excess of 20%, as the impact of the Great Depression was felt across America (Lombardi, 1976).

During times of economic contraction, marked by increases in unemployment, community colleges are often called on to offer training that can get the unemployed back into the workforce quickly (Katsinas, D'Amico, & Friedel, 2011). Frequently this means offering more short-term programs, generally one year or less, targeted to business and industry needs. But also, as a more general matter, short-term certificates are becoming a growing component of community college program offerings. Between the 1989–90 and 2009–2010 academic years, the number of short-term certificates (those of one year or less) increased 429% at community colleges, from 46,494 to 259,705 (Mullin, 2011).

In some cases, the training required could be met with non-credit workforce development training. Noncredit courses can often be developed and offered more rapidly than credit offerings. The Maricopa (Arizona) Community College district, for example, responded to decreases in state fiscal support by establishing the Maricopa Corporate College, which caters to the needs of business (Fain, 2014). Its offerings are generally noncredit courses.

Increasingly, however, there is a push from policymakers to have this training provided as credit-bearing courses leading to an educational certificate. This push toward credit-bearing education aims to support the policy goals of the federal and state governments to have a more formally educated workforce. (While noncredit workforce training has substantive value and may result in an industry-recognized credential, it is not counted as increased educational attainment for policy purposes, as it is not currently quantifiable, nationally or internationally. However, industry certifications are becoming increasingly aligned with formal academic credentials.)

For institutions supported by tax dollars, there is a direct connection between economic performance and funding. Reduced funding in periods of economic downturn impacts community colleges in a number of ways and often creates extreme challenges bordering on chaos. First, institutions attempt to plan financially a few years into the future and, to the extent possible, tend to use projections built upon prior funding. Economic jolts substantially outside of an institution's budget forecast lay carefully laid plans to waste, as discussed in more detail in Chapter 13. Another response to these shocks can be an increase in tuition and fees, a topic discussed further in Chapter 12. Economic shocks can also influence the decisions of institutional leadership in terms of the type of faculty hired, the nature of their contracts, and influence other personnel decisions. Furthermore, the type and scope of programs that can be offered also come under more exacting assessment. Finally, and perhaps most important to our current conversation, recessions alter the trajectory of future funding, as the funding for the current year is always informed by previous funding (Katsinas, Lacy, Adair, Koh, D'Amico, & Friedel, 2013).

The Origin of Public Resources

The U.S. Congress, all state legislatures, and all local government agencies raise money for a vast number of interests, ranging from courts, policing, imprisonment, and national security to social programs, environmental protection, emergency actions, defense, and education. These revenues come from taxes, as raising revenue is *the* primary function of taxation, although it has come to play a much broader policy role as well. Simply put, a tax is a payment authorized by and paid to a governmental agency to be used either *as* a revenue source to perform operations deemed necessary and appropriate by the agency; to redistribute wealth by various means; *or* to regulate and protect the general welfare.

Whether it is a tax based on consumption or production (personal or corporate income, Social Security and payroll, sales, property, excise, licensing, and tolls) or a tax on wealth and unearned income (estate, gifts, and capital gains), it is important to note that all taxes are paid by individuals. Even the taxes paid by major and small corporations are paid based on the profit from sales (manufactured goods and services) paid for by individuals at some point. The origination of taxes at the individual level reinforces the public good expected from all sectors of higher education while also raising issues related to how tax revenues are realized. The former is the focus of this book, whereas the latter addresses related issues of public finance (the appendix provides information on the principles of taxation).

Government revenue originating from income taxes paid to the federal and most state governments, sales taxes paid to the states and many local authorities, or property taxes paid to local governments all are essential to the operation of all sectors of higher education. Tax-based funds generated at all levels are the primary revenue source for community colleges and all of public higher education, with tuition revenues a close second. In their FY2013 State Higher Education Finance Report (SHEF), the State Higher Education Executive Officers (SHEEO, 2014) reports that for FY 2013 states contributed $72.4 billion or 51% of current operating monies to higher education institutions in the United States. Net tuition accounted for $61.8 billion or 43%, and local sources contributed $9.2 billion or 6%. The total for FY 2013 was $143.4 billion.

Competition for Public Resources

Community colleges compete with other entities for revenue. These include other sectors of higher education and a panoply of programs.

State Resources

A number of activities are funded through state budgets, including public services, higher education institutions, and state student higher education aid programs.

Public Entities

Broadly speaking, public service activities are grouped by the U.S. Department of Commerce into eight categories: General Public Service (executive, legislative, tax collection, financial management and interest payment expenditures), Public Order and Safety (police, fire, law courts, and prisons), Economic Affairs (transportation, agriculture, industry, and others), Housing and Community Services, Health, Recreation and Culture, Income Security, and Education. Between 1959 and 2012, the percentages of state expenditures for these categories have, not unexpectedly, altered (see Figure 1.5). As a percent of total expenditures, the areas of Health (13%), General Public Service (2%), Public Order and Safety (2%) increased, Recreation and Culture remained at the same percentage of state expenditures, and Economic Affairs (–8%), Income Security (–5%), Education (–4%), and Housing and Community Services (–1%) decreased.

The trends illustrated in Figure 1.5 show that education spending experienced an initial growth period as a share of state spending

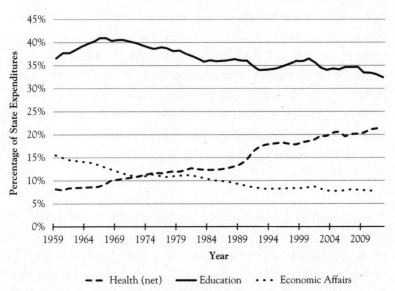

Figure 1.5   Distribution of State Expenditures for Health, Education, and Economic Affairs: 1959 to 2012

Source: Adapted from U.S. Department of Commerce (n.d.).

in the early 1960s, peaked in 1966, and then steadily declined. Within that education category, state expenditures for elementary and secondary education decreased 7% between 1959 and 2012, but decreased 10% from the peak year of 1966 to 2012. For higher education, there was a 2% increase in the allocation of state expenditures between 1959 and 2012, from 4% to 6%. However, the highest percentage of state budgets allocated to higher education (7%) came in the mid- to late 1970s, rather than in the 1960s as was the case for compulsory education.

Higher education exists in a unique place in relation to government funding. While K–12 education is compulsory, neither the United States nor state constitutions require the provision of free public higher education. From a practical standpoint at the state capitols, the funding of higher education—be it public, private, four-year, or two-year—is fundamentally a discretionary activity. Zumeta (1995) referred to this tentative, discretionary position for higher education as that of a budget balancer. Analysis of state budgets by Delaney and Doyle (2011) reinforces the budget balancer concept and suggests one obvious reason why, in times of retrenchment, budgets for higher education are cut more than those for other public services: colleges and universities can raise revenue from tuition and fees. Or perhaps higher education is simply not a top budget priority. Reporting on a series of surveys of state directors of community colleges, Katsinas, Lacey, Adair, Koh, D'Amico, and Friedel (2013) noted that K–12 was perceived to be the largest state budget driver in 2007 and 2008, followed by the recession in 2009 to 2011 and then Medicaid in 2012 and 2013.

Student Financial Aid

State resources for public institutions are also diminished by channeling state funds to student aid programs, and thereby private and for-profit institutions, rather than sending it directly to public colleges. New York was at the forefront of this practice. During the establishment of the State University of New York in 1948, the commission leading its development adopted the perspective of a member who stated, "While recognizing that there was a place in our [SUNY] system for community colleges, I could not quite see why community colleges should be placed, as proposed, at the very core of our system of higher education. The community college would thus become the major recipient of the state's higher education funds … we should strengthen the state's private universities and colleges through an expanded scholarship program" (cited in Carmichael, 1955, p. 170). In 2011 and 2012, students attending publicly controlled institutions of higher education received 70.8% of all state student aid funds, with students at private institutions receiving 22.4% and students at for-profits receiving 5.5% (National Association of State Student Grant and Aid Programs [NASSGAP], 2005). The share of funds going directly to community college students was not reported; however, analysis by NASSGAP staff found that while 29% of students attending community colleges received state-based student aid, just 15% of all state aid program funds went to those students (Solomon, 2011), far less than their proportion of the overall undergraduate population.

Within state allocations to higher education, community colleges also compete, more or less explicitly, with their public four-year counterparts. Over time, community colleges have received, on average, approximately 20% of state tax appropriations for postsecondary education (Mullin, 2010a). The persistent funding disparities stem in part from the political and practical realities that do not allow for an abrupt shifting of resources. Another reason is the program mix at different institutions and the varying associated costs of running the program. For example, it is generally, though not always, the case that educating a graduate student costs more than educating a student pursuing a subbaccalaureate degree. But some of the disparity is doubtless due to the profile of the students served in the various sectors.

Private Sectors of Higher Education

Community colleges are just one of four primary sectors of higher education (colleges and universities); the other three are public four-year, private four-year, and for-profit institutions. All sectors of higher education reinforce the importance of higher education writ large, but the private sector institutions take different approaches with respect to themselves and each other.

Private Non-Profit Institutions

Private non-profit institutions, of course, consist of more than just the likes of Harvard, Princeton, and Yale. The sector has a wide range of member institutions, represented by groups such as the National Association of Independent Colleges and Universities and the Council for Independent Colleges. In the nineteenth and twentieth centuries, private colleges received public appropriations. Chambers (1968) noted that between "1880 to 1920 Pennsylvania similarly made direct appropriations to several denominational colleges, but in 1921 its supreme court declared that practice unconstitutional" (p. 88). Concern regarding private institutions receiving state appropriations centered on the denominational nature of private colleges, as that public support violated the separation of church and state. With the ability to receive direct appropriations or other revenues from public sources restricted, policy options to support those colleges—which by mid-twentieth century had gained a high profile—were limited. Symposia, convenings, articles, and books captured the tenor of the conversations; see, for example, Harris's (1960) *Higher Education in the United States: The Economic Problems*. A key issue during this time was the widening difference in tuition and fee prices between public and private institutions and, more specifically, what to do about it. (Callan [2002] suggests this focus continues in the modern era.)

Keeney (1960) pondered, "What will happen if the privately supported institutions double tuition and consequently double salaries? The state institutions will be forced to increase their salaries and will, therefore, need a considerably increased income" (p. 42). (This perspective is informed by the recognition, true today, that private and public four-year institutions compete for the same faculty.) The question would be how to pay for it. As the reauthorization of the Higher Education Act of 1965 approached in early 1970s, two options gained traction—should Congress increase federal appropriations to institutions of higher education or expand student financial aid to support increases in tuition and fees?

During the establishment of federal student aid on a broad scale at the beginning of the 1970s, public universities favored institutional grant aid rather than student financial aid in order to keep tuition low and reduce the administrative complexity and budgetary outlays necessary to implement complex student aid programs (Gladieux & Wolanin, 1976). Conversely, private liberal arts colleges advocated for federal student aid as "a means of enabling them to compete with low-cost public institutions" (ibid., p. 47) for students.

In the end, an expansion of the student aid system won out over institutional grant aid during the debates and ultimate enactment of the 1972 Educational Amendments to the Higher Education Act of 1965, as detailed by Gladieux and Wolanin (1976) in *Congress and the Colleges*. This decision had momentous implications for public policy, with most university advocates, including those in the public sector, now being thankful that the legislature endorsed student aid over institutional support. Some of the resulting dynamics of this choice are discussed in Chapter 5, focusing on student aid.

As part of the debate leading up to the decision to expand student financial aid, Chambers (1968) commented that increases in tuition, supported by student aid, would make it more difficult for low-income students to attend college. To him, student financial aid was simply a mechanism to redirect public funds to private entities. In commenting on the debate between institutional grant aid, favored by public institutions, and an expanded student aid program, favored by private institutions, Chambers (1968) suggested the application of the following question regarding any proposed financing scheme, to get at the core of the proposal: was the funding scheme designed to (1) indirectly channel tax dollars to private colleges or (2) shift the cost of education away from the public and therefore to the student?

The substantial role and amount of public tax-oriented funds going to private non-profit institutions was not lost on Breneman and Finn (1978); they observed "it is ironic that the private sector has recently chosen to rename itself the 'independent' sector when the data show *financially* these institutions are anything but independent of government" (emphasis in original, pp. 25–26). This observation continues to hold true 40 years after the Educational Amendments of 1972, as the plurality of Federal Supplemental Educational Opportunity Grant (FSEOG) and Federal Work Study funds went to private colleges, while more than half of federal Perkins Loans went to students attending private institutions (College Board, 2013a).

Mensel (2013), leader of the American Association of Junior Colleges' federal relations effort in 1972, commented that the community college sector did not fully support the institutional aid program because it was inequitably structured; he noted "The grants would [have been] made in this order: $1,200 per FTE in graduate work, $400 per upper-division FTE, and $100 per lower-division FTE" (p. 52). The primary—and ultimately unsuccessful—focus for community colleges during the 1972 reauthorization was on the establishment of state postsecondary systems, otherwise known as 1202 Commissions, in which community colleges would be incorporated with universities rather than be governed by a state's K–12 system. The primary drivers behind the push for 1202 Commissions were the introduction of accountability measures, increased government regulation, and a concern for equity and efficiency (Tillery & Wattenbarger, 1985).

Private For-Profit Institutions

For-profit institutions are businesses that have a responsibility to owners (including shareholders) to generate profit. Rather than compete head-on with traditional higher education institutions, for-profit colleges have largely focused on markets underserved by traditional higher education institutions, though this population includes many of the nontraditional students whom community colleges aim to serve. Hentschke (2010) identified five actions that for-profit institutions were considering in order to expand into new markets:

- Shifting focus from the employer to the worker

- Increasing competition with traditional colleges and universities

- Developing partnerships with traditional colleges and universities

- Reaching down an educational level to high schools

- Aggregating coursework from various institutions to develop a coherent program of study or to award a credential

It also must be acknowledged that for-profit colleges have reached some students that non-profit higher education has not.

The for-profit sector of higher education has grown dramatically over the past 30 years, in large part because of the availability of student aid funds: they diverge from community colleges in certain fundamental aspects. These include governance, tuition, reliance on student aid, profits, and expenditures on operations such as advertising (Mullin, 2010b). These differences were highlighted in the debates surrounding the 2010 gainful employment regulations and their second finalization in October 2014. However, we can expect the for-profit sector to continue as a source of competition for community colleges in the coming years. There is too much overlap in program offerings and student population for it be otherwise.

Conclusion

This chapter examined trends that influence community college finance including enrollments, unemployment, and other state funding commitments in order to portray the factors that allow us to consider what the future portends.

Questions

Identify two community colleges and complete the following questions. Community colleges may be located by using the College Navigator tool of the National Center for Education Statistics at http://nces.ed.gov/collegenavigator/.

1. Examine trends in enrollment at two community colleges from the 2007–08 to the 2011–12 academic year. Are they similar or different? Why or why not?

2. Do the unemployment trends in the state(s) in which the colleges are located run counter to enrollment trends between the 2007–08 and 2011–12 academic years?

3. How much state student financial aid, as reported by NASSGAP in their annual report, went to nonpublic institutions in the state(s) in which the colleges are located in 2007–08 and 2011–12?

Chapter Two

The Shifting Balance of Revenue

While sharing some characteristics with their private and for-profit peers, public institutions obviously differ in one key way: they are financed by state and, in some instances, local appropriations. This funding is inevitably accompanied by oversight and accountability requirements. As a result, colleges are beholden to individual policymakers who may or may not share their perspectives. At the same time, however, external public support can be a huge institutional benefit. Whatever the case, the shifting composition of institutional revenues toward students (that is, tuition and fees), even as state policymakers diminish their support (often while increasingly exerting greater institutional control), presents significant challenges.

Over the past 50 years, the percentages of funding for higher education from its three primary sources have changed dramatically. Figure 2.1 illustrates the proportion coming from state and local funding and that coming from tuition and fees. These shifts are of the highest substantive importance to colleges and have critical political and policy ramifications as well.

This chapter focuses on the implications of the shifting balance of institutional revenues at community colleges by examining three individual states. Each state revenue configuration highlights aspects of the primary funding sources for community colleges. The chapter concludes with suggestions for stabilizing future revenue.

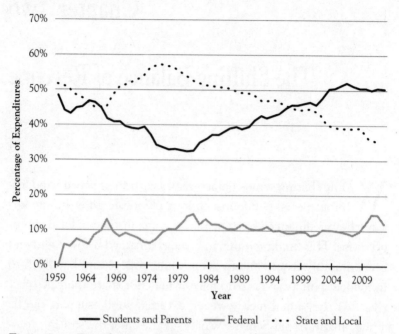

Figure 2.1   Distribution of Expenditures to Finance Higher Education: 1959 to 2012

Source: Adapted from U.S. Department of Commerce (n.d.).

The Balance in Three States

The balance of revenues among state, student, and, where applicable, local sponsors varies within each state. In some respects this dynamic precludes a single national portrait of community college financing. It is fairly well understood that colleges rely upon diverse-sized revenue streams, but it is less clear, even to researchers, how these disparate sources interact.

Community college funding policies (explicit or implicit) often delineate assigned "shares" of support from the primary funding sources. These policies are underpinned by the recognition that postsecondary education is of benefit to both society and students.

This section examines the different funding dynamics of primary revenue sources in three states, each with a different balance: Virginia, California, and Illinois.

Virginia

Despite numerous studies in the 1950s about the future of postsecondary education in Virginia, at the end of the decade the state remained without a community college system. In 1964, Virginia's level of postsecondary participation was among the lowest in the country; 25% of the college age population was enrolled, compared to 32.4% for the South overall and 43.7% nationally (Vaughn, 1987). Noting the implications of this situation for the future of the state, and building upon the numerous previous studies, in 1966 the Virginia Community College System (then named the State Board for Community Colleges) was created. In the following year a master plan for community colleges in the state was developed.

While local support and involvement in planning contributed to the development of the community college system, concern about local control and funding of the colleges resulted in the establishment of a centralized community college system without local community support (Vaughn, 1987). Funding for the community college system came from the state's first sales tax (Virginia Community College System, 2014) and tuition and fees.

Trends in the balance of revenue between the state and students in Virginia from the late 1960s to present illustrate, over time, a narrowing of the gap between what was historically a high level of state support (nearing 70% until the 1990s) until a decrease to nearly half of historical levels in 2012–2013 (see Figure 2.2). The students' share increased from 10% at the beginning of the community college system to over 30% in the 2012–13 academic year.

California

California became the first state to establish local junior colleges through legislation with the 1907 enactment of an amendment to the California State Political Code (Center for the Study of Higher Education, n.d.). The first community college in California was established in 1910 as Fresno Junior College, and in 1917 the California legislature provided funding for the creation of junior

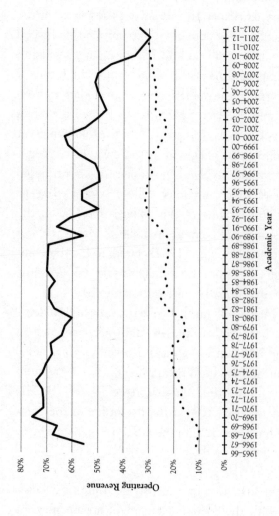

Figure 2.2   Percent of Operating Revenues for Virginia Community Colleges, by Source: 1966–1967 to 2012–2013

Note: Data were originally obtained from annual reports of the Virginia Community College System. Missing data were provided by the Virginia Community College System; however, data definitions may or may not have changed over time. The authors attempted to ensure consistency in the data and accept responsibility for any errors. Additionally, the community colleges received a fair amount of federal support that is not captured in this figure, which is focused on the relationship between the state and student shares of funding.

Source: Adapted from Virginia Community College System, personal communication.

colleges throughout the state. Over the next 50 years, community colleges expanded to serve the state's growing population. In 1960, with the passage of the Donahoe Higher Education Act, the master plan was developed. The master plan created a tripartite system, which articulated a structure for the enrollment of students in community colleges as an efficient way to educate individuals prior to transfer to one of the senior institutions (California Legislative Analyst Office, 2004; Coons, 1960). The major features of the master plan included differentiation of functions among the public segments; differentiation of admissions pools for the public segments (University of California or UC = top 12.5%; California State University or CSU = top 33.3%; Community Colleges or CCs admit any student capable of benefiting from instruction); establishment of the principle that students should pay fees for auxiliary costs (such as dormitories); and establishment of governance structures for each of the public segments. This system allowed the state to serve burgeoning enrollments while staving off the need to construct new or enlarge existing UC or CSU campuses, which are far more costly.

Embracing the low-to-no-tuition philosophy, the state initially did not charge tuition for residents at community colleges and only assessed fees. The result was and continues to be a reliance on state revenue sources, with some contributions from local entities (Figure 2.3).

The relationship of state to local operating revenues at California's community colleges changed in the 1970s. The rapid increase in home values and the subsequent hike in property tax bills created a public cry to lower property taxes. In 1978, Proposition 13 limited property tax rates to 1% of assessed value of a home at the time of purchase. Proposition 13 also created the requirement that all state tax increases need a two-thirds vote (super majority) of the legislature and that local special taxes must be approved by two-thirds of voters. Proposition 13 reduced local property taxes overnight by 57%, effectively destroying the power of local boards

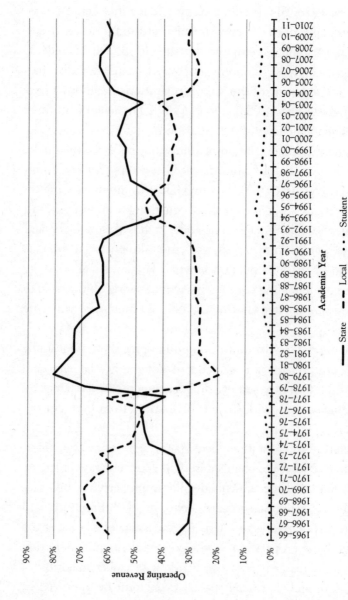

Figure 2.3 Percent of Operating Revenue for California Community Colleges, by Source: Fiscal Year 1965–1966 to 2010–2011

Note: Most recent data available. Starting in 1985–86 California's lottery contributed between 2.3 and 5.4% of operating revenue, with a lesser proportion in more recent years.

Source: Adapted from California Postsecondary Education Commission (2010).

to raise ad valorem taxes, which significantly reduced local property tax revenues available to cities, counties, and schools (Public Policy Institute of California, 2008). Needless to say, this proposition dramatically affected community college financing, and it also became a catalyst for an increased state legislative role in community college policy activities.

In 1983, California's community colleges were able to charge an enrollment fee, set at $11 a unit. The imposition of the student fees for 1984 resulted primarily from the deep recession of the early 1980s, passage of Proposition 13 (which resulted in lower property tax revenues for community colleges and strained state budget/reserves to make up for the lost local revenues), and related state budgetary problems.

Proposition 98 was passed in 1988 as an amendment to the state constitution. Prop 98 was meant to establish a guaranteed, minimum annual funding level (at least 39% of general fund revenues) for K–14 districts (K–12 and community colleges); this funding formula generated roughly two-thirds of total community college funding (California Legislative Analyst Office, 2005). This funding comes through a combination of state general fund and local property tax revenues, which is supposed to grow each year in accord with the economy and K–12 enrollment; however, through the use of three different formulas, the state suspends this formula when it cannot meet the funding goal, resulting in uncertain community college support.

The recession of the early 1990s impacted California significantly. Between 1990 and 1994, California lost 868,000 jobs and the state's income rate growth slowed to 2%, far below the state's rate of inflation and population growth. With its passage in 1990, Prop 111—like its predecessor, Prop 98—modified the State Appropriations Limit (SAL), which "places annual limits (or ceilings) on the appropriations of tax proceeds that can be made by the state, school districts, and local governments in California" (California Legislative Analyst Office, 2000). The legislation decreased state support for community colleges to such an extent that the state was contributing less than the local governments between 1992 and 1995, which was unprecedented. While student fees increased in the first decade of the twenty-first century, the percentage of operating revenues paid by students remained below 10%, with the state again paying the largest share.

Illinois

The first junior college in America was established in 1901 at Joliet, IL. William Rainey Harper, president of the University of Chicago, advocated for these institutions as "lower schools" that would have curricula and instructional forms that reserved "higher order scholarship" to universities. The community college concept found firm ground in Illinois, and various local governments and private entities developed junior/community colleges across the state. The state itself began to formally govern community colleges in 1951 when they were included as part of the public school system. In 1955 they first received state support. Their status as "higher education" institutions was formally refuted in 1961 by the state's attorney general, only to be reversed in 1963 when the attorney general agreed that community colleges provided education services equivalent to degree programs. This change in their status was important, as it allowed them to be placed within the master plan for postsecondary education (Hardin, 1975).

In 1961, the newly created Illinois Board of Higher Education was charged with developing a master plan for the state (Erickson, 1969). As it pertained to community colleges, the recommendations by committee members—who favored, among other things, a two-year branch campus approach to expanding access—were ultimately overturned in favor of maintaining a system in which local entities continued the colleges they had established under a one-third funding arrangement. The master plan recommendations informed the development of Illinois' *Junior College Act of 1965*

(Public Act 1965), which removed the junior college from the system of common (K–12) schools and put a ceiling on how much revenue could come from students in the form of tuition—colleges could charge up to one-third of the cost of instruction—as well as how much could come from the state (50 percent of operating expenses).

The trends in Figure 2.4 show that Illinois has increasingly depended on students to fund public community colleges. While the one-third philosophy has been in place since 1965, the student share of revenues has increased from approximately 11% to nearly 33%. In the same time period, the state share has decreased from a high of approximately 40% in 1976–77 to a low of less than 20% in 2006–07. Over the past 20 years the local contribution has somewhat stabilized at approximately 40%.

Observations on Different State Funding Arrangements

These three state examples highlight some of the different community college funding arrangements, tying them to relevant political, historical, educational, and other variables. In Virginia, the lack of a local contribution forces colleges to rely heavily on student enrollments to generate needed revenue. Although California students pay fees, their share is minimal; the colleges operate primarily on state and local contributions. In Illinois, the philosophy of the community college system since its inception is that the state has expected the student to be a substantial contributor to institutional funding. This funding arrangement allows community colleges to enact a tuition and fee charge up to one-third of the per-capita cost of education. Deeply rooted in local control and interest, and countering recommendations to significantly reduce the fiscal burden placed upon students, the one-third funding philosophy at the state level has been maintained over time. Mullin and Frost (2011) noted that although this approach was maintained in Illinois, it was less successful for the community colleges of the State University of New York, which clearly demonstrates that a funding philosophy

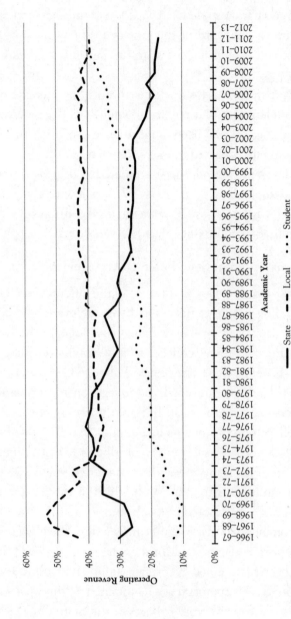

Figure 2.4 Percent of Operating Revenue for Illinois Community Colleges, by Source: Fiscal Year 1966–1967 to 2012–2013

Source: Adapted from Illinois Community College Board (1967 to 2013).

is not worth the paper it is written on without requisite fiscal and policy support. Additionally, it is worth noting that, even in Illinois, the one-third model applies to statewide totals, with shares at individual community colleges not always hewing to that apportionment.

In states where both the student and state contribute their respective shares to fund community colleges, enrollment is the binding factor, as appropriations are largely based upon the number of students enrolling (or completing), and tuition and fees are the direct result of enrollment.

In states where there is a local contribution to community college funding, revenues are diversified by a revenue source not tied to enrollments. Local funding is the result of local taxes that can be a powerful source of stability as enrollments ebb and flow. This was seen in the Great Recession of 2008–09. However, funds from local sources have their own cycles as well.

Balancing Interests

The financing of higher education extends beyond the allocation of revenue to the exertion of authority or control that is not explicitly about dollars. So it is useful to understand some of the dynamics and priorities animating each of these external funding sources.

Local

Approximately 25 states have a local property tax contribution to fund community colleges (see Chapter 3). The benefits of local control/funding generally carry with them an increased interest in the activities of the college. This is especially important for community colleges, as they are, by definition, connected to the communities in which they are located. In every identifiable case, community colleges have a defined service area, although distance or online education adds a new dimension to that reality. Most local governments provide community colleges with financing through property taxes, like their K–12 counterparts. Local control therefore acts as a quality monitor, as voters and taxpayers remain keenly interested in the wise investment of public resources.

That said, the local control of educational funding and related oversight opens the potential for the abuse of power, exertion of personal priorities not shared by the college administration or the local community, and an inequitable provision of services to stakeholders in the service area. Trustees are political creatures, whether elected or appointed. It should also be noted that even in states without local funding, local college trustees may be vigorous advocates for the college.

States

While not constitutionally required to fund higher education, states do promote it by providing financial support. The reasons for doing so are many: historical, political, and economic reasons, and a desire to enhance equity, among others. Historically, the state has served as the leading revenue source for public colleges, and politically, a college education is not only a common aspiration of much of the population but also signals to business and industry that the state has the infrastructure for and commitment to providing an educated workforce.

A challenge inherent in the state funding of institutions is the fact that its officials can impose, through that funding, controls, conditions, and so on that are problematic to the college and may be disproportionate to its investment as well. That said, the affiliation with "state" provides a powerful symbol of the nature and commitment of the college.

Students

Both students and their families want to find the right education at an affordable price. They often are unclear about the role that public subsidies play in community college tuitions. Vigorous efforts are under way to provide better consumer information to students, but there are challenges in terms of developing a clear, accurate set of metrics that allow for apt comparisons among institutions. This is the case in part because the full value and implications of higher education are so difficult to quantify, and also because a student's choice of an institution or program is an inherently personal, subjective decision. And that decision may have nothing to do with any information the prospective student may have received.

Generally speaking, students' payments come from two sources: the student and his or her family and student aid programs and related outside providers. These will be discussed in greater detail in Chapter 5.

Harmonizing Financing Policy Actions

Ideally, the revenues that flow to institutions reinforce the importance of each and enhances the whole. However, coordinating policy across different governmental levels can be a challenge. And as indicated in the preceding discussion about the funding of different state systems, there is no single right way to integrate this funding and the policies that attach to it.

Pffefer and Salanick (1978) identified three factors to use in analyzing the level of dependence between entities, and this can be related to community college funding. They include the extent to which an outside entity serves as a resource for the other, the extent to which an outside entity controls the allocation of resources, and whether there are other outside entities that also provide resources. These are all factors to consider when developing funding systems that are designed to work together.

Collaborative Approaches

Although they are not commonly employed, there are policy options available to government or institutions to stabilize funding streams. The first, maintenance-of-effort provisions, are constructed to ensure that a certain level of funding is maintained as a prerequisite to receive funding from a different source. For example, the American Recovery and Reinvestment Act (Pub. L. No. 111–5, 2009) incorporated a maintenance-of-effort provision in its State Fiscal Stabilization Fund that required states to maintain funding for K–12 and higher education at 2006 levels for the 2009–2011 fiscal years in order to receive significant fiscal support. However, maintenance-of-effort provisions are challenging, as they limit the flexibility that legislative or other bodies traditionally retain, and the entity that imposes the maintenance of effort needs some sort of leverage. However, as states have reduced their commitment to postsecondary education, federal policymakers have increasingly discussed creating state maintenance-of-effort policies, largely in the context of the reauthorization of the Higher Education Act (HEA). Arguments for and against maintenance-of-effort provisions are presented in Table 2.1.

Table 2.1.   Arguments for and Against Maintenance-of-Effort Provisions

Arguments for	Arguments against
Enables the entity from which the funds come to pursue their policy priorities on a sustained basis	Undermines sovereignty and control of entity overseeing impacted revenue source
Leverages a revenue source, incentivizes actions by the other	Is vulnerable to reluctance of the entity overseeing the impacted revenue source to be committed to a certain level of funding
Stabilizes revenue needs from other sources	Runs the risk that the other entity may claim hardship or pursue a waiver
Mitigates cyclical funding, thereby allowing for more stability and better planning	Commits governmental funds during times when continued support may be challenging to provide
Respects sovereignty by not incentivizing rather than mandating action	Shifts power over policy to an entity that may not have constitutional authority or responsibility

Note: These arguments were both expanded and adapted from Alexander, Harnish, Hurley, and Moran (2010), who spoke directly to the relationship between federal and state governments. The information provided in this table removes the specific entity from the discussion to get to the underlying arguments that may occur between any two entities, such as state and local governments.

A second funding philosophy that is used to stabilize community college budgets, and make them more efficacious, derives from K–12 finance: equalization funding. Equalization funding addresses funding differences between two or more educational institutions and aims to use state funding to offset this difference. The goal is to provide some sort of minimum or foundational funding for all colleges. The Illinois community college funding mechanism continues to maintain an equalization component, detailed in Exhibit 2.1.

Exhibit 2.1 State Statute for Illinois Community College Equalization Funding

Equalization grants shall be calculated by the State Board by determining a local revenue factor for each district by:

(A) adding (1) each district's Corporate Personal Property Replacement Fund allocations from the base fiscal year or the average of the base fiscal year and prior year, whichever is less, divided by the applicable statewide average tax rate to (2) the district's most recently audited year's equalized assessed valuation or the average of the most recently audited year and prior year, whichever is less,

(B) then dividing by the district's audited full-time equivalent resident students for the base fiscal year or the average for the base fiscal year and the two prior fiscal years, whichever is greater, and

(C) then multiplying by the applicable statewide average tax rate.

Note: This statute has additional language that provides greater detail.

Source: 110 ILCS 805/2–16.02 (2013).

Not surprisingly, equalization funding is politically challenging within states, as well-resourced institutions tend to lose state revenue to less-resourced institutions. In Nebraska, where the legislature developed interdependence between the state and local contributions in their 2007 community college funding model, the resulting tension over the revised funding model was a factor in motivating the largest college in the state to "stop paying its dues to an association of the six schools and prompted that group to expel [the college]" (Hammil, 2011).

Coercive Approaches

The classification of an institution as eligible for federal student aid funds (Title IV eligibility) is an enduring and powerful example of what might be termed coercive funding—using "strings" that accompany funding to leverage institutional practice. It is, in essence, the primary policy lever available to the federal government to alter institutional actions. This is discussed in more detail in Chapter 5, on student financial aid.

Another approach is to use matching funds provided by one government entity to incentivize action by another. Baker and Bergeron (2014) proposed one such program, titled the Public College Quality Compact. Under this plan, a state would have to meet certain conditions—namely, to promise students from low-income families that college will be affordable, develop a plan to make funding streams sustainable, implement strategies to improve institutional performance, standardize credit transfer and admission requirements, and raise high school learning standards—in order to receive matching funds from the federal government.

Proposals such as the two provided here underscore the tension between government control and institutional flexibility. Kerr (1968) noted that Congress would not be willing to simply hand over funds to states for higher education, because in doing so they would lose control over how the money was spent. Nearly 50 years later his observation holds true. The question for states, and for colleges, is whether the requirements of any federal program are sufficient disincentive to eschew federal funds. In practice that has not proven to be the case.

Conclusion

While it is clear that community colleges rely upon diverse revenue streams, their impact on institutions is enormous, and changes. This chapter examined funding arrangements that have emerged in three states. It also discussed dynamics related to the relationships between funding sources.

Questions

One community college needs to be identified before completing the following questions. Community colleges may be located by using the College Navigator tool of the National Center for Education Statistics at http://nces.ed.gov/collegenavigator/.

1. Does the state in which the colleges you chose to study are located have an explicitly stated funding philosophy? If so, what is it? If not, what should it be and why?

2. Would you advocate for a maintenance-of-effort provision for states? Why or why not?

3. Do you think it is plausible to have an equalization funding model in all states where there is local funding? Why or why not?

Chapter Three

Institutional Support

As we have discussed, community colleges receive support for operations from a multitude of sources, ranging from tuition and fees, as other sectors of higher education are supported, to, in some cases, local appropriations, as K–12 school districts are funded. This diversity of revenue sources makes community college finance challenging to understand and analyze.

Without a firm grasp of some of the dynamics that lie behind the various sources of revenue, it becomes even more challenging for leaders to be effective fiscal stewards and to advocate effectively for funding. To help current and future institutional leaders better understand the sources of institutional support, this chapter examines revenue sources as well as their trends. Some of this discussion is necessarily technical. The chapter closes with a discussion to enhance a general understanding of financial data.

Community College Revenues

For an institution to be eligible to participate in federal student aid programs (Title IV of the Higher Education Act), it must report data to the U.S. government's Integrated Postsecondary Education Data System, known most commonly by its acronym, IPEDS. These data are then presented to the public through a number of publication vehicles of the U.S. Department of Education—such as *College Navigator*, the *Digest of Education Statistics*, or the *Condition of Education*—and are made public for use by analysts (prominently by the Delta Cost Project), professors, institutional researchers, the media, and so on. (The Delta Cost Project presents national data and accounts for the changing classification of institutions by providing ten years of data for a matched set of institutions, or a set of the same institutions, over a given period of time.)

Nationally, community college revenues totaled $56. 2 billion for 2011–12, the most recent year for which data were available. These revenues and the source from which they were derived, as presented in Table 3.1, provide necessary context for examining community college revenues.

Table 3.1.   Community College Revenues, by Category: 2011–2012

Revenue Category	Amount (in thousands)	Percent or Total	Amount per Student
Total Revenues	$56,153,074	—	$13,542
Tuition and Fees	$9,407,634	16.8%	$2,269
Federal Appropriations	$120,279	0.2%	$29
Federal Grants and Contracts	$1,931,982	3.4%	$466
Federal Nonoperating Grants	$11,941,246	21.3%	$2,880
State Appropriations	$13,034,033	23.2%	$3,143
State Grants and Contracts	$1,477,802	2.6%	$356
State Nonoperating Grants	$1,161,061	2.1%	$280
Local Appropriations	$9,697,357	17.3%	$2,339
Local Grants and Contracts	$570,728	1.0%	$138
Local Nonoperating Grants	$101,569	0.2%	$24
Other	$6,810,952	11.9%	$1,618

Source: Adapted from Snyder and Dillow (2014).

Tuition and Fees

Tuition and fees accounted for 16.8% of all community college revenues in 2011–2012. The composition of this increasingly important source of funding is slightly more complex than may at first appear. This section endeavors to provide some clarity about this funding stream, examining what is and is not counted in the category.

For public community colleges reporting on this category of revenues, institutions were instructed to "[r]eport all tuition & fees (including student activity fees) assessed against students for education purposes. Include revenues for tuition and fees net of discounts & allowances from institutional and governmental scholarships, waivers, etc. (report gross revenues minus discounts and allowances). Include here those tuition and fees that are remitted to the state as an offset to state appropriations" (National Center for Education Statistics [NCES], 2013a, page number not provided).

Therefore, there is a difference between tuition and fee revenue and tuition and fee prices per se. Whereas tuition and fees can be multiplied by a number of students to estimate total revenues, the source of those revenues is not always the student. For the purposes of IPEDS, data used nationally, institutions are instructed to report tuition and fees net of discounts and allowances as opposed to the gross amount. This means that there are additional, tuition-based revenues that flow into the institution's coffers but are not reported in this category. Many of them are reported under federal and state nonoperational grants, as will be discussed later. Many of these sources are provided in Table 3.2.

For public community colleges, the largest source of financial support was the Federal Pell Grant Program; 38% of community college students received a Pell grant. This was followed by federal subsidized loans (15% of students) and institutional need-based grants (12% of students). Table 3.2 also illustrates the extent to which students in the three other sectors of higher education used

Table 3.2.   Sources of Support for Students, by Sector: 2011–2012

Source of Support	Sector			
	Public two-year	Public four-year	Private	For-profit
Federal Pell Grant	38%	38%	36%	64%
Federal Direct Subsidized Loan	15%	41%	53%	69%
Institutional Need-based Grant	12%	12%	37%	1%
Federal Direct Unsubsidized Loan	11%	40%	53%	66%
State Need-based Grant	8%	16%	18%	4%
Private Grant	4%	11%	17%	3%
Employer Aid (Students and Parents)	4%	6%	9%	6%
Employer Aid (includes staff)	4%	6%	10%	6%
Federal Supplemental Educational Opportunity Grant (FSEOG)	3%	5%	10%	14%
State Merit-only Grant	3%	6%	4%	*
Veterans' Benefits and Dept. of Defense	3%	3%	4%	8%
Veterans' Benefits	3%	3%	3%	8%
Federal Work Study	2%	5%	21%	1%
Private Loan	2%	7%	12%	12%
Institutional Merit-only Grant	1%	9%	37%	*
Institutional Tuition and Fee Waiver	1%	3%	4%	*
Vocational Rehabilitation & Training	1%	0%	*	*
Athletic Scholarship	0%	1%	4%	*
Federal Non Title IV Grant	0%	1%	1%	*

Table 3.2. *(continued)*

Source of Support	Sector			
	Public two-year	Public four-year	Private	For-profit
State Work Study	0%	*	*	*
Federal Direct PLUS Loan	0%	7%	12%	5%
State Non-need Grant	*	1%	2%	0%
State Loan	*	0%	0%	*
Institutional Work Study	*	1%	4%	*
Institutional Tuition Waiver for Staff	*	0%	*	*
Institutional Loan	*	0%	1%	*
Federal Perkins Loan	*	3%	8%	2%

Note: Denotes unstable estimate. These data illustrate a representative sample of all undergraduate students in each sector for the given year. Sources of support were presented in descending order for percentage of students participating in the program at community colleges.

Source: Authors' analysis of National Postsecondary Student Aid Study 2012 data (National Center for Education Statistics, 2014d).

these student aid sources. Student financial aid is discussed in more detail in Chapter Five.

Federal Revenues

In total, federal funds accounted for 24.9% of all community college revenues in 2011–2012. These revenues were reported to IPEDS in three categories: appropriations, grants and contracts, and nonoperating grants. This section examines the federal funding categories.

Appropriations

Federal appropriations accounted for less than 1% of all community college revenues in 2011–2012. For this category of revenues, institutions were instructed to "[r]eport all amounts received by the institution through acts of a federal legislative body, except grants and contracts. Funds reported in this category are for meeting current operating expenses, not for specific projects or programs. An example is federal land-grant appropriations" (National Center for Education Statistics, 2013a, page number not provided). Clearly, these direct appropriations are not a significant source of community college funding.

An analysis of IPEDS data by the authors found that 31 community colleges received federal appropriations in 2011–2012. Northern Oklahoma College in Tonkawa, Oklahoma, received the largest appropriation ($10,182,007), and Middlesex Community College in Bedford, Massachusetts, had the distinction of receiving the smallest ($776).

Federal Grants and Contracts

Federal grants and contracts accounted for 3.4% of all community college revenues in 2011–2012. For this category of revenues, institutions were instructed to "[r]eport revenues from federal governmental agencies that are for specific research projects or other types of programs and that are classified as operating revenues. Examples are research projects and similar activities for which amounts are received or expenditures are reimbursable under the terms of a grant or contract. Include federal land grant appropriations if considered operating revenue. Do not include Pell Grants or other federal student aid here" (National Center for Education Statistics, 2013a, page number not provided).

An analysis of IPEDS data by the authors found the vast majority of community colleges received federal operating contract and grant funds in 2011–2012. Of those institutions receiving funds, Fox Valley Technical College in Appleton, WI received the largest amount ($36.5 million) and James Sprunt Community College in Kenansville, NC received the smallest amount ($343).

Federal Nonoperating Grants

Federal nonoperating grants accounted for 21.3% of all community college revenues in 2011–2012. For this category of revenues, institutions were instructed to "[r]eport all amounts reported as nonoperating revenues from federal governmental agencies that are provided on a nonexchange basis. Include Pell Grants and other Federal student grant aid, including Veterans Education Benefits here. Do not include revenues from the Federal Direct Student Loan (FDSL) Program. Do not include capital grants & gifts" (National Center for Education Statistics, 2013a, page number not provided). Ivy Tech Community College, which reports to IPEDS as a system, received the largest amount, at $246.4 million. Many of these funds are based on federal student aid in the form of grants, as detailed in Table 3.2.

State Revenues

In total, state revenues accounted for 27.9% of all community college revenues in 2011–2012. These revenues were reported by colleges to IPEDS in three categories: appropriations, grants and contracts, and nonoperating grants. This section clarifies state revenue funding categories by examining what is included in each category.

Appropriations

State appropriations accounted for 23.2% of all community college revenues in 2011–2012. For this category of revenues, institutions were instructed to "[r]eport all amounts received by the institution through acts of a state legislative body" (National Center for Education Statistics, 2013a, page number not provided).

State contributions to community colleges revenues have not been large compared with those provided to other sectors. State tax appropriations received by community colleges the 1974–75 to

2009–10 academic years made up approximately 20% of revenues to higher education (Mullin, 2010a).

State Grants and Contracts

State grants and contracts accounted for 2.6% of all community college revenues in 2011–2012. For this category, institutions were instructed to "[r]eport revenues from state governmental agencies that are for specific research projects or other types of programs and that are classified as operating revenues. Examples are research projects and similar activities for which amounts are received or expenditures are reimbursable under the terms of a grant or contract" (National Center for Education Statistics, 2013a, page number not provided).

State Nonoperating Grants

State nonoperating grants accounted for 2.1% of all community college revenues in 2011–2012. For this category of revenues, institutions were instructed to "[r]eport all amounts reported as nonoperating revenues from state governmental agencies that are provided on a nonexchange basis. Do not include capital grants & gifts" (National Center for Education Statistics, 2013a, page number not provided).

Local Revenues

In total, local revenues accounted for 18.5% of all community college revenues in 2011–2012. These revenues were reported by colleges to IPEDS in three categories: appropriations, grants and contracts, and nonoperating grants. This section outlines what is included in each category.

Appropriations

Local appropriations accounted for 17.3% of all community college revenues in 2011–2012. For this category of revenues, institutions were instructed to "[r]eport all amounts received from property or other taxes assessed directly by or for an institution below the state level. Include any other similar general support provided to the institution from governments below the state level, including local government appropriations" (National Center for Education Statistics, 2013a, page number not provided).

The varying degree to which local sponsors fund community colleges has led to the distinction between what are termed state-aided community colleges and state community colleges. Palmer (2008) defined state-aided community colleges as "states in which local tax appropriations account for at least 10% of total government funding for all community colleges in the state," whereas state community colleges received little or no local tax appropriations. Yet as state support continued to decline, Garrett (1999) made the observation that "Now, more than ever before, it can be said that public community colleges have changed from being state-supported to being state-assisted" (p. 10).

Local Grants and Contracts

Local grants and contracts accounted for 1.0% of all community college revenues in 2011–2012. For this category of revenues, institutions were instructed to "[r]eport revenues from local governmental agencies that are for specific research projects or other types of programs and that are classified as operating revenues. Examples are research projects and similar activities for which amounts are received or expenditures are reimbursable under the terms of a grant or contract" (National Center for Education Statistics, 2013a, page number not provided).

Local Nonoperating Grants

Local nonoperating grants accounted for 0.2% of all community college revenues in 2011–2012. For this category of revenues, institutions were instructed to "[r]eport all amounts reported as nonoperating revenues from local governmental agencies and organizations that are provided on a nonexchange basis. Do not include capital grants & gifts" (National Center for Education Statistics, 2013a, page number not provided).

Other

In total, revenues from other sources accounted for 11.9% of all community college revenues in 2011–2012. These revenues originate from disparate sources.

Sales and services of auxiliary enterprises and other operating revenues accounted for 3.63% and 1.69% of total community college revenues, respectively. In addition, gifts (0.47%), investment income (0.31%), other nonoperating revenues (1.25%), other revenues (0.97%), and 0.2% from additions to permanent endowments were included in the "Other" category.

Some of these categories are more reflective of the revenue sources of other sectors of higher education. And in that vein, there are surely opportunities to increase the importance of gifts and permanent endowments at community colleges. It is from these sources that institutional grant aid for students often originates, which, as was illustrated in Table 3.2, has become an increasingly important source of support for community college students.

The last two categories that contributed to the "Other" category were capital appropriations (2.96%) and capital contracts and grants (0.65%). The acquisition of these funds is often a challenge, as state funding for capital projects faces direct competition with K–12 and university projects, as well as the fact that the projects themselves are so expensive.

Trends in Revenue

Figure 3.1 illustrates trends in total revenues per student at public community colleges and four-year institutions, compared to total revenues in 2005–2006 (the year to which the data are indexed). These seven years of data allow for a couple of observations. First,

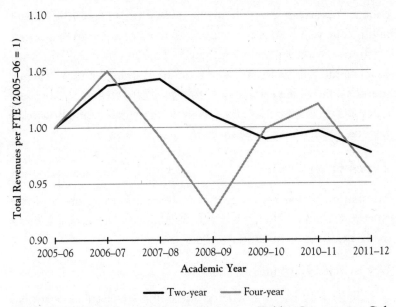

Figure 3.1   Total Revenues per Student at Public Community Colleges and Four-Year Institutions Indexed to 2005–2006: 2005–2006 to 2011–2012

Note: Expenditure data were adjusted for inflation by NCES, making them comparable from year to year. The data were also contextualized by providing an amount per student, rather than a total amount that does not take into account the number of students enrolled.

Source: Adapted from Snyder and Dillow (2014).

community colleges received fewer total revenues per student in 2011–2012 than they did in 2005–2006, at $13,860 and $13,542 in inflation-adjusted dollars, respectively. The same holds true for public four-year institutions, where total revenues were 96% of what they were seven years earlier. Second, the economic downturn of 2008–09 was experienced more immediately by community colleges than by four-year institutions, as total revenues exhibited a downward trend starting in 2008–09. Conversely, revenues at public four-year institutions first exhibited sharp decreases, then increases, then decreases in total revenues. From these trends it appears that the initial shock to the economy impacted community colleges negatively throughout the downturn, whereas the impact public four-year institutions exhibited more of an erratic pattern.

Total revenues per student may be broken down into the various revenue sources to gain a better understanding of each revenue source's relative importance to a college. Doing so may also provide an opportunity for colleges to focus efforts to understand how their revenue sources may compare to those of their peers.

Types of Revenue

In addition to various categories of revenues, there are multiple *types* of revenues. The type of revenue may dictate how the funds may be utilized by institutional leadership.

Unrestricted Revenues

A college may use unrestricted funds for any legal educational purpose. Tuition is an example of unrestricted revenue. The strength of unrestricted funds for institutional leaders is that, by definition, they provide maximum flexibility. Unrestricted revenues, of course, do not allow the originating source—the state, federal, or local government—to use funding as a lever to change institutional behavior.

Restricted Revenues

Restricted funds are provided to the institution only for their designated purpose, such as benefiting specific populations. Fees, as discussed further in Chapter Four, serve as an example of restricted revenues. Restricted revenues carry with them the assurance that a given program or service is being provided, with the targeted nature of the revenue ensuring accountability. The challenge with restricted revenues for college leaders is that they pay for only certain activities, and even related necessary expenditures may not be covered. For example, if a college operated on only restricted revenues in the form of fees for instruction, then the administration would face a challenge providing related services such as registrars or the student aid office.

Endowment Revenues

Endowment funds are intended to be invested so that the institution can utilize the investment returns. They are usually the result of a gift or grant that is required to be held in perpetuity by the donor or granting agency. In their truest form, the principal balance is not spent—only the income from the interest. There are, however, various types of endowment funds.

Term Endowments

In the case of term endowments, the principal may be expended after a stated period or when a certain event occurs. For example, a donor may have left a term endowment that provides investment returns for 20 years, after which time the principal may be applied to a college priority.

Quasi-Endowments

Quasi-endowment funds may be treated like an endowment or expended at any time that the college, or controlling entity, deems it appropriate. For example, a donor may have given a campus art gallery an endowment stipulating that the investment income was to be used to fund community art opportunities, only to be liquidated four years later to purchase a piece of art for the gallery.

Perspectives on Funding

Financial data can be presented in any number of ways. Prior to concluding this chapter, it is worth noting a few key ways in which financial data are used to make campus decisions.

Total and Per-Student Funding Levels

There is frequent disagreement between state policymakers and institutional officials regarding postsecondary funding levels. State officials generally suggest that they increase funding; institutional representatives often disagree. Who is right? As Hauptman (2013) notes, it depends on the data you are using to discuss the issue, as in some senses funding can both decline and increase simultaneously.

In terms of absolute dollars, states generally do increase higher education funding. However, when examined on a per-student basis, funding does not necessarily increase. This occurs when the increase in full-time equivalent students results in expenditures per student that are less than that for the prior year, even though the total amount appropriated for college increased. Any analysis of trends in higher education funding needs to account for both the total amount of spending and a contextualized amount, such as funding per student, that speaks to its purchasing power.

In Table 3.1, both the total amount of state spending along with the proportional share of funding and revenue per student were provided to allow for a complete understanding of the data. If a prior year's data were provided in a similar fashion, one could make meaningful year-to-year comparisons.

Different Accounting Practices

IPEDS data collections are generally standardized across all institutions, with some variance in financial data contingent upon whether the institution is controlled publicly or by a private entity or is for-profit, as the financial accounting standards vary across these sectors. This variance in how data are reported makes annual cross-sector comparisons of what appears to be similar information difficult. In practice, this means that comparing an institution to another in a particular geographic area, such as a neighboring for-profit college, is not recommended. The U.S. Department of Education describes why:

> Different institutions may classify certain funds differently as a scholarship or fellowship or as a pass-through. One common area of differences is Pell Grants. Private institutions (and a few public institutions) operate under accounting standards adopted by the Financial Accounting Standards Board (FASB). The vast majority of public institutions use accounting standards adopted by the Governmental Accounting Standards

Board (GASB). Public institutions using current GASB accounting standards are required to treat Pell Grants as scholarships, using the logic that the institution is involved in the administration of the program (as evidenced by the administrative allowance paid to the institution). *FASB standards give private institutions the option to treat Pell Grants as scholarships or as pass-through transactions, using the logic that the federal government determines who is eligible for the grant, not the institution.* Because of this difference in requirements, public institutions will report Pell Grants as federal revenues and as allowances (reducing tuition revenues), whereas FASB institutions may do this as well or (as seems to be the majority) treat Pell Grants as pass-through transactions. *The result is that in the case where a FASB institution and GASB institution each receive the same amount of Pell Grants on behalf of their students, the GASB institution will appear to have less tuition and more federal revenues, whereas the FASB institution treating Pell as pass-through will appear to have more tuition and less federal revenues* [emphasis added]. (National Center for Education Statistics, 2010)

However, within sector (that is, public two-year), comparisons should result in an apples-to-apples comparison, as all public community colleges report the data the same way (a few public four-year universities use the same accounting standards as private four-year institutions). For fiscal data, public community colleges report using the GASB accounting standards and common definitions when they complete the IPEDS finance data survey forms.

Adjusting for Inflation

Usually, but not always, monetary values are adjusted for inflation using one of three leading inflation indices. When financial values are not adjusted for their changing value their utility is limited, because of the changing purchasing power of the dollar over time. The three primary price indices applied in higher education finance are the Consumer Price Index (CPI), the Higher Education Cost Adjustment (HECA), and the Higher Education Price Index (HEPI). Those external to colleges generally favor the CPI, whereas some colleges prefer the HEPI, as it represents a basket of goods the college consumes, rather than those of the average consumer. The HECA is a compromise of sorts between both indices. Details of the indices are described in greater detail in McKeown-Moak and Mullin (2014).

Matched Sets

Year-to-year variances in fiscal data may also be attributable to a differing number of institutions that report data. By using matched sets, the same number of colleges is used for each year of a given study. At the state level this is not usually an issue. Classification schemes at the national level raise complications in the classification of community colleges, in particular those offering bachelor's degrees. In fact, national community college revenues have appeared to be decreasing when in fact they are not; rather, the number of institutions the data represent has changed and thereby influenced the data one is relying on.

Conclusion

This chapter outlined the types of revenues flowing to community colleges. It first focused on the various sources of institutional revenues, then continued to trends in and types of revenue. It discussed general financial data within the community college.

Questions

Two community colleges need to be identified before completing question one. Data for community colleges may be located by using the College Navigator tool of the National Center for Education Statistics at http://nces.ed.gov/collegenavigator/.

1. How does the distribution of revenues differ between the two community colleges you selected to study? If there is a substantial difference, why do you think it occurred? If there is not a substantial difference, why not?

2. Compare total community college revenues in 2005–06 to 2011–12 for a community college in Georgia. Explain why there is a difference.

Chapter Four

Tuition and Fees and the
Cost of Attendance

The student role in community college finance has become increasingly important. First, the price students are being asked to pay is increasing much faster than inflation, and second, tuition is increasing as a percentage of revenue.

In this chapter, we examine community college tuition and fees in detail, including defining exactly what they are, the guiding philosophies regarding tuition, and trends in tuition and fees. The chapter also examines the calculation of the total "cost of attendance," which in turn is connected to student aid policies. This discussion is built on in the discussions of pricing and student financial aid, examined in Chapters Twelve and Five, respectively.

Tuition

Tuition and fees are often lumped together as if they were one and the same, but they are not. Tuition is a charge for instructional purposes; this makes the revenues a college receives from tuition flexible, in that they may be used in ways that the college determines best to provide instruction. Community college tuition is usually charged on a per-credit basis, in contrast to a lump sum that covers all courses taken over a given period. Credit-based pricing supports the open access mission of community colleges by allowing students with different enrollment intensity patterns (that is, full-time or less than full-time) to pay their proportional share (Lombardi, 1976). There are many reasons for adopting a credit-based system of paying for higher education (Wellman & Ehrlich, 2003), but it also has some complexities (Laitenen, 2012). Suffice it to say that a credit-based framing of higher education contributes to the way we look at community college fiscal data now and likely will for the foreseeable future.

Why Tuition?

Why do we have tuition at all? This may appear to be an odd question to those who have paid tuition or to those coming into institutional leadership roles from private entities. The expectation that students pay for their higher education is engrained in our national ethos, right? The answer is, not necessarily.

Take, for example, Governor William Haslam of Tennessee. In 2014 he introduced and steered to enactment a proposal to make community college tuition in Tennessee free to graduating high school seniors. California maintains a low-cost community college system, and other state policymakers, such as Massachusetts Governor Deval Patrick in 2007, have floated the idea of making community college free (Bullock, 2007; Lu, 2014).

While the current political environment has been conducive to discussions of charging no tuition to very low tuition at community colleges, the debate is not new. It has occurred from the expansion of public higher education in the mid-twentieth century, to the focus on developing a federal student financial aid system in the 1960s and 1970s, to current positions and practices reinforced by the enrollment and economic cycles examined in Chapter One.

Perspectives on Tuition Levels

Three prevailing perspectives inform the setting of prices. First is the no-to-low tuition position. Second is the position that argues against no to low tuition but not necessarily for a specific tuition level. The third argues for the highest tuition possible, with the understanding student aid should be available to make college affordable—the so-called "high tuition, high aid" policy.

The No-to-Low Tuition Perspective

The notion that community colleges should be free or nearly free arises from both precedent and perspective. The belief in a tuition-free community college in part reflects the colleges' evolution, in some states, from K–12 systems (Koos, 1924). In other cases, the existence of free universities expanded the notion of free education as an extension of free K–12 education (Eells, 1931). This led some, including Eby (1927), to question that if K–12 and universities were free, why not community colleges?

Other justifications followed, including the argument that there were additional costs students incurred when enrolled in college. This idea is an extension of studies on human capital, which places a monetary value on one's time. This is to say that for every hour a student is in class, studying, or commuting to class, an hour's wage is lost. Economists refer to this as opportunity cost or forgone earnings (Johnson, 1960). Related to this (and a consideration given more attention later in this chapter) are the prices paid for books, supplies, and other needed materials. Textbooks have become increasingly expensive in recent years, amounting to a solid third of the average community college tuition, but creative solutions to their pricing have shown some good results. These costs are part of the price (or cost) of attendance.

A third justification for no or low tuition and fees holds that price serves as a barrier to educational opportunity. There is a body of research literature, examined later in this chapter, which suggests that the price of college influences a student's decision to enroll or even consider enrolling.

A fourth justification for no to low tuition and fees is grounded in the social ideals of equal opportunity. In discussing the price of college, Johnson (1960) noted, "[w]hile some are trying to bring racial barriers [to higher education] down, others are trying to put economic barriers up" (p. 44). Increased educational attainment's association with higher wages, greater economic opportunity, and upward social mobility has repeatedly been documented and is examined further in Chapter Ten. By pricing students out of college, it is argued, the opportunity for all potential students to improve their standing in society is substantially limited.

A fifth justification is also an economic one. Simply put, states can save money if they encourage students to access higher education first through a community college (Ruppert, 2001). While the efficiency of community college as an entry point to a four-year degree is contested, Mullin (2012c) estimated that $22 billion was saved by students in nine consecutive cohorts of students who first started at a community college and then transferred to a four-year institution, when the number of credits accepted at the four-year institutions were multiplied by average prices and summed together. The tension related to encouraging students to start at the community college may be approached from various perspectives, with the crux of the issue focused on the unsettled question of whether or not the community college diverts students from reaching their full academic potential (Brint & Karabel, 1989; Rouse, 1995; Clark, 1960).

In sum, the no-to-low tuition perspective was outmoded not by an alternative that would more broadly provide educational opportunity, but rather because other ideas were more persuasive or fiscal revenue sources could not be maintained for such a commitment (Lombardi, 1976).

Against No to Low Tuition

Discussions of tuition and fee policies have a middle ground of sorts, which acknowledges that students should have some "skin in the game" but does not aspire to set prices as high as a student can pay.

The first justification, espoused as early as 1928 by Brothers, is that students should have a financial stake in their learning, and that students who attend college for free do not appreciate or take seriously the investment being made in them. This perspective is countered by those who point to costs outside of tuition and fees that students pay to attend college, including forgone earnings and related costs of attendance.

The second justification relates to the fact that tuition and fees are a revenue source for institutions. The President's Commission on Higher Education (1947), noted for coining the term "community college," identified tuition and fees as a funding source for colleges. State and local governments also recognized that tuition and fee revenue can support public colleges where other public entities competing for public funds cannot.

A third justification for the establishment of tuition and fees of some amount is grounded in the belief that an extremely low-cost option is inherently low quality. From this perspective, "less expensive" is equated with, among other things, less desirable faculty, and therefore provides an inferior learning opportunity. The quality argument is an emotional one. It is countered in part by those who point to the tremendous documentable benefits of community college education, as well as the problems associated with calculating and so comparing institutional costs at the program level—not an activity that is commonly undertaken and shared with the public.

A fourth justification for having a tuition and fee policy is that students are the primary beneficiaries of education and should therefore be responsible for paying for it. This perspective is supported by data that illustrate the substantial individual economic and noneconomic returns to education. However, it does not acknowledge the public economic and noneconomic returns to increased educational attainment.

The fifth justification for a tuition and fee policy is grounded in the belief that significantly subsidizing college is a blunt policy instrument with unintended consequences. It holds that no to low tuition allows wealthier students to take unfair advantage of a public good that they are able to pay for themselves. This justification serves as the foundation of a high-tuition, high-aid pricing model—the third tuition and fee philosophy.

High Tuition, High Aid

A third approach to setting tuition and fees suggests that colleges should make students pay for the full cost of their education to the extent they are able, while at the same time providing generous student financial aid to accommodate individual differences in the ability to pay full tuition. Under this approach, colleges maximize their revenue from more affluent students while still being able to enroll lower-income students.

This approach requires accurately estimating the amount a student, and possibly his or her family, can afford to pay for their education. In short, the high tuition and high aid model relies on a fairly simple calculation—total tuition and fee price minus the expected family contribution—to arrive at an amount of "unmet need." The student aid framework and philosophy are discussed later.

The basic justification for this approach is that it is inefficient for the public to subsidize, through the reallocation of tax dollars in the form of low tuition, students who do not need to be subsidized.

A second justification for the high-tuition, high-aid approach is that colleges need control over how much tuition they collect to meet institutional expenditures, particularly for the attraction and retention of faculty. Restricting access to potential revenues through higher tuition limits the ability of colleges to fund projects and initiatives.

A third justification is that most people think "more expensive" equals "better." Although they acknowledge that learning obviously can take place with very limited resources, they believe that creating the optimal learning environment requires substantial expenditures.

A fourth justification is that public expenditures for higher education have essentially reached a limit and alternative revenue sources are needed. As data in Chapter One noted, the high water mark for higher education funding by state governments was the 1970s. At that time, a need to accept higher tuition and offset it with student aid (while also providing greater opportunity) took root, with the passage of the 1972 Educational Amendments to the Higher Education Act.

Whether a governing entity adopts the no-to-low tuition approach, or the high-tuition, high-aid approach, or something in between, it is reasonable to suggest that the awareness of previous tuition and fee debates has likely had one effect: it has served to keep tuition lower than it would have been without the debate.

Fees

In addition to tuition, colleges charge students fees, of which there are two varieties: required and nonrequired. An example of a required fee is a laboratory fee that provides fiscal support for lab supplies and materials used in a particular course. A nonrequired fee could be a student activity fee that supports cocurricular or nonacademic activities that a student may opt out of paying.

In 1931 Eells noted that with tuition often set by states or other government entities, fees emerged as an alternative revenue source. This continues to hold true. In Florida, for example, boards of trustees of Florida colleges can also set an out-of-state differential fee, an activity and service fee (not to exceed 10% of tuition), a fee for student financial aid purposes of up to 5% (or 7% if $500,000 was not raised with the fee), a technology fee (not to exceed 5%), a capital improvement fee (which may be up to 20% of tuition but cannot exceed an increase of $2 per credit from the previous year), and other fees for services such as transcripts, installment payments, and a convenience fee for students paying online (43 F.S. 1009.23).

The student activity fee does in fact have to be used only for such activities and not for other operations, such as instruction. This distinction is often overlooked, which is problematic, as the common perception is that tuition and fee revenue represents an unrestricted amount of dollars that institutional leadership has at its disposal. An increasing percentage of total tuition and fee revenue is becoming restricted to meet particular purposes that the fees were developed to serve (such as debt service). Examples of the types of required fees charged by community colleges are provided in Table 4.1 for a (convenience) sample of community colleges.

It appears that most fees are no longer charged, or reach a maximum level, when a student registers for 18 credit hours per semester or when the total fees charged for a particular purpose reach a set amount. Furthermore, fees that are specific to a course are not included in national statistics, which should be kept in mind. In addition, some institutions allow students to opt out of paying certain fees if there is a justifiable objection and notice is provided within a certain time frame.

Table 4.1. Required Fee Types for Five Select Colleges: 2013–2014

Required Fee Type	Community College				
	A	B	C	D	E
Institutional	X				
Student Activity	X	X	X	X	
Technology	X	X			
Out-of-District			X	X	X
Campus Revitalization	X				
Facility/Capital Outlay	X		X		X
Sustainability			X		
Access		X			
Accident Insurance		X			
Health				X	X

Note: Colleges were kept anonymous. The data provided were not meant to be representative of national trends; rather, they were selected to show the similarities and differences across colleges as highlighted in the text.

Source: Institutional websites.

Trends in Tuition and Fee Prices

The first national portrait of tuition and fee prices each year has historically been provided by the College Board with its October release of a publication titled *Trends in College Prices* (College Board, 2014a). The publication is widely anticipated in the higher education policy community, as among other things it allows for the benchmarking of state tuition and fee levels to national averages and provides year-over-year comparisons of the sectors that often inform discussions of federal student aid policy.

Less noticed by the policy community, but critical for analysts and researchers, is the spring release of national tuition and fee data by the National Center for Education Statistics (NCES) of the U.S. Department of Education. A comparison of the two shows slightly different values (see Figure 4.1). This is due, in part, to the fact that the College Board data are enrollment-weighted; for example, it adjusts its averages to account for the fact that California has low tuition and fees and a lot of students, whereas Vermont has high tuition and fees and fewer students. The NCES does not weight the data, preferring to treat all institutional tuition and fee values the same. An analysis of the data indicates that the NCES tends to report a lower price than the values presented by the College Board, with differences being between 5% on the low end and 23% on the high end in 1987–88 to 2000–01, respectively.

These values are, of course, the sticker price and do not always reflect the price the student pays when attending college. They do provide a national average tuition and fee price that has, after adjusting for inflation, roughly doubled between the 1991–92 and 2011–12 academic years.

In 2012–2013, the national average tuition and fee price at community colleges was $3,527, with 86% reflecting the amount charged for tuition and the other 14% reflecting the amount

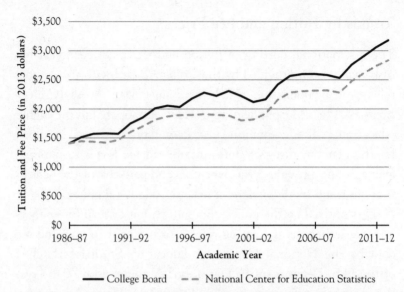

Figure 4.1   Trends in Inflation-Adjusted Tuition and Fee Prices for Public Two-Year Institutions Published by the College Board and the National Center for Education Statistics: 1987–1988 to 2012–2013

Notes: Values reflect 2013 dollars, adjusted by the Consumer Price Index for all Urban Consumers (CPI-U). 1987–88 was the first year the College Board reported data that differed from the National Center for Education Statistics.

Sources: Adapted from College Board (2014a) and Snyder and Dillow (2014).

charged for required fees. While it is well known that tuition prices are increasing, fee prices are increasing as well (Figure 4.2). After controlling for inflation, required fees increased 67% over the 1999–2000 to 2012–2013 span, from $291 to $486, respectively.

Additionally, in 1999–2000, the percent of total tuition and fees derived from required fees was 11%. By 2012–2013 this had increased to 14%. The increase in the total amount of fees and the proportional share of tuition and fees coming from fees (which are, as stated, sometimes more controllable by institutions than tuition) is a trend worth watching.

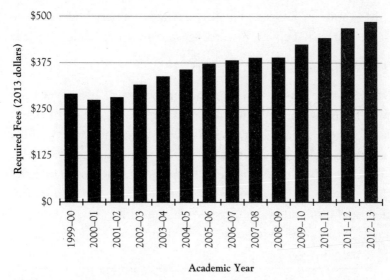

Figure 4.2   National Average Required Fees Amount: 1999–2000 to 2012–2013

Note: Data reflective of degree-granting, Title IV eligible, public two-year colleges in the United States only. These data reflect annual snapshots and as such were not calculated using a matched set of institutions.

Source: Authors' analysis of Integrated Postsecondary Education Data System (National Center for Education Statistics, 2014c).

Cost of Attendance

From the congressionally mandated publication of "shame lists" of the most expensive colleges and those with the highest percentage increases in tuition and net price, to the Obama administration's evolving focus on consumer information, culminating most currently in its Postsecondary Institution Rating System (PIRS), the issue of college price, or affordability, continues to be front and center in higher education policy discussions. These conversations rehash long-standing considerations of exactly what elements constitute the price of college to the student. Is the price simply the required tuition and fees? Does it include books and supplies? And also room and board? What about the earnings students forgo while enrolled?

The Well-Intentioned Construct

While the debate surrounding these perspectives has never been fully settled (McKeown-Moak & Mullin, 2014), federal student financial aid programs in the Higher Education Act powerfully operationalize one definition, the "cost of attendance." Cost of attendance for federal student financial aid purposes includes tuition and fees, books and supplies, room and board, transportation, and other allowable expenses, along with considerations for students in different situations (see Exhibit 4.1).

Exhibit 4.1 Federal Definition of Cost of Attendance

§ 1087II. Cost of attendance

For the purpose of this subchapter and part C of subchapter I of chapter 34 of title 42, the term "cost of attendance" means—

(1) tuition and fees normally assessed a student carrying the same academic workload as determined by the institution, and including costs for rental or purchase of any equipment, materials, or supplies required of all students in the same course of study;

(2) an allowance for books, supplies, transportation, and miscellaneous personal expenses, including a reasonable allowance for the documented rental or purchase of a personal computer, for a student attending the institution on at least a half-time basis, as determined by the institution;

(3) an allowance (as determined by the institution) for room and board costs incurred by the student which—

    (A) shall be an allowance determined by the institution for a student without dependents residing at home with parents;

(B) for students without dependents residing in institutionally owned or operated housing, shall be a standard allowance determined by the institution based on the amount normally assessed most of its residents for room and board;

(C) for students who live in housing located on a military base or for which a basic allowance is provided under section 403(b) of title 37, shall be an allowance based on the expenses reasonably incurred by such students for board but not for room; and

(D) for all other students shall be an allowance based on the expenses reasonably incurred by such students for room and board;

(4) for less than half-time students (as determined by the institution), tuition and fees and an allowance for only—

(A) books, supplies, and transportation (as determined by the institution);

(B) dependent care expenses (determined in accordance with paragraph (8)); and

(C) room and board costs (determined in accordance with paragraph (3)), except that a student may receive an allowance for such costs under this subparagraph for not more than 3 semesters or the equivalent, of which not more than 2 semesters or the equivalent may be consecutive;

(5) for a student engaged in a program of study by correspondence, only tuition and fees and, if required, books and supplies, travel, and room and board costs incurred specifically in fulfilling a required period of residential training;

(6) for incarcerated students only tuition and fees and, if required, books and supplies;

(7) for a student enrolled in an academic program in a program of study abroad approved for credit by the student's home

institution, reasonable costs associated with such study (as determined by the institution at which such student is enrolled);

(8) for a student with one or more dependents, an allowance based on the estimated actual expenses incurred for such dependent care, based on the number and age of such dependents, except that—

(A) such allowance shall not exceed the reasonable cost in the community in which such student resides for the kind of care provided; and

(B) the period for which dependent care is required includes, but is not limited to, class-time, study-time, field work, internships, and commuting time;

(9) for a student with a disability, an allowance (as determined by the institution) for those expenses related to the student's disability, including special services, personal assistance, transportation, equipment, and supplies that are reasonably incurred and not provided for by other assisting agencies;

(10) for a student receiving all or part of the student's instruction by means of telecommunications technology, no distinction shall be made with respect to the mode of instruction in determining costs;

(11) for a student engaged in a work experience under a cooperative education program, an allowance for reasonable costs associated with such employment (as determined by the institution);

(12) for a student who receives a loan under this or any other Federal law, or, at the option of the institution, a conventional student loan incurred by the student to cover a student's cost of attendance at the institution, an allowance for the actual cost of any loan fee, origination fee, or insurance premium charged to such student or such parent on such loan, or the average cost of any such fee or premium charged by the Secretary, lender, or

guaranty agency making or insuring such loan, as the case may be; and

(13) at the option of the institution, for a student in a program requiring professional licensure or certification, the one-time cost of obtaining the first professional credentials (as determined by the institution).

Source: 20 U.S.C. § 1087ll.

The cost of attendance is of substantial importance, as it is the value from which a student's expected family contribution (the amount it is determined that a student can pay) is reduced by to arrive at a financial need amount. This financial need amount is the maximum amount of federal financial aid a student may receive in the form of grants or loans. (States or institutions may have their own definitions and calculations to determine unmet need.)

The community college sector is the only one in which, at least at present, average tuition and fees are below the federal need-based Pell Grant maximum amount ($5,730 for the 2013–14 award year). This allows low-income students to receive grant funds to cover items beyond tuition and fees but included within the cost of attendance, and among other things has the effect of reducing the amount the student would need to borrow. It also allows a student—depending on his own circumstance—to limit the need to work.

Finding the right balance between work and studies is delicate for college students, and has become a major policy issue. The annual (median) earnings for a high school graduate in 2012 were $33,904 (note, 8.3% were unemployed [Bureau of Labor Statistics, 2014]). If, for example, in 2012 a student enrolled full-time at Wake Technical Community College in Raleigh, North Carolina, she would not only forgo $33,904 in earnings but would be responsible for the cost of attendance of roughly $8,280 if she lived off campus with family (the cheapest option), for a total expense of $42,184. Assuming the student was low-income and eligible for federal grant aid, we could subtract $5,730 (Pell Grant maximum to arrive at a new total "cost" of $36,454. Again, this reflects the personal costs to a low-income student to enroll full-time and not work. (This cost differs from viewing college as an investment that yields higher lifetime earnings gained by completing a credential, as discussed in Chapter Ten.) Given this cost, it is not surprising, then, that 84% of community college students work or that 60% of community college students work full-time (Mullin, 2012a).

It may be said that the Title IV cost-of-attendance calculation is a student-friendly construct, as it increases well beyond tuition and fees the amount of financial support a student is eligible to receive. At the same time, the construct is not so friendly to institutions. For nonresidential institutions, it inflates the perception of what institutions actually charge students. For example, while nearly a quarter of community colleges had a residence hall in 2012, only 1% of the community college student body lived in on-campus housing (Tekle, 2013). When room and board are included in the cost-of-attendance calculation, it makes an institution seem much more costly than it is to an unfamiliar observer, such as a student or policymaker. Additionally, because the Pell Grant maximum amount has consistently been higher than the average tuition and fees amount, not all revenue assumed to reach community colleges from the Pell Grant program in fact makes it to the institution.

The Tension

This situation, wherein the cost of attendance helps students but hurts community colleges can create misperceptions of their costs, is leading to heated discussions about college affordability. Some of these aspects follow.

A Misapplied Metric

The previously mentioned "shame lists" use the cost of attendance and its sister, net price, to rank institutions in terms of affordability.

Some think that this is done inappropriately. Again, the net price formulation can cause institutions to be perceived as being much more expensive than they really are. For example, although its tuition and fee rate of $3,276 was close to the national average $2,834 in 2012, Florida Keys Community College was ranked as one of the most expensive institutions in the community college sector (National Center for Education Statistics, 2014a). This was due in part to the high living costs in the Florida Keys, resulting in a cost of attendance ranging between $12,707 for students living off campus with family to $24,617 for a student living independently off campus (National Center for Education Statistics, 2014b).

A Subsidy and a Surplus

The gap between tuition and fees and the Pell Grant maximum award, intended in part to make college more affordable, led to its becoming a target for budget cuts as the program became ever more costly in the Great Recession. This was the case in the proposed elimination of living expenses for Pell Grants for students solely enrolled in online programs—a move that would have hurt only those community college students studying in online programs. Fortunately, from the community college perspective, the proposal never cleared Congress, although it was included in legislation approved by the Senate Appropriations Committee.

However, we may expect a heightened focus on the impacts of cohort default rates in the future as community college students rely more on federal loans to offset rising costs of attendance. In 2012, 18% of all community college students borrowed for college, up from 9% in 2004 (Phillippe & Tekle, 2013b). Given that the population attending community colleges are more likely to default, and subsequently to put that college's federal Title IV student aid eligibility in jeopardy, colleges may be forced to reconsider the implications of student borrowing. This would protect institutions in some ways, but it has the potential to erode the last vestige of the low-cost higher education system for many students—federal student financial aid.

Conclusion

This chapter discussed practical and policy/theoretical aspects of tuition and fee prices and how they relate to the cost of attendance. This allows for further treatments of affordability, indebtedness, opportunity, and social mobility—central issues of current higher education policy debates that also have tremendous practical campus impacts. Other chapters in this book will build upon these concepts.

Questions

One community college needs to be identified before completing the questions two and three. Community colleges may be located by using the College Navigator tool of the National Center for Education Statistics at http://nces.ed.gov/collegenavigator/.

1. Which of the three tuition perspectives aligns with your way of thinking? Explain why.

2. What percentage of the total tuition and (required) fees amount for the college was for fees?

3. What is the college's cost of attendance?

Chapter Five

Student Financial Aid

Student financial aid provides a passport to community college education for millions of students each year. The campuses would have an entirely different face and character without it. While student financial aid has always played a critical role in facilitating broad access to community college, this assistance is more important than ever, as institutions derive ever more of their revenues from tuition—a full 36%, according to the College Board (2014a)—and students are forced to rely on outside sources to finance their education. Unfortunately, this trend is unlikely to abate, as in the United States education is increasingly viewed as a private good for which public subsidies are unnecessary, rather than a social good that benefits all.

Broad access to higher education in America is largely a post–World War II phenomenon. The GI Bill (formally known as the Servicemen's Readjustment Act of 1944 [Pub. L. No. 78–346]) created opportunities for college attendance among segments of the population that previously would not have contemplated it. This landmark legislation, which helped 2.2 million service members attend college and whose impact reverberates today, was followed by the National Defense Education Act (NDEA) of 1958 (Pub. L. No. 85–864). The NDEA was widely viewed as America's response to the launching of Sputnik by the Soviet Union, with its implied threat to America's scientific preeminence. This in turn was followed by enactment of the Higher Education Act of 1965, one of the numerous Great Society initiatives that have had an extraordinarily long reach. Each of these pieces of legislation has evolved but largely remained whole, cumulatively reaching the point at which close to 60 of all undergraduates receive some form of federal assistance. Federal aid represents 69% of all student aid awarded (which includes state, institutional, private, and employer [College Board, 2014]).

This chapter will focus largely on the federal student financial aid programs, which provide the bulk of such funding to students, but veterans' benefits, tax incentives, state, and institutional aid are also extremely important and will be examined as well.

Higher Education Act and the Federal Role

The Higher Education Act of 1965 (HEA; Pub. L. No. 89–329) is the single most important piece of federal legislation impacting community colleges. It is difficult to imagine higher education without it, much as it is now difficult to contemplate retirement in America without Social Security. Some 43% of all credit community college students receive some form of federal aid (Authors' analysis [National Center for Education Statistics, 2014d]).

It is always important to remember that the student aid programs are just that: aid to students. When the HEA was originally being debated in Congress many parties believed that the emerging federal assistance should be provided directly to institutions. In retrospect, the decision to tender the aid in the form of a voucher, to individuals, was a stroke of brilliance. This approach sparked strong political support for the programs, as it emphasized the concept of giving individuals an opportunity to achieve academic and corresponding life success through their ability and effort. It also was advantageous to colleges because it provided the federal government with less justification to become engaged directly in the academic and other activities of colleges—again, student aid was largely about students, not institutions. As discussed in the next section, over time this demarcation has eroded but generally prevailed.

Applying for Federal Aid

Students wishing to receive Title IV aid must complete a Federal Application for Student Financial Aid, better known as the FASFA. Underlying the FASFA are the complex formulae used to evaluate student and family need for financial assistance (though because of their complexity these will not be discussed here).

Despite the obvious importance of ensuring that all students complete the FASFA, a disturbingly high percentage of community college students, far more than one-quarter, fail to do so. A majority of these students are part-time. The oft-cited complexity of the application form, and the required accompanying materials, are no doubt reasons why many students do not apply. However, many students are aware of neither the true costs of attending community college nor the fact that substantial federal is available (Advisory Committee on Student Financial Assistance, 2008). Consequently, it behooves administrators to devote needed resources to ensuring that all students apply for aid. Community college leaders will always want to devote their first—and last—dollar to teaching and related academic activities, but much is lost when their student financial aid offices are not adequately supported. Fortunately, a variety of innovative approaches—including administering aid at the state level, engaging in systematic funding of aid offices, and making greater outreach efforts to high schools—have shown promising results. First Lady Michelle Obama has also made FASFA completion a personal, high-profile priority.

The Pell Grant Program

The Federal Pell Grant Program provides fundamental and far-reaching opportunity for low- and moderate-income students to attend community college. It is the building block upon which all other student financial aid rests.

Pell Grants have been revised repeatedly since their establishment in 1972 as the Basic Educational Opportunity Grant (BEOG) program. Until the 2008–09 award year the size of grants awarded to community college students were limited by links to the cost of attendance and, later, tuition. These statutory restrictions have been eliminated, and community college students are now eligible to receive the same size grants as those attending the most expensive colleges in the nation. This is evidence of the ongoing recognition of the value of community college education.

As with other federal student aid programs, Pell Grants are awarded on the basis of need—the grant that a student receives is calculated by subtracting the student's expected family contribution (EFC) from the maximum grant level. Therefore a student with a zero EFC receives the maximum annual grant, which is largely set by appropriators. Funding and student eligibility for the Pell Grant program was expanded dramatically by a spate of legislation: the College Cost Reduction and Access Act (Pub. L. No. 110–84, 2007), the Higher Education Opportunity Act of 2008 (Pub. L. No. 110–315, 2008), the American Recovery and Reinvestment Act (Pub. L. No. 111–5, 2009), and the Health and Education Reconciliation Act (Pub. L. No. 111–152, 2010).

The impact of these bills, plus ongoing support for the program, was evident in the 2012–13 award year, when Pell Grants reached 3.3 million community college students—37.7% of all community college credit students. (In contrast, in 2003–04 only 23.1 percent of community college students received a federal grant of any kind, including Pell Grants [Authors' analysis; National Center for Education Statistics, 2014d]). Pell Grant awards to community college students amounted to $10.5 billion, 32.8% of all Pell Grant funds. To give some point of reference, this $10.5 billion represents almost 20% of all the revenues received by community colleges in 2012–13 (though not all Pell Grant funds go directly to colleges, since funds can be used for books, transportation, living expenses, and so on). Pell Grant funds awarded to students attending community college increased by 99% in just the three years between FY 2008–09 and FY 2012–13. (This dramatic increase is slightly understated because of changes in the number of colleges classified by ED as community colleges; that is, those for whom the highest degree awarded is the associate's.)

However, the rapid expansion of the Pell Grant program in recent years has created pressing fiscal problems for the program. In a funding environment ruled by overall caps on annual appropriations, the nonincremental expansions mentioned earlier have created extraordinary fiscal pressures on the program, whose program costs in FY 2014 represented 42% of the entire funding of the Department of Education (U.S. Department of Education, 2014a). The program has also been subject to periodic shortfalls (Pell Grants operate like an "entitlement" program, in which anyone qualifying for a given grant receives one, yet the program is funded through annual spending bills, in which a set amount of money is provided), and recent shortfalls have led to limitations on program eligibility that had a particularly negative impact on community college students. This includes cancellation of the year-round Pell Grant as well as eligibility for Ability-to-Benefit students (that is, those without a high school diploma or General Educational Development diploma). These changes and others that have been contemplated by those interested in curbing program expenditures demonstrate the vulnerability of populations served disproportionately by community colleges at a time when student *success* is being emphasized at least as much as *access*.

The Federal Student Loans Programs and Student Borrowing

As with students in other sectors of higher education, borrowing by community college students continues to increase. In recent years, the increases in the relatively low tuition and fees at community colleges have outstripped the Consumer Price Index; for example, they increased by 18% *after* inflation for the five years ending in 2014-–15 (College Board, 2014a), and median family income continues to decline, making loans a necessary and/or attractive option for many community college students. More than 17% of all community college credit students take out federal loans (National Postsecondary Student Assistance Survey, 2011–12), and 33% of all full-time students borrow (Authors' analysis [National Center for Education Statistics, 2014d]). The federal definition of "cost of attendance," which includes books, transportation, and living expenses, usually allows students to borrow the maximum amount provided by the federal government. This ready access to loan capital has major implications for students and institutions alike.

Fortunately, and unlike the situation in other sectors of higher education, community college students still are able to use grant aid as their primary form of assistance. The number of Pell Grants awarded to community college students is nearly twice that of loans made to them. By contrast, students attending four-year public institutions are almost twice as likely to take out a federal loan as to receive a Pell Grant (Authors' analysis [National Center for Education Statistics, 2014d]).

The primary loan programs accessed by community college students are Stafford Loans. These are both subsidized and unsubsidized; the former type, based on need, carries a lower interest rate than unsubsidized loans, and students are not charged interest while they are enrolled at least half-time and for a six-month grace period following graduation. Parental Loans for Undergraduate Students (PLUS) are another important source of capital, with a higher interest rate. Under current law, dependent undergraduate students generally may borrow a total of $12,000 in their first two years under the two Stafford loan programs, and independent students can borrow $20,000. PLUS loans have a limit of the student's cost of attendance, minus other aid received.

Although community college student borrowing does not reach the sometimes staggering levels accrued in other sectors of higher education (much less that seen for graduate and professional school), managing student debt is a major challenge for students and institutions, and a top concern of policymakers. About 33%

of all community college degree or certificate earners had debt in 2011–12, and they had borrowed, on average, $12,260 (Authors' analysis [National Center for Education Statistics, 2014d]). Forty-one percent of all associate degree recipients had some debt. Helping students manage this debt is an increasing challenge for institutions.

Community college loan default rates are on the rise. The federal government now uses a three-year cohort default rate measure (essentially, the window of measured defaults is at most three years), and the most recent official default rate (FY 2011) for two- to three-year public institutions was 20.6%. Although the causes of student defaults are complex, and community colleges themselves currently have few tools to limit student borrowing, there is no avoiding the fact that this level of default—more than one out of five borrowers—is simply unacceptable. Campuses, the government, and the government's loan servicers are intensively focused on ways to reduce these defaults, but the underlying problem remains. Community college advocates in Washington continue to seek policies that would place additional limits on student borrowing, particularly by those who are less well prepared for higher education, as there is, understandably, a high correlation between dropping out and nonrepayment of loans.

A new emphasis on Income-Based Repayment (IBR), which has been championed by the Obama administration, does hold promise for getting at the heart of defaults by creating a repayment structure in which default basically cannot occur. As the name implies, IBR links a student's monthly loan payments to their resources at hand. After 20 years of repayment, the balance of the loan is forgiven. This policy has major implications for the financing of higher education—it has been argued that it facilitates overborrowing and runs the risk of hampering the ability of college graduates to use their incomes for supporting their families and other purposes—but the stark financial realities of the cost of college attendance probably ensure that the use of IBR will continue to expand.

Campus-Based Student Aid Programs

An important component of federal student aid is the three "campus-based" programs: Federal Work-Study, Supplemental Educational Opportunity Grants (SEOG), and Perkins Loans. They are referred to as "campus-based" because funds are allocated by formula to institutions, which then award them to qualifying students. Campuses have some flexibility in determining who receives awards; therefore they become critical components of many students' overall financial package, particularly at higher-priced institutions. Of community college students, 4.9% receive campus-based aid (Authors' analysis [National Center for Education Statistics, 2014d]).

Very briefly, Federal Work-Study gives students a chance to help finance their education through employment either by their institution; by a federal, state, or local public agency or private non-profit organization; or by a private or for-profit organization. Ideally, these opportunities are integrated into the student's course of studies, and 7% of the funds must be awarded for community service purposes.

The SEOG program augments Pell Grants and provides up to $4,000 annually. Institutions must give first priority for awards to students with demonstrated "exceptional need" (students with the lowest EFCs at the institution) who are also Pell Grant recipients. Perkins Loans are low-interest loans that were established before the major federal loan programs. Community colleges have little involvement with this program.

Both inadequate funding and the allocation formulas limit the impact of the campus-based programs for community college students. Institutions that entered the programs in their early years are guaranteed funding, and community colleges did not aggressively pursue these funds at that time. Dramatically increased enrollments have brought some additional funds to campuses, but only in relatively small amounts, because of static appropriations. Also, despite strong political support for the programs from independent colleges among others, Congressional appropriators have favored Pell Grants over the campus-based programs.

Nevertheless, community colleges awarded $160.7 million in SEOG funds in 2011–12 (U.S. Department of Education, 2014b), 16.6% of all funds, and $153.1 million, 13.0% in Federal Work-Study funds, so the funding remains a critical component at many institutions.

Federal Tax Incentives for Higher Education Attendance

Federal higher education tax provisions do not receive the same attention as the major federal student financial aid programs, but they remain an extremely important source of financing. The most important item is the American Opportunity Tax Credit (AOTC), which was created out of the Hope Scholarship Tax Credit in the 2009 American Recovery and Reinvestment Act (Pub. L. No. 111–5 [2009]). In 2014 more than 9 million undergraduate students, about half of all, are projected to receive an AOTC. Aggregate AOTC funding was $21 billion in 2012 (Consortium on Higher Education Tax Reform, 2013), more than 60% of the cost of the Pell Grant program. Unfortunately, sector breakouts, and so the community college student receipt of these funds, are not available.

The AOTC provides up to $2,500 each year for four years, covering tuition and fees and required course materials. It is 40% refundable, which helps deliver assistance to low-income students who do not have a tax liability. However, and most unfortunately for community college students, the credit is structured such that Pell Grant recipients often do not qualify for the credit, as it can be claimed only after any nontaxable grant funds are subtracted from eligible expenses.

Many community college students, particularly noncredit students, qualify for the Lifetime Learning Credit and take advantage of it. The credit covers 20% of qualified tuition expenses. Large numbers of community college students also benefit from Section 127 of the Internal Revenue Code, which allows individuals to receive up to $5,250 of educational assistance from their employers tax-free.

Despite this, the tax provisions tend to be used by a relatively low proportion of community college students. First, the incentives are both complicated and numerous. The Government Accountability Office has found that there were "sub-optimal" filing outcomes in a shockingly high number of instances, and that in 2009 14% of filers (1.5 million of almost 11 million eligible returns) failed to claim a credit or deduction for which they appear to be eligible (Government Accountability Office [GAO], 2012). There is broad consensus that the higher education tax incentives, only some of which are mentioned here, need to be streamlined and simplified. Another factor that limits the visibility of these tax benefits is that colleges are not directly involved in delivering the assistance to students, though substantial reporting requirements accompany the provisions. Finally, and perhaps most important, tax code benefits are delivered to students mainly *after* they have incurred education expenses, which limits their utility for those with extremely limited incomes. A number of analysts have looked at ways to deliver AOTC benefits in advance of students' incurring educational expenses, but this change would carry with it great administrative complexity.

Veterans' Benefits

Community colleges have a long and proud history of serving the veteran population. The propensity of veterans to enroll in their local community college is natural, given their experiences and the common predilection to return home to begin a new phase of life. This historic engagement has been given greater, impetus and urgency through the swelling numbers of separated service members enrolling in college as the military conflicts in Afghanistan and Iraq have wound down.

Federal veterans education benefits are relatively generous. Under the Post-9/11 GI Bill, qualifying veterans have 100% of their public college tuition and fees paid for up to 36 months. A monthly housing allowance is provided, as is up to $1,000 per year to cover books. This legislation accounts for 56% of all VA educational benefits (Government Accountability Office, 2013). The Montgomery GI Bill-Active Duty program covers tuition for active duty service members, also for 36 months. In this context, distance education is a common means of delivery. Community colleges are learning to be savvier in providing course offerings for this population; for-profit institutions have certainly taken the lead.

Substantial numbers of community college student have accessed these benefits. The average annual benefit for community college students is $5,600 (including benefits provided to dependents). However, public institutions receive just 38% of these benefits, only a shade more than for-profit institutions.

Administration of programs serving veterans as well as defense personnel has often been an uneasy task for colleges. The VA and DOD have tended to promulgate regulations and administrative processes that do not dovetail neatly with those guiding the Title IV student aid programs. Administrators at these agencies also have less familiarity with campus practices, making for clumsy regulatory requirements. This problem has been compounded by substantial public and Congressional concern over for-profit institutions' aggressive recruiting practices with this population. Indeed, while for-profit institutions enroll approximately 12% of all the students in higher education, their students receive 34% of all the VA benefits (Government Accountability Office, 2013). The public is understandably concerned about potential manipulation of this population, and community colleges have borne some of the administrative brunt of this concern.

State Student Financial Assistance

States continue to provide substantial direct student financial assistance to community college students. Overall, the students received $1.592 billion in grant aid in award year 2011–12 (Authors' analysis [National Center for Education Statistics, 2014d]), which was 18% of the total awarded.

State student financial aid policies, however, are all over the map; some states provide robust support for all students, whereas in other places support is much less generous and the terms and conditions of that aid are unfavorable to community college students. States are now awarding approximately one-third of their student aid in the form of merit aid, although this proportion has recently decreased, albeit slightly. Numerous policy analysts have criticized merit aid because it runs counter to the long-held tenet that large government student financial aid should be need-based. (Substantial research continues on the impact of merit-based aid on college success.) In any case, merit-based aid programs tend to be less favorable to community college students because of their relative lack of academic preparation and achievement compared to students in other sectors.

State student aid is often structured in ways that work against community college students, including limiting funding to full-time students. Some states simply stop providing any aid to students once a year's annual funding for grants has been exhausted, and this practice can work against community college students, who frequently apply for aid late in the enrollment process. In addition, private non-profit colleges have been very effective in securing grant aid for their students; indeed, they receive more in state student financial assistance than community college students—a reflection, in part, of their higher tuitions, but also of their political clout.

Institutional Aid

A small but in many cases important component of community college student aid is institutional assistance—that is, aid awarded, and therefore controlled, by the college. The advantage of this form of aid is obvious, in providing maximum flexibility for institutions to serve particular populations or individual students who may have particular financial needs or be particularly meritorious. As community colleges become more aggressive and savvy in their fund-raising efforts, colleges have more of this aid to distribute, reaching $1.166 billion in 2011–12 (Authors' analysis [National Center for Education Statistics, 2014d]), roughly one-tenth of Pell Grant funding. It is just 4% of all institutional aid (more than two-thirds is awarded at private non-profit colleges) but can be expected to grow over time, as financial pressures on students increase and community college fundraising grows savvier.

Federal Student Aid, Institutional Policy, and Administrative Costs

Lastly, any discussion of student aid, particularly federal student aid, needs to examine its broader campus impact and institutional context. The reality is that, due to their nature and importance, the student aid programs influence the structure and operations of a variety of campus activities, including academic programs. This dynamic has a "tail wagging the dog" aspect because, at least in concept, the Title IV student aid programs are designed to simply provide financing to students. In any case, the government's administration of the student aid programs, with more than 7,000 participating institutions, currently entails an accompanying battery of requirements. These requirements constrain institutions and add substantial cost to their operations.

Key from the administrator's point of view is the fact that the Title IV regulations extend well beyond the student financial aid office. In fact, virtually all administrative activities of a college are responsible for ensuring compliance, to some extent. This includes the registrar's office, student affairs, business office, campus security, institutional research, athletic department, bookstore, counseling services, and others. Ensuring that each of these campus entities stays abreast of complex and often fluctuating federal requirements is an ongoing challenge.

Traditionally and by statute, the federal government does not become involved in campus academic affairs. Despite periodic bouts between college lobbyists and both Congress and the executive branch, this demarcation, while moving in the direction of government regulation over time, has generally been observed, or at least potential perceived encroachments on it are subject to heated debate. These include a federal regulatory definition of credit hour, mandated state procedures for the licensure of distance education programs, and the accreditation process. But the federal government retains all the leverage—it can basically require a campus to do *anything* as a condition of participation in the student aid programs.

Without question, the programmatic eligibility requirements for federal student aid (as opposed to those for students) shape the structure of academic programs, particularly in regard to length and, to some extent, how academic credit is awarded. And although Congress and regulators are attempting to adapt the student aid programs to changing modes of delivery, assessment, and course design, these efforts clearly lag institutional and state innovations.

The overt cost of compliance with federal regulations, particularly in the student aid area, continues to receive warranted attention. In late 2013, four U.S. senators (Lamar Alexander [R-TN], Barbara Mikulski [D-MD], Michael Bennet [D-CO], and Richard Burr [R-NC]) established a high-profile Task Force on Government Regulation of Higher Education to examine ways to reduce the expenditures of campuses required for complying with student aid regulations. This effort has been a cooperative effort with all of higher education and shows real promise.

Community colleges are uniquely challenged by federal regulations. It's basically a matter of money. The institutions strain to identify the resources needed to ensure compliance with byzantine, ever-fluctuating federal rules. Quite naturally, the first impulse of institutional leaders is to put additional resources into areas, usually teaching, that more directly benefit students, rather than devoting dollars to administration of federal student aid. But given the liabilities that noncompliance can bring, rigorous attention to the regulatory labyrinth is mandatory. Student financial aid officers have extremely difficult and important jobs to do, and they seldom receive the recognition and compensation that might be expected to accompany them.

Conclusions

Student financial aid is an essential source of support for community college students—the colleges are almost inconceivable without it. This support comes primarily from the federal government, but there are other important sources. The student aid programs have evolved over time and continue to evolve, but their basic feature of enabling students to meet college expenses also continues and is not expected to change in this fundamental respect.

Questions

1. How can institutions ensure that all eligible students receive student financial aid and other benefits?

2. How can the Pell Grant program remain optimally vital for community college students?

3. What can colleges do to ensure that students borrow only needed funds?

4. What role might merit aid play in encouraging community college students to come to school better prepared?

5. How can community colleges better serve veterans, who often have generous federal support?

6. What are the primary administrative obligations that accompany receipt of student financial aid?

Chapter Six

Infrastructure and Funding Issues

Infrastructure needs, expenditures, and financing are of enormous consequence for community college leaders. New or improved buildings can jump-start a campus or serve as a profound legacy, or both. Managing campus facilities needs, with the stakes so high for institutional health, deserves special focus. This is particularly the case because community colleges continue to struggle to receive a reasonable share of public funding for infrastructure.

In the publication *Policy Matters*, distributed by the American Association of State Colleges and Universities (Hurley & Harnish, 2014), the authors indicated that two of the most important issues for the coming year were state capital outlay and deferred maintenance for educational facilities. The authors of this annual policy brief stated:

> With states' fiscal pictures improving markedly in the aftermath of the Great Recession, state policymakers will consider bills designed to address capital outlay and deferred maintenance needs of community colleges and public universities. Aging campus facilities and diminished state monies due to the economic downturn has led to pent-up demand for significant state investment in campus construction needs. While so-called "deferred maintenance" needs are often not obvious to the casual observer, the costs associated with these critical

upgrades are significant and increase with each passing year. The need for state monies for campus infrastructure improvement will vary for items including but not limited to enhancing classroom capacity; developing 21st century laboratories and research facilities; and updating, retrofitting or replacing critical campus infrastructure such as roofs, power plant-affiliated equipment, and water and electrical substructures. The higher education community, along with the construction and labor lobbies, will advocate for state funding capital outlay funding measures during this year's legislative sessions. In some states, taxpayer investment in campus construction and infrastructure improvement will be determined by taxpayers themselves at the ballot box via referendums that will take place concurrent with the November midterm elections. [p. 4]

The Concern for Educational Facilities

The buildings and grounds of a community college reflect that school's commitment to the educational experience for students, faculty, and the community at large. Modern architecture, renovated and modernized older buildings, outstanding athletic complexes, beautiful landscaping, and modern signage are what is most frequently seen and remembered by students, patrons, visitors, neighbors, and individuals passing by. These appearances do help define the institution and provide its tone and setting.

The facilities are also long-term assets of the institution, but building them entails substantial capital costs. Total college and university construction completed in 2013 totaled $10.9 billion. Of that amount, 68%, or $7.5 billion, was spent on new construction. The remaining $3.4 billion went to expansion of existing buildings or to major repair and renovation of others. It was expected that colleges and universities would spend $10.6 billion on construction starts in 2014 (Abramson, 2014).

There are also major costs associated with maintenance and improvement. In addition, there are the costs of operating the facility—climate control, light, computer services, janitorial services, and so on. Higher education institutions paid from $4.72 per gross square foot (GSF) of facility space in 2007 to operate their facilities. This was a 9.4% increase over five years. In many parts of the country these cost increases were not matched by corresponding funding increases; this resulted in staff downsizing and reductions in maintenance and improvements (Kadamus, 2013).

Energy Conservation

An additional concern at community colleges involves energy conservation and the cost of fossil fuels. As part of the "Green Campus" movement, many colleges have made improvements to their infrastructure to reduce their dependency on these fuels, such as adding wind generators and electric monitoring equipment for temperature and lighting control, and the construction of green buildings following the Leadership in Energy & Environmental Design (LEED) requirements. LEED is a green building certification program that gives credit for best practices meeting guidelines for the use of energy-efficient building strategies. Other innovative projects, such as green cafeteria operations to reduce the use of plastic utensils and reduce or eliminate the costs of washing tons of dishes with hot water, have reduced energy consumption on campuses across the country by approximately 14%. With an estimated reduction in energy costs of $0.30 per GSF (from $2.54 per GSF in 2009 to $2.24 per GSF in 2012) for the estimated 140 million GSF of campus buildings built from 2009 to 2012, the resulting saving would exceed $42 million (Kadamus, 2014). Efforts of this nature are clearly the wave of the future.

Safety

Safety is another critical concern for all educational institutions, and colleges are responsible for providing a safe learning environment. There is broad awareness of mass school shootings.

The first that captured national attention was the Texas Tower Massacre at the University of Texas, Austin, in August 1966; this tragedy and the shootings at Columbine High School in Colorado in April 1999, Virginia Tech in April 2007, and Sandy Hook Elementary School in Connecticut in December 2012 are some of the worst in terms of lives lost. However, these incidents are but a few of the totality of school, community college, and university violence. In 2013 there were 31 reported shooting incidents on educational campuses across the country. Twenty shootings were reported in elementary and secondary schools, 5 at community and technical colleges, and 6 at universities. There were 26 deaths and 35 injuries. As this book went to press, in November 2014 in Marysville, Washington, a high school shooting left the shooter and four others dead, and at Florida State University in Tallahassee, Florida, three students were wounded in a library shooting, and the shooter was killed by campus security.

In the twentieth century and through 2005, 2 to 3 shooting incidents were reported each year. In 2006 and 2009 there were 7 reported each year; in 2008 and again in 2011 there were 9. In 2012 there were 14 reports; in 2013, 31 reports; and during the first 4 months of 2014, 34 reported incidents. Proper planning and improvement for facilities and grounds are important factors to consider in preventing incidents. Colleges throughout the United States have initiated safety and security plans for their campus and its buildings and grounds. Safe walkways, lighting, and security devices for parking areas and dormitories, and safety awareness programs for students, faculty, and staff are but a few of the initiatives being taken to increase safety on our college campuses. All of this comes at a cost.

Unfortunately, dangers include more than incidents of violence. Potential natural and man-made disasters must be considered on every campus. In many Western states, colleges must be prepared for forest fires, earthquakes, avalanches, and mudslides. Flooding and tornadoes are an issue for the Great Plains, the Midwest, and parts of the East and South, and hurricane preparedness is a crucial concern along many of our coastal regions. Access to and egress from dormitories and other buildings in the event of a fire are a concern everywhere. Every aspect of preparedness and the safety of all individuals on campus involves facilities.

This is especially important when renovating an existing building or planning new construction. Issues to be addressed include wind load calculations for roofs in high wind and hurricane areas, properly clearing landscaping and developing land use plans to prevent forest fires and mudslides, and incorporating new and innovative structural components and fire detection and suppression technology in a new structure, which can reduce damage and injury from fires and earthquakes.

Problems with Community College and Higher Education Facilities

There are five major categories of problems with college facilities: age, condition, adequacy, deferred maintenance, and funding.

Age

It has often been reported that the age of a campus building is the best indicator of current or future facility needs. For the large multidimensional campus or group of campuses, looking at the age of facilities can help guide the institution in determining priorities. To understand the effect of age, many authorities use the Five Stages of Age for Educational Facilities. These rough benchmarks have proven to have ongoing utility.

Stage 1

Stage 1 describes a building for the first 20 years of its existence. During this time period there is minimal need for maintenance or change. The building will in all likelihood more than adequately meet the goals and expectations of the purpose for which it was designed and built. The classroom building will function properly to help deliver contemporary instruction, and the dormitory will support student life in a modern and safe environment.

Stage 2

Stage 2 describes buildings aged 20 to 30 years. These structures begin to need capital equipment replacement. Building systems like windows, doors, and roofs; heating, ventilation, and air conditioning (HVAC) units; and basic electrical and plumbing fixtures are becoming worn out from the effects of the external environment—the weather—as well as routine use.

Maintenance and, eventually, replacement are essential. Caulking doors and windows, painting, and making repairs to roofs and heating and air conditioning systems all can update the appearance and extend the useful life of the building.

Stage 3

Stage 3 occurs when buildings are 30 to 40 years old. Absent complete and thorough preventive maintenance, there will be the beginnings of total systems failure. Leaking roofs will allow water to infiltrate the walls and other structures, resulting in structural deterioration and mold generation that can result in the need to close the structure while removal and repairs are made. Poorly maintained windows and doors allow outside air infiltration that can stress HVAC systems, often rendering them useless. Boilers and other plumbing fixtures can break, electrical systems can fail, and the facilities generally begin failing to fulfill the purpose for which they were designed and built—whether that be instruction, research, administration, service, or student living.

Stage 4

During the time period 40 to 50 years after initial construction— known as Stage 4—the deterioration process has continued and systems show significant signs of failure. Even with the most advanced preventive maintenance, replacement of failing systems or total renovation of the facility is often the most feasible option.

Stage 5

Stage 5 describes a building at the end of its useful life, greater than 50 years old. Several questions enter the discussion of whether to renovate or replace the building. Is the building capable of maintaining its original purpose? Can the building be repurposed to meet new and expanding campus needs? Is the building of historical or social value to the college and its surrounding community or state? What are the relative costs of renovation compared to new construction?

A college building boom occurred in the 1960s and early 1970s. This was a reaction to the flood of post-war baby boomers entering postsecondary education after high school. In addition, there was a major push from the federal government for new and expanded research and development facilities for science and math and agriculture. Today, despite the building of many new facilities on college campuses, many buildings are also at or past the 50-year mark. A 2013 study reported that an estimated 58% of all college space is more than 25 years old. In addition, it has been noted that the amount of space more than 50 years old grew from 18% in 2007 to 22% in 2012 (Kadamus, 2013). The nagging problem remains that within the next 10 to 15 years, a majority of these facilities will reach the end of their useful life—50 years. Laboratories, dormitories, sports complexes, and teaching classrooms may no longer be appropriate for modern, contemporary applications.

Condition

Campus leaders and board members are constantly asking about the condition of their buildings—after all, it's a key asset. Several metrics are used to assess the condition of an educational facility or group of facilities, in addition to the benchmarks outlined earlier. Some campus administrators and facility managers use an age profile whereby the oldest buildings are assumed to need the most help. Others use a "renovation age" concept that resets the life-cycle age of a given building following renovation or other capital improvements (Kadamus, 2013). The U.S. Department of the Interior (DOI) uses a facility condition index (FCI) to classify their facilities throughout the United States. The DOI policy manual for facilities states:

> Articulating asset condition enables bureau managers to address a major asset management question, "What is the condition of my portfolio?" The relative condition of owned assets is measured using the FCI which is an accepted industry metric for determining the condition of assets. FCI is used to measure the condition of all buildings and structures in the DOI real property portfolio that is reported into the government-wide Federal Real Property Profile (FRPP). Facility Condition Index is calculated for assets by dividing the cost of Deferred Maintenance by the Current Replacement Value. The result of this formula is a value that is never less than zero and never greater than 1.0. An asset with an FCI of 0 is in excellent condition and an asset with a rating of 1.0 is in very poor condition. [Department of the Interior, Department of the Interior, DOI, 2008, p. 16]

Another index used to track the condition of campus facilities is the replacement cost index (RCI). First developed and reported in the 1980s, the RCI calculations looked at public pre-K to high school facilities initially in rural and small school districts throughout the United States (Honeyman, Wood, Thompson, & Stewart, 1988). These original studies were intended to compare a measure of the condition of school buildings in different size school districts with different tax bases and district wealth. Two formulas were developed. RCI_1 takes the original cost of the building, OC, adds the total value of all major/capital improvements to that building, I_1 to I_N, and divides this amount by the building's estimated current replacement cost, CRC. The formula is given as:

$$RCI_1 = \frac{OC + (I_1 + I_2 \ldots I_N)}{CRC}$$

The second formula, RCI_2, factors in the level of deferred maintenance (LDM) accumulated during the life of the building. This formula articulates the effect of deferred maintenance on the building by indicating the change in the RCI because maintenance had been deferred:

$$RCI_2 = \frac{OC + (I_1 + I_2 \ldots I_N)}{CRC + LDM}$$

Both the RCI_1 and the RCI_2 will have a value between 0 and 1. The higher the value, presumably, the better the condition of the building. For example, a building originally built for $1 million has an estimated replacement cost of $10 million. With no improvements made to the building, the RCI_1 is 0.10. If the same building had $3 million in renovations and upgrades over its useful life the RCI_1 would be 0.40. For this building, if it also had a level of deferred maintenance, possibly for a new roof, windows and doors, or new HVAC system at $1 million, the RCI_2 drops to 0.09. Each of these values indicates a possible level of the condition of the building. In our example, if these were three different buildings with the values of 0.09, 0.10, and 0.40, the building with the 0.09 value (no improvements over time and a high level of deferred maintenance) should be the first evaluated for repair, renovation, or replacement.

Adequacy

The concept of building adequacy relates to whether the building is adequate for its designated purpose; for example, are there enough classrooms with the appropriate design, specialized equipment, and technology to meet the needs of the instructional programs being offered? Are the libraries, music and arts centers, athletic facilities, laboratories, and parking areas adequate for the needs of the community, faculty, staff, and students? Are there enough rooms, and are dormitories modern and conducive to healthy and safe living? Are all the buildings adequate and accessible for individuals with disabilities, as mandated by the Individuals with Disabilities Education Act (IDEA)? Do the buildings and grounds meet all local, state, and federal guidelines for safety defined by local and state building codes and by the Occupational Safety and Health Administration (OSHA)? The answers to these and other questions will guide the decision whether to renovate or rebuild a given building.

Deferred Maintenance

The concept of deferred maintenance refers to the number and scope of repairs that are realized and budgeted for but never actually undertaken. These projects become part of an institutional facilities backlog. As reported in the 2013 *The State of Facilities in Higher Education*:

> From 2007 to 2012 project backlogs (on higher education campuses across the country) have increased by 15%. Furthermore, the rate of increase in the backlog is accelerating from 2010 to 2012, a direct result of aging campuses and reduced capital investment. At the current rate, overall project backlogs will hit $100/GSF (Gross Square Footage) by 2015 and maybe sooner. Most facility experts cite the threshold of a $100/GSF backlog as a level where facility operations can no longer be proactive because so many building components are breaking; reactive work orders take up all of their staff time. [Kadamus, 2013, p. 17]

The institutional backlog is detailed by the component parts of all buildings in each of the five stages described here. By listing the buildings and their maintenance/renovation and repair needs according to the expected useful life of the components of each building, the backlog can indicate those buildings are most in need of immediate help.

The Governmental Accounting Standards Board (GASB) describes the estimated useful life of the component systems of the building such that:

> The purpose of building component depreciation is to more accurately measure the annual depreciation of multi-functional academic buildings with significant investments in fixed equipment and infrastructure. Buildings are made up of components with each component having its own useful life. Depreciation is more accurately measured when based on the useful life of each component. [Governmental Accounting Standards Board, 2006, p. 1.]

As part of this GASB document the authors indicated the useful life of college building components to be used in the state of Oregon. These values ranged from 50 years for most of the building's shell, exterior walls, and support structures to 10 years for computer and office equipment and information technology (IT) systems (see Table 6.1).

The analysis of these components can be employed to determine levels of deferred maintenance and therefore used in the RCI_2 calculation. For example, an academic building 27 years old would be in need of repair/maintenance for all aspects of the structure except the building shell. However, if all fixed equipment had been replaced 5 years previously, these components would

Table 6.1.   Useful Life of Building Components

General Building Components	Building Component	Estimated Useful Life (in years)
Building Shell		
	Site Preparation	50
	Foundation	50
	Steel Frame	50
	Construction Exterior	50
	Floor Structure	50
	Walls—Exterior	50
	Roof Structure	50
Building Finishes		
	Roof Cover	20
	Construction Interior	20
	Floor Cover	20
Building Services Systems		
	Electric	23
	Heating, Ventilation, and AC	23
	Plumbing	23
	Fire Protection	23
	Elevators	23
Fixed Equipment		
	Fixed Equipment 20 year	20
	Fixed Equipment 15 year	15
	Fixed Equipment 10 year	10
	IT and Network Infrastructure	10

Source: Adapted from the General Accounting Standards Board (2006).

not be included in the estimated cost to bring the building up to currency. By estimating and summing the costs of these component improvements, an approximation of the total deferred maintenance level can be used for the RC_2 calculation for that building. When all buildings in the campus or institutional portfolio are presented in such a manner, those buildings with the lowest RCI_2

(with the greatest need and of most immediate concern) can be targeted for improvement.

Funding Facility Needs

In 2008 the American Association of Community Colleges issued a report titled *Funding Issues in U.S. Community Colleges: Findings from a 2007 Survey of National State Directors of Community Colleges* (Katsinas, Tollefson, & Reamey, 2008). The authors note that 33 states indicated they had experienced either an increase or a significant increase in their levels of deferred maintenance since fiscal year 2002. Forty-four states reported science labs as their most pressing space need, 34 states reported the need for academic classroom space, 20 states reported the need for computer labs, and 16 states reported needing all three (Katsinas, Tollefson, & Reamey, 2008).

How were college leaders hoping to pay for these facilities? In 2008, 37 states reported that state-issued bond proceeds (which required a statewide referendum) were available for community college construction efforts. Thirty-four states allowed local colleges to issue bonds. Twenty-seven states provided funding via special legislative appropriation, and 20 states provided funds from the state's general fund. Fifteen states allowed the use of local government-issued bond proceeds to help community college construction needs (Katsinas, Tollefson, & Reamey, 2008).

What are bonds? Just as individuals can borrow money for a house or car, governments have the means of borrowing money for large-scale projects that they presently need but cannot afford to pay out of annual operating funds. Bonds are to state and local government agencies (the issuers) what a mortgage is to individuals. Investors in bonds expect a return from the issuers for the use of their money. This return is in the form of interest (known as the coupon) to be paid by the issuer within a determined length of time (the maturity date).

There are many types of bonds used in financial transactions in the United States and abroad. "Municipal bond" describes a bond issued by states, cities, local government, and educational entities. These bonds are primarily used to address infrastructure needs. The key feature of these bonds is that the investor is usually exempt from federal taxes, and in most states the revenue earned by the investor is exempt from state and local taxes as well. When the tax consequences of the bond issue are considered, the tax break to the investor and the pronounced security of the governmental agency result in lower coupon rates. There are two basic types of tax-exempt municipal bonds—general obligation bonds and revenue bonds. For general obligation bonds, whatever level of government issues the bond is responsible for paying the principal and interest to investors. These payments are provided through the agency's ability to tax. For educational issuers, the payment of bond obligations is usually funded by increases in local property tax levies or, in many locations, additional local-option sales tax revenue. Revenue bonds are also issued primarily to fund infrastructure projects. The difference is that the principal and interest are paid from fees for services from the project built by the bonds. These projects include water and sewage treatment facilities, toll roads, bridges, airports, hospitals, and subsidized housing. It is important to note that the process of initiating, selling, and managing a bond issue is tightly controlled in state statute and federal Internal Revenue Service rules, regulations, and laws. Usually the voters in the municipality that is responsible for repaying the debt must approve these bonds in a public referendum.

In 1992, Miami Dade Community College in Florida issued one of the first billion-dollar bond offerings for a community college. In 2008, for the Los Angeles Community College District, local taxpayers passed a $3.5 billion bond referendum. At the same time, the L.A. Unified Public School District had local property owners pass a $7.0 billion bond referendum for public school needs (Blume, 2008).

What Is Coming in College Construction?

It has been reported that the private sector is powering a new wave of public school, college, and university infrastructure construction (Jackson, 2013). Public-private partnerships have been in existence in one form or another for more than 200 years (National Council for Public-Private Partnerships, 2012a). These partnerships take different forms. Outsourcing is one form of a partnership. Many colleges outsource landscaping, custodial, IT, and maintenance operations to private companies specializing in the appropriate field. This form of partnership allows colleges to budget for whatever services are needed without employing and training individuals to perform these duties.

Another form of partnership is referred to as P3—a true public-private partnership. P3 agreements are defined as follows:

> A Public-Private Partnership (PPP) is a contractual arrangement between a public agency (federal, state or local) and a private sector entity. Through this agreement, the skills and assets of each sector (public and private) are shared in delivering a service or facility for the use of the general public. In addition to the sharing of resources, each party shares in the risks and rewards potential in the delivery of the service and/or facility. [National Council for Public-Private Partnerships, 2012b]

P3 agreements continue to grow in the United States because organizations are seeing how successful they can be. Examples from transportation, bridge and toll highway construction, environmental concerns, power and water authorities, and K–12 public schools abound. In almost every instance the public sector is seeing savings in taxpayer money, higher quality, and more efficient construction. Colleges and universities are seeing the benefits as well. New dormitories, classroom buildings, and athletic facilities are being developed using the P3 model. A college in New Jersey is working with a solar energy company to reroof several of their campus buildings and add solar energy—electricity—that they will purchase from their partner. Recently a small college in Pennsylvania contracted with a developer to build small restaurants, shops, and a student-housing complex on land not being used by the college. Student fees for the housing and rent from the businesses occupying the site will help the partners recoup their investment.

As colleges throughout the country face declining resources from state and local sources, budget reductions have forced hiring freezes and reductions in many capital expenditures needed to repair or replace facilities on their campuses. Many of these same colleges are seeing substantial growth in their student enrollment numbers. As Bernstein reports in a paper for the National Association of College and University Business Officials (NACUBO) (2006):

> Public-private partnerships can offer advantages to both sides. For student housing developers, these arrangements can result in a mitigation of project-related risk, much of which is minimized by the favorable location of student residential projects. PPP's also can provide developers with access to otherwise unobtainable locations, which can offer better risk-adjusted returns over the long run. When institutions are simply seeking to tap the private sector's expertise, the developer may not be required to put any equity at risk, but will instead earn a fee for providing development services.

For colleges and universities, PPP's can substantially reduce a project's impact on debt capacity. As of this writing, it is this particular benefit that is largely driving administrators to explore these partnerships. Other college and university benefits include expedited development timelines, reduced construction costs, and the opportunity to follow the latest trends in student housing design (Bernstein, 2014, p. 8).

Conclusion

This chapter examined community colleges' educational facilities and the challenges that may be associated with maintaining facilities. It closed with a consideration of identifying facility needs and the future of approaches to college construction and renovation.

Questions

1. What is the condition of all or at least some of the buildings in your institution's facility portfolio? Estimate the replacement cost indices for those facilities. Considering the adequacy of each facility and the future needs of the campus, compare the results and make recommendations for future actions.

2. Investigate your state's rules, regulations, and statutes concerning the building of college facilities. Describe the steps necessary to construct a building on your campus.

3. Investigate the rules, regulations, and statutes that govern public-private partnerships in your state.

4. Describe a possible partnership that would benefit your institution.

Part Two

Expending Fiscal Resources

Chapter Seven

Institutional Expenditures

While revenues are obviously critical to an institution, their deployment is equally critical. Institutional objectives are realized through expenditures, and using revenues well earns trust from those providing them and underscores effective leadership.

All too often, a college's operations and attendant expenditures are misunderstood by outside observers and at worst stir the ire of critics of higher education. We live in a technology-rich world that requires the use of state-of-the-art equipment, infrastructure, and related information resources to effectively educate students. Sadly, the standard is not always maintained. This chapter focuses on aggregate expenditures, then examines the various expenditure categories, and then looks at their trends. The chapter closes with an examination of budgeting. All of these expenditures feed into colleges' ongoing work to increase educational attainment.

Community College Expenditures

Nationally, community college expenditures totaled $54.0 billion in 2011–12, the most recent year for which data are available. They are presented in Table 7.1. This table serves as the foundation for this examination of community college expenditures; each section will examine each of the various expenditure categories.

Education and General Funds

College expenditures traditionally have a subset, Education and General (E&G) funds. These expenditures are most directly related

Table 7.1.   Community College Expenditures, by Category: 2011–2012

Expenditure Category	Amount (in thousands)	Percent of Total	Amount per Student
Total expenditures	$54,030,554	100.0%	$12,817
E&G subtotal	$48,050,998	89%	$11,398
Instruction (total)	$18,660,082	34.5%	$4,426
Research	$20,281	0.0%	$5
Public service	$759,781	1.4%	$180
Academic support	$3,649,257	6.8%	$866
Student services	$4,526,015	8.4%	$1,074
Institutional support	$6,714,618	12.4%	$1,593
Operation and maintenance of plant	$4,475,080	8.3%	$1,062
Depreciation	$2,364,242	4.4%	$561
Scholarships and fellowships	$6,881,643	12.7%	$1,632
Non-E&G	$5,979,556	11%	$1,418
Auxiliary enterprises	$2,371,079	4.4%	$562
Hospitals	$0	0.0%	$0
Independent operations	$0	0.0%	$0
Interest	$1,358,824	2.5%	$322
Other	$2,249,654	4.2%	$534

Source: Adapted from Snyder and Dillow (2014).

to instruction and therefore are the most researched and debated by policymakers.

In 2011–2012, E&G funds accounted for 89% of all expenditures at community colleges nationally. The following discussion examines what is included in each category. All quotations are from the National Center for Education Statistics (2013a); no page numbers were provided.

Instruction

In 2011–2012, community colleges spent $18.7 billion on instruction, accounting for 34.5% of total expenditures. For this category of expenditures, institutions were instructed to report as follows: "Expenses of the colleges, schools, departments, and other instructional divisions of the institution and expenses for departmental research and public service that are not separately budgeted should be included in this classification. Include expenses for both credit and noncredit activities. Exclude expenses for academic administration where the primary function is administration (e.g., academic deans) ... The instruction category includes academic instruction, occupational and vocational instruction, community education, preparatory and adult basic education, and remedial and tutorial instruction conducted by the teaching faculty for the institution's students."

Table 7.2 provides an overview of the faculty composition at community colleges in the fall 2012 term; 53.3% were either tenured or on the tenure track, with another 51,512 working under some form of contract with the college.

Faculty who are on the tenure track have the potential to earn significantly more than those who are not. On average, a professor on 9- to 10-month contract makes $69,671 a year, whereas a lecturer makes $49,591. These data vary by state (Table 7.3), from a low of $47,276 for a professor in Oklahoma to $94,600 for a professor in Alaska, for example.

Table 7.2.   Faculty Composition of Community Colleges: Fall 2012

Faculty Status (All ranks)	Total	Mean	Median
With faculty status, total	110,379	119	90
Tenured	45,143	82	62
Tenure track	13,724	26	18
No tenure system	51,512	67	36
Multiyear contract	4,313	69	30
Annual contract	40,434	61	30
Less-than-annual contract	6,765	31	8
Without faculty status	1,558	21	5

Source: Authors' analysis of National Center for Education Statistics (2014c).

Table 7.3. Average Salary for Faculty on 9- or 10-Month Contracts, by Faculty Status and State: 2011–2012

State	No. Colleges	9- or 10-Month Contract					
		Professor	Associate Professor	Assistant Professor	Instructor	Lecturer	No. Rank
Alabama	25						$53,206
Alaska	2	$94,600	$64,736	$67,301			$50,750
Arizona	20	$50,689			$57,063		$67,962
Arkansas	22		$47,260	$41,765	$40,965		$45,495
California	114	$90,456	$80,453	$76,875	$82,999		$78,359
Colorado	14	$48,948	$42,649	$40,196	$43,992		$44,437
Connecticut	12	$82,932	$66,151	$56,179	$48,990	$53,087	
Delaware	3						$64,206
Florida	6	$66,021	$59,235	$55,850	$49,835		$49,814
Georgia	36	$60,528	$48,704	$41,904	$41,379	$40,702	$44,983
Hawaii	6	$81,081	$70,816	$63,625	$54,387		
Idaho	4	$56,456	$47,769	$43,671	$45,478		$42,704
Illinois	48	$80,803	$70,780	$61,392	$56,907		$57,143
Indiana	1	$55,421	$49,535	$44,224	$39,055		
Iowa	16	$62,060	$52,762	$49,574	$49,301		$47,439
Kansas	25	$56,396	$49,284	$46,076	$42,991	$38,016	$38,101
Kentucky	16	$60,170	$48,574	$42,254	$38,674		
Louisiana	18	$53,581	$48,490	$44,940	$38,033	$26,333	$39,627

Maine	7	$61,920	$49,268	$50,717	$52,139		$51,465
Maryland	16	$76,449	$62,748	$54,422	$48,298	$53,520	$70,748
Massachusetts	16	$66,100	$53,947	$50,510	$47,712		$65,413
Michigan	31	$77,111	$72,850	$66,291	$63,314	$53,299	$60,524
Minnesota	31				$42,336		$53,072
Mississippi	15				$47,282		
Missouri	18	$62,652	$55,087	$48,848	$43,526	$40,700	$50,422
Montana	11	$51,635			$39,047		$45,451
Nebraska	8	$57,476	$57,219	$43,127	$57,279		$51,384
Nevada	1	$68,588			$52,128		
New Hampshire	7	$56,817	$48,042	$42,518	$39,907		$56,662
New Jersey	19	$92,415	$74,044	$61,083	$51,054	$46,952	$45,776
New Mexico	19	$60,155	$52,900	$47,637	$44,888	$50,592	$54,377
New York	35	$83,680	$68,066	$58,373	$48,585	$56,992	$47,221
North Carolina	59				$48,755		
North Dakota	5	$58,767	$52,932	$50,629	$44,404	$49,322	$46,131
Ohio	25	$67,934	$59,925	$52,579	$45,298	$46,402	$46,163
Oklahoma	12	$47,276	$57,305	$52,922	$41,798		$42,863
Oregon	17	$67,739	$57,631	$48,801	$58,996		$57,556
Pennsylvania	17	$71,566	$60,635	$53,192	$46,194	$48,891	$40,250

(continued)

Table 7.3. *(continued)*

State	No. Colleges	9- or 10-Month Contract					
		Professor	Associate Professor	Assistant Professor	Instructor	Lecturer	No Rank
Rhode Island	1	$74,894	$56,777	$49,045			
South Carolina	20	$64,009	$55,806	$46,671	$42,021		$44,561
South Dakota	5				$44,638		$44,054
Tennessee	13	$60,267	$50,089	$42,775	$38,876		
Texas	63	$58,282	$51,497	$47,660	$43,673	$39,946	$52,576
Utah	1	$59,462	$52,771	$48,191	$41,589		
Virginia	24	$64,502	$59,707	$53,088	$48,606		$48,008
Washington	26	$54,714			$56,499		$55,757
Wisconsin	17	$62,382	$50,760	$44,882	$71,188	$41,180	$77,573
West Virginia	10	$65,885	$55,680	$46,370	$40,088	$39,454	$46,372
Wyoming	7	$72,469	$62,466	$56,537	$51,627		$59,294

Notes: The number of institutions used in this analysis was based on criteria utilized to create the group. Specifically, the parameters used here include U.S., Title IV eligible, degree-granting, public 2-year institutions. Applying these filters arrived at a total of 945 colleges. A result is that community colleges that offer a bachelor's degree are not included, as is common to nationally reported data for the public 2-year sector. Also not included in this table are faculty on 11- or 12-month contracts and part-time faculty. Data for Vermont were not available and therefore are missing from this analysis.

Source: Authors' analysis of Integrated Postsecondary Education Data System (IPEDS) data (National Center for Education Statistics, 2014c).

In 2010–11, the most recent year for which data were available, total expenditures for salary for full-time faculty on a 9- or 10-month contract were $6,625,128. This does not include an additional $1,937,412 in expenses for benefits, including retirement plans, health care plans, disability, tuition plans, worker's compensation, or other benefits.

In addition to full-time instructional faculty, institutions rely heavily on part-time instructional staff or adjunct faculty. National compensation data for this population are not yet available from the National Center for Education Statistics, so comparisons are not made.

Research

In 2011–2012, community colleges spent $20.2 million on research, accounting for 0.04% of total expenditures—an obvious reflection of community colleges' focus on instruction. For this category of expenditures, institutions were instructed to report "expenses for activities specifically organized to produce research outcomes and commissioned by an agency either external to the institution or separately budgeted by an organizational unit within the institution. Do not report nonresearch sponsored programs (e.g., training programs)."

Public Service

In 2011–2012, community colleges spent $759.8 million on public service, accounting for 1.4% of total expenditures. For this category of expenditures, institutions were instructed to report "expenses for all activities budgeted specifically for public service and for activities established primarily to provide noninstructional services beneficial to groups external to the institution. Examples are seminars and projects provided to particular sectors of the community. Include expenditures for community services and cooperative extension services."

Academic Support

In 2011–2012, community colleges spent $3.7 billion on academic support, accounting for 6.8% of total expenditures. For this category of expenditures, institutions were instructed to report "expenses for the support services that are an integral part of the institution's primary missions of instruction, research, and public service. Include expenses for museums, libraries, galleries, audio/visual services, ancillary support, academic administration, personnel development, and course and curriculum development. Include expenses for veterinary and dental clinics if their primary purpose is to support the institutional program." As the completion agenda takes root, these expenditures may grow, or at least grow in prominence, as there is increasing emphasis on the importance of these expenditures in getting students to graduation.

Student Services

In 2011–2012, community colleges spent $4.5 billion on student services, accounting for 8.4% of total expenditures. For this category of expenditures, institutions were instructed to report "expenses for admissions, registrar activities, and activities whose primary purpose is to contribute to students' emotional and physical well-being and to their intellectual, cultural, and social development outside the context of the formal instructional program. Examples are career guidance, counseling, and financial aid administration. This category also includes intercollegiate athletics and student health services, except when operated as self-supporting auxiliary enterprises."

Institutional Support

In 2011–2012, community colleges spent $6.7 billion on institutional support, accounting for 12.4% of total expenditures. For this category of expenditures, institutions were instructed to report "expenses for the day-to-day operational support of the institution.

Include expenses for general administrative services, executive direction and planning, legal and fiscal operations, and public relations/development."

Operation & Maintenance

In 2011–2012, community colleges spent $4.5 billion on operations and maintenance, accounting for 8.3% of total expenditures. For this category of expenditures, institutions were instructed to report "expenses for operations established to provide service and maintenance related to grounds and facilities used for educational and general purposes. Also include expenses for utilities, fire protection, property insurance, and similar items."

Depreciation

In 2011–2012, community colleges spent $2.4 billion, accounting for 4.4% of total expenditures, on depreciation. For this category of expenditures, institutions were instructed to report "the amount of depreciation allocated to each functional [expenditure] category."

Scholarships & Fellowships

In 2011–2012, community colleges spent $6.9 billion on scholarships and fellowships, accounting for 12.7% of total expenditures. For this category of expenditures, institutions were instructed to report "expenses in the form of outright grants to students selected and awarded by the institution. This is the amount that exceeds fees and charges assessed to students by the institution and that would not have been recorded as discounts & allowances. This classification will include the excess of awards over fees and charges from Pell grants and other resources, including funds originally restricted for student assistance. Do not include loans to students or amounts where the institution is given custody of the funds but is not allowed to select the recipients." The primary point of distinction for these funds is the fact that the institution awards the funds. This amount, for private institutions, is referred to as net grant aid—or aid in excess of that applied to tuition and fees and room and board.

Non-E&G

In addition to direct education expenses, other expenditures indirectly contribute to the education function. In 2011–2012, Non-E&G funds accounted for 11% of all expenditures at community colleges nationally. This section outlines the expenditure categories.

Auxiliary Enterprises

In 2011–2012, community colleges spent $2.4 billion on auxiliary enterprises, accounting for 4.4% of total expenditures. For this category of expenditures, institutions were instructed to report "expenses of essentially self-supporting operations of the institution that exist to furnish a service to students, faculty, or staff, and that charge a fee that is directly related to, although not necessarily equal to, the cost of the service. Examples are residence halls, food services, student health services, intercollegiate athletics, college unions, and college stores, when the activities are operated as auxiliary enterprises."

Hospitals & Independent Operations

In 2011–2012, community colleges did not spend any money on hospitals or other independent operations, as they do not operate hospitals and are not engaged in the operation of major, federally funded research and development centers.

Interest & Other

In 2011–2012, community colleges spent $1.4 billion on interest paid for each functional expense category, accounting for 2.5% of total expenditures. An additional $2.5 billion, reflecting 4.2% of expenditures, was spent on other expenses and deductions for each functional expense category.

Expenditure Trends

Figure 7.1 illustrates trends in E&G expenditures per student at public community colleges and public four-year institutions in 2011–2012 as compared to expenditures in 2005–2006 (the year to which the data are indexed).

These data for seven years allow for a few observations. First, community colleges are receiving fewer E&G dollars per student in 2011–2012 than they did in 2005–2006. This is not the case for public four-year institutions. Second, the economic downturn of 2008–2009 was experienced more severely by community colleges than by other sectors of higher education. (In fact, during that period revenues at public four-year institutions increased on a

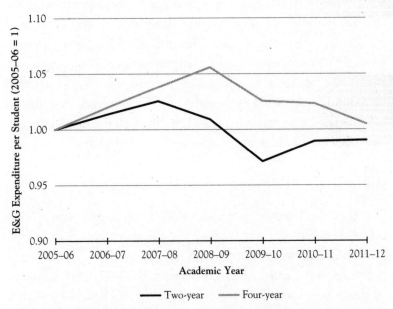

Figure 7.1   E&G Expenditures per Student at Public Community Colleges and Four-Year Institutions Indexed to 2005–2006: 2005–2006 to 2011–2012

Note: Expenditure data were adjusted for inflation by Snyder and Dillow, making them comparable from year to year.

Source: Adapted from Snyder and Dillow (2014).

per-student basis.) Third, during the post-recession recovery, community college E&G expenditures per student increased, whereas those for public four-year institutions decreased.

Hurlburt and Kirschstein (2012) noted that community colleges were the only sector of higher education to spend less than they had ten years previously on education and related expenses (E&R funding per full-time equivalent). E&R is a subset of financial data that focuses only on the educational mission of the college and includes expenditures for instruction, student services, and a portion of institutional support, academic support, and operations and maintenance. Specifically, they found that E&R spending increased at all private institutions by double digits, between 4% and 8% at public four-year colleges, whereas it declined 9% at community colleges. A reason provided for this decline was that enrollment at community colleges increased 9% during this time period, offsetting any increase in funding gains that the colleges may have experienced. It also reinforced a perspective all too common among policymakers requesting that community colleges do more with less. Some colleges were able to cushion the blow of funding reductions through the use of reserves, but these were insufficient to counter the general trend.

Budgeting

The process of setting institutional budgets is obviously a complicated and fraught exercise, as it is all about setting priorities. Budgeting requires extensive knowledge of the college, state policies and priorities, and at times even the federal government. Adding to the complexity is the fact that various budgeting models or approaches may be used on a campus at various times; there is no single "correct" way to tackle the activity.

An Integrated Activity

The annual budget is the institution's guiding blueprint. Boards of trustees have an integral role in providing guidance on, and input into, the budget. It is always important to review outcomes from prior years, assessing the annual plan of the budget as its cycle continues into the following year. Also, given the fluctuating nature of state budgets and the need for those budgets to be balanced, institutional leaders typically have to alter the budget during a particular fiscal year. Almost always, the alterations involve reductions in activity.

A college's budgeting occurs in the context of the state's higher education governing/coordinating boards, its legislature, and the campus community. Each of these parties impacts the budgeting decisions. This makes budgeting an integrative activity with an intricate sequence of steps, fluid timelines, and rapidly changing information.

Budgeting Models

Barr and McClellan (2011) present a thorough overview of budgeting models in higher education and practical steps to developing a budget. Rather than recreate their work, a review of budget models are presented in Table 7.4. It is helpful to note that each of these budget models may be used at a college at the same time, be it in a department or college or for a grant program. Identifying which budget process is appropriate for a particular unit requires an understanding of both the operating models as well as how the task to be budgeted for aligns with unit, department, and/or college goals.

There is, of course, no single appropriate budgeting model for every situation. For example, developing a budget for a grant program may be an exercise in either initiative-based or zero-base budgeting.

Budgeting for Outcomes

Performance-funding is discussed in other portions of this work. Key to understanding its impact throughout a college is the assertion of Burke and Minassians (2003) that performance-funding stops at the vice presidential level and does not necessarily change

Table 7.4.   Budget Models

Budget Model	Highlights
All funds	Emphasizes a holistic goals-oriented perspective.
	Takes into account all sources of revenue and expense.
Formula	Relies on the use of specific criteria in allocation resources.
	Development of the formula is critically important.
	Retrospective in nature.
	Most commonly employed in higher education.
Incremental	Establishes across-the-board percentage changes in expenditures over current budget based on assumptions regarding revenues for coming year.
Initiative-based	Requires units return portion of their budgets for the purposes of funding new initiatives.
	May be one-time or recurring adjustments.
	Units apply to the pool to support new initiatives.
Performance-based	Allocation of resources premised on attainment of performance measures.
Planning, programming, and budgeting systems	Premised on tightly integrating strategic planning, budgeting, and assessment.
	Decision a function of identified challenges and opportunities, weighing risk-reward ratios, and monitoring performance.
Responsibility-centered	Locates responsibility for unit budget performance at the local level.
	Units are seen as revenue centers or cost centers.
	Units are allowed to retain some portion of end-of-year budget surplus.

Table 7.4. (*continued*)

Budget Model	Highlights
Zero-based	Each item in the budget must be justified at the time the budget is developed.
	Assures active monitoring of the link between institutional activities and institutional goals.

Note: The original table also provides the strengths and weakness of each approach.

Source: Adapted from Table 5.3 in Barr and McClellan (2011).

institutional behaviors at the program level. This is a critical observation, as institutional leaders need to develop strategies for integrating their external funding with the actions of a broad swath of campus personnel, particularly faculty. Surely the levels and terms under which colleges allocate revenues internally may have the greatest impact on institutional practices and therefore on outcomes.

In an effort to recognize community colleges that align their budgets with positive student outcomes, the Government Finance Officers Association (GFOA) was supported by the Bill and Melinda Gates Foundation to develop and elevate an award program to be administered by GFOA, titled *GFOA Best Practices in Budgeting for Community Colleges*. This program focused on how colleges demonstrate budget process excellence. As part of the process, guided by community college finance practitioners, a budget framework was developed. The resulting budget process framework had five parts that are highly instructive for effective community college finance (Government Finance Officers Association, 2014).

- *Develop Principles and Policies.* The first step is to prepare and develop inputs into the budget process. This includes adopting and reinforcing budget principles and policies. These principles and policies in turn guide the budget process. Additionally, it is necessary to examine how internal and external forces may impact the budget.

- *Define Goals.* The second step is to define goals for the college and its various subunits. It is then possible to identify gaps between the goal and the current status of the college and subunits. Prior to moving on to the next step, colleges are advised to identify root causes of the gaps, to the extent possible.

- *Identify Strategies.* After the guiding principles, lines, and goals have been set and gaps identified, the college should develop strategies to address the gaps. Effort should be made to identify research-based actions rather than those supported with anecdotes or less systematic information.

- *Prioritize Strategies.* The fourth step is to prioritize which strategies should be implemented after determining the spending associated with each. Funds should then be allocated and a document developed to communicate the purpose of the allocations.

- *Monitor Implementation.* The final step is to incorporate monitoring into the process. The information gathered during this step should inform future allocation decisions.

This framework is but one that may be applied to the development of an institution's budget. It has the benefit, at present, of the opportunity for national recognition via a forthcoming awards program and, in addition to its inherent benefits, may be of interest to community college leadership.

Conclusion

This chapter detailed the types of expenditures employed by community colleges and further examined how the process of setting a budget extends beyond routine actions of a short-term exercise. Budgeting requires extensive knowledge of the college, the state, and even the federal government. Further, various budgeting models may be employed in different segments at a college campus at any given time. In closing, perhaps the wisest piece of advice one can receive as it relates to budgeting is this: "Beware of recurring expenditures without recurring revenues."

Questions

Two community colleges in two different states need to be identified before completing question 1. Community colleges may be located by using the College Navigator tool of the National Center for Education Statistics at http://nces.ed.gov/collegenavigator/.

1. How does the distribution of expenditures differ between the two community colleges you selected to study? If there is a substantial difference, what do you think accounts for it? If there is not a substantial difference, why not?

2. Which budget process, in your opinion, would be best received by the leadership in your college?

Chapter Eight

Aligning Mission and Money

This chapter focuses on the issue of community college completion and appropriate ways to measure the mission in the context of resource allocation. It is critical that institutional leadership understands the metrics being used to evaluate the outcomes of a community college education, whether the mechanism is a performance funding formula, a state report card, a federal rating system, or any other presentation about an institution's "performance" that directly or indirectly influences the allocation of revenues or the expenditure of funds.

Community College Completion

Institutions of higher education are accountable to many stakeholders, each with their own expectations of relevant information and indicators of performance. Over time, institutions, states, accrediting agencies, and the federal government have all developed intricate accountability systems that rely, at least in part, on data to hold institutions accountable (McKeown-Moak & Mullin, 2014). The well-known think tank the Education Trust stated in a 2013 paper that "institutions of higher education strenuously resist accountability efforts" (Dannenberg & Voight, 2013, p. 9). This is a harsh assessment that is far from true (accountability also being in the eye of the beholder), but the perceptions, or at least the allegations, continue.

Prior to examining the metrics that may be used to align the community college mission to money, we probe three specific measures that have been used to suggest that higher education is failing and hence in need of new incentive structures. They include educational attainment trends, international comparisons, and graduation rates.

Attainment Trends

The educational attainment of the U.S. population has grown dramatically in recent decades. In 1950, 65% of the population aged 25 and over had not completed high school; in 2010, that figure was just 13%. Because high school completion is a precursor to postsecondary attainment, it is not a surprise that postsecondary attainment has increased as high school completion has increased. In 1950, only 13.2% of the population aged 25 or higher had completed a year of college, compared to 55.9% in 2010 (see Figure 8.1).

Given the surge in attainment depicted in Figure 8.1, it appears that U.S. colleges and universities have improved in their ability to help students attain additional higher levels of education. To those familiar with the policy conversations, the data presented in these two trends—substantial decreases in high school dropouts and increased postsecondary participation and completion—run counter to the notion that the institutions that make up the American higher education system and, in particular, the institutions that cocreate educational attainment have fallen from grace (Smith & Mullin, 2014).

International Comparisons

To better understand the widespread, and paradoxical, perception that higher education is failing at a time of substantial increases in attainment, it is important to understand international comparisons between systems of higher education, as this is the primary data point used to corroborate the "failure" perspective.

The last time the United States led the world in educational attainment was 1991. Nearly 20 years later, in 2010, the United States was ranked fourth in educational attainment

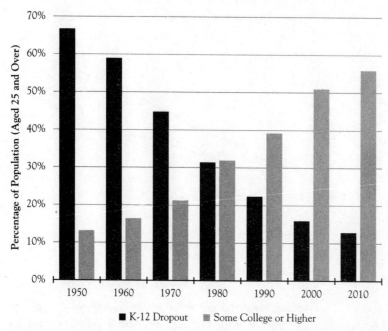

Figure 8.1   Comparing Changes in Two Measures of Educational Attainment

Note: Original data table note: 1947 and 1952 to 2002 March Current Population Survey, 2003 to 2011 Annual Social and Economic Supplement to the Current Population Survey (noninstitutionalized population, excluding members of the Armed Forces living in barracks); 1950 Census of Population and 1940 Census of Population (resident population).

Authors' notes: Data for 1960 were not available; data for 1959 were used instead. The use of a bachelor's degree or higher classification is the result of a lack of associate degree and postsecondary certificate data. Associate degrees have begun to be counted of late, yet as mentioned in this chapter, certificates are not counted. Data for high school graduates were not included in this adaptation of the data.

Sources: Author's analysis of U.S. Census Bureau (2013).

behind Canada, Israel, and Japan (Organization for Economic Co-Operation and Development [OECD], 2012) (see Figure 8.2). Although Israel and Japan did not provide data to OECD for comparison in 1991, trends in the data suggest that Israel, whose

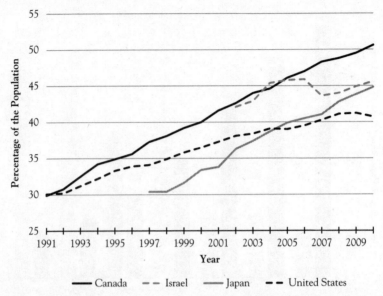

Figure 8.2   Educational Attainment Levels in Countries for 25- to 64-Year-Olds (Percentage of the Population), with Top Four Countries Ranked: 1991 to 2010

Source: Adapted from Organisation for Economic Co-Operation and Development (OECD) (2004, p. 72, Table A3.4a), (2012, p. 38, Table A1.4).

attainment has remained fairly stagnant over the time period for which data are provided, might have contended for the lead in 1991, whereas Japan has made substantial gains in attainment.

While the percentage of the population that has attained some level of higher education—the central metric in international comparisons—is assumed to be a direct measure of a nation's educational productivity, attainment levels are also a function of other factors. For example, Canada's level of attainment growth is due in part to immigration policy that sought to increase the number of immigrants with higher levels of educational attainment (Preston, Damsbaek, Kelly, Lemione, Lo, Shields, & Tufts, 2010).

Additional data from the OECD speaks to the educational attainment level of the United States' younger population (25 to 34 years old), which lags further behind other countries than our total population. In essence it shows that younger populations in other countries are achieving higher levels of educational attainment than their older peers, while the United States is fairly stagnant. It shows we are much further behind other countries, and that the need for more college graduates, from an international competitiveness perspective, requires that we more fully educate the younger generation. Policymakers are right to be highly concerned about this situation.

Of some solace is the fact that international comparisons do not include postsecondary certificates, hindering comparisons. The data clearly indicate that community colleges are offering ever higher numbers of certificates (Mullin, 2011). In addition, students of color—who are becoming a larger proportion of the U.S. population—are trending heavily to certificates (Horn & Li, 2009). An analysis by Carnevale, Rose, and Hanson (2012) suggests that the nation's educational attainment would increase by 5% if certificate earners (who have earnings 20% above those of the average high school graduate) were counted. If we did this, America would assume second place in 2010 for 25- to 64-year-olds. This is important not just because it would depict a more accurate picture of education attainment in the U.S. population, but also because nearly 40% of awards earned at community colleges are certificates. If we adjusted the younger population rate by accounting for certificates, using the conservative parameters set forth by the researchers from Georgetown and assuming that other countries do not have the same practice of overlooking credentials, our international ranking substantially improves: from being tied for twelfth to being tied for fifth.

Graduation Rates

The Committee on Measures of Student Success, mandated by the Higher Education Opportunity Act of 2008, was charged with examining graduation metrics for community colleges and came to the conclusion, "Although federal graduation rates provide important comparable data across institutional sectors, limitations in the data understate the success of students enrolled at two-year institutions and can be misleading to the public" (2011, p. 4). This conclusion derives from the fact that the graduation rates include only full-time students, omit transfers out, and do not reflect the actual time it takes community college students to complete programs. In light of this finding about this highly prominent metric—used to hold community colleges accountable and present their performance to the public—it can be fairly said that the federal graduation rate distorts more than it enlightens.

It is also the case that students do not always interpret data the way it was intended. One reason may be that three of the purposes of consumer information—protection from abuse, better student selections through providing comparative information, and assurances about program quality (El-Khawas, 1976)—were rarely made explicit when developing the data that underpins higher education consumer information frameworks. Furthermore, the author noted that "the introduction of a consumer perspective into postsecondary education has been at once confusing, challenging, and welcome. So far, however, lack of clarity among three distinct purposes has hampered the design of effective approaches to consumer reform" (p. 45). Nearly 50 years later, her words still ring true. More recent studies of how students perceive metrics utilized by the College Navigator (MacAllum & Glover, 2012), the College Scorecard (Morgan & Dechter, 2012), and the Shopping Sheet (National Association of Student Financial Aid Administrators & JBL Associates, 2013) drew the same conclusion.

Measuring the Mission

Fortunately, some metrics do provide an accurate portrayal of higher education. These data can be used not only to tell a more accurate story about higher education than do federal graduation rates, but also to drive institutional improvement (Mullin, 2012b).

Further, indicators of performance are influencing the allocation and awarding of funds through performance funding mechanisms.

Student Progress Outcomes and Success

Although outcomes and success are often conflated in conversations related to college performance, they are distinctly different. The term "outcomes" refers to a range of all possible observations, whereas "success" refers to the subjective selection of one or more observed outcomes to evaluate the various outcomes. For example, Figure 8.3 presents data for a cohort of students who enrolled at a community college and their status six years later.

The outcomes for this cohort of students include six categories, from earned a bachelor's degree to not enrolled and no credential. These six categories reflect the range of possible outcomes for the cohort. Alternatively, the same information could be recast to speak to success by counting only those students who earned either a bachelor's degree or an associate's degree. This practice would be consistent with the previous discussion of international comparisons of educational attainment. However, once one realizes that an additional 8.5% of students earned a certificate, the concept

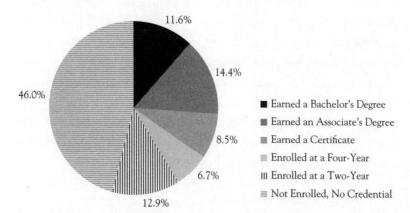

Figure 8.3   Six-Year Outcomes for Students Beginning at a Community College in Fall 2003

Source: Adapted from Mullin and Phillippe (2013).

of "success" may change. Further, there are the additional 19.6% of students who are still enrolled, and it is clearly not accurate to label these students—many of whom are persisting in light of various risk factors that research has identified as more common among community college students than their four-year student counterparts—as failures.

Some analysts have used this nonsuccess portion of a cohort to run analyses that calculate the "wasted" cost of college simply because they did not attain a degree within a given time period. While degree attainment is undoubtedly important, the students are not failures and the funds are not wasted.

For institutional leaders engaged in generating the funding and running colleges, it is imperative that a clear understanding of the range of possible outcomes, rather than a narrowly tailored definition of "success," be understood and appropriately employed. This is worth knowing when developing performance-focused reports or funding formulas, because a failure to appropriately classify outcomes may result in, at best, the loss of revenues and, at worst, a narrowing of opportunity as colleges enroll only those students who are statistically predicted to graduate.

Before closing this conversation, it is fair to say that 46% of students not completing a credential or still enrolled after six years, as depicted in Figure 8.3, should spur further inquiry and action by institutional leadership. Examining outcomes rather than subjective measures of student success is not an excuse for inaction, rather a call for the institution to be more targeted in the actions it takes, in order to have the greatest impact and to be most efficient. From a financial viewpoint, the loss of that many students has substantial impacts on a college's budget.

Acknowledging Differences

Expecting all students to reach the same goal—that is, a degree—in the same amount of time may be understandable, but it is not practical. Students are different from each other in the paths they take as well as their level of academic preparation. In the previous example, the outcomes provided reflected the traditional collegiate experience. There is another set of outcomes that is more broadly defined.

Milestone Events

Research by Ewell (2007) and Leinbach and Jenkins (2008) identified momentum points and milestone events that have a clear value. Leinbach and Jenkins (2008) define milestone events as "measurable educational achievements that include both conventional terminal completions, such as earning a credential or transferring to a baccalaureate program, and intermediate outcomes, such as completing developmental education or adult basic skills requirements" (see Figure 8.4; p. 2).

This research takes into account the obvious reality that, based on where a student starts, the outcomes will likely vary; those entering ready to earn college credits will likely earn a degree faster than students who first have to earn a high school diploma equivalency, and the latter in many cases will not ever attain a degree. In addition, even when students enter college at the same time and the same level, the course load they are able to take each semester will influence their ability to graduate at the same time. This method of accounting for student differences is taking hold in state accountability and performance funding metrics and is spurring new lines of thinking about efficiency and productivity in community colleges.

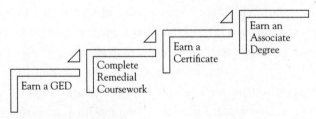

Figure 8.4   Milestone Events
Source: Adapted from Leinbach and Jenkins (2008).

Input-Adjusted Metrics

As stated, students come to college with differences in their life experience, educational background, and level of preparedness. Community colleges traditionally enroll students with a greater number of risk factors that negatively influence the likelihood that they will earn a degree.

Aside from acknowledging the progress students make by using outcome metrics that take into account student progress, like the aforementioned milestone events, there are statistical methods to account for individual differences through the development of input-adjusted metrics. Input-adjusted metrics begin as regular metrics but are altered through the application of statistical analyses that include risk factors known to influence the metric.

HCM Strategists' (2012) review of the research suggests that the metrics utilized in accountability systems need to be adjusted to account for some key risk factors. These factors include, but may not be limited to, race, gender, high school background, standardized test scores, grades, class rank, academic attitudes and behavior, and goals. HCM cites research findings revealing that when these student differences were taken into account, a 52% difference in graduate earnings between two institutions in Texas was reduced to just 4%.

Their work in this area has come to find that "as more information about students is taken into account, differences in outcomes tend to diminish (or even reverse), and any *remaining* differences are more likely to be attributable to institutions" (p. 1; emphasis not in the original). This statement was recently reinforced by a study of transfer students in Illinois that found when student characteristics were considered, the "community college penalty"—a moniker for a research finding that students starting at a community college are less likely to earn a bachelor's degrees and are therefore better off starting at a four-year institution—disappears (Lichtenberger & Dietrich, 2013).

Given the multiple risk factors associated with noncompletion that characterize a large portion of the community college student body, any method of accounting for differences in students certainly increases the measured "performance" of community colleges. Yet, while those who work at or champion community colleges would likely be supportive of portraying their college in a more positive light, there are widespread concerns over the use of input-adjusted metrics. Primary among them is the concern that input-adjusted metrics explain away poor performance and, to some, reinforce the idea that students with risk factors should be held to a different standard. This last concern evokes memories of separate but equal educational systems and concomitant expectations—ideals that are not in keeping with the values of the community college movement. At the same time, a number of leading publications are starting to use input-adjusted metrics, including the *Washington Monthly's* annual college guide and the *U.S. News & World Report* rankings of colleges (Blumenstyk, 2014). Further, as it relates to the community college, at present these metrics focus on a "success" metric of graduation and ignore other outcomes, such as transfer, discussed earlier in the chapter.

Certifications and Educational Certificates

One other outcome of particular importance to the community college sector is the industry-recognized certification. This credential differs from a certificate awarded by a college, though they are frequently confused. As with certificates, the production of industry-recognized certifications at community colleges is growing.

To assist in providing clarity as well as to measure the prevalence of certificates, certifications, and licenses in the U.S. population, the federal Interagency Working Group on Expanded Measures of Enrollment and Attainment (GEMEnA) was formed in 2009. One result of this working group was the establishment of definitions for certifications, licenses, and educational (college) certificates, as follows:

- **Certification.** A credential awarded by a certification body based on an individual demonstrating, through an examination process, that he or she has acquired the designated knowledge, skills, and abilities to perform a specific job. The examination can be written, oral, or performance-based. Certification is a time-limited credential that is renewed through a recertification process.
- **License.** A credential awarded by a licensing agency based on predetermined criteria. The criteria may include some combination of degree attainment, certifications, certificates, assessment, apprenticeship programs, or work experience. Licenses are time limited and must be renewed periodically.
- **Educational certificate.** A credential awarded by a training provider or educational institution based on completion of all requirements for a program of study, including coursework and tests or other performance evaluations. Certificates, as an academic award, are not time limited and do not need to be renewed. Most educational certificates are awarded at the subbaccalaureate level, but a small number are awarded after the completion of a post-secondary degree. Certificates of attendance or participation are not in the definitional scope for educational certificates (Bielick, Cronen, Stone, Montaquila, & Roth, 2013, p. 5).

These definitions were used as part of the thirteenth wave of the 2008 Survey of Income and Program Participation (SIPP) administered by the U.S. Census Bureau (http://www.census.gov/sipp/). An analysis of the resulting data suggests that while certifications and licenses are held by students with some college and associate degrees, they are more prevalent for those with higher levels of educational attainment (see Figure 8.5).

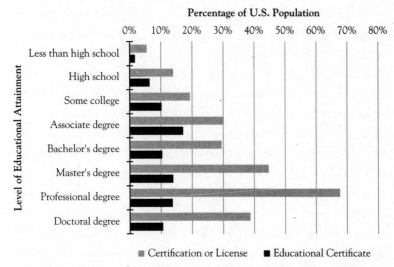

Figure 8.5   Percentage of the U.S. Population Aged 18 and Older with a Certification, License, or Educational Certificate, by Level of Educational Attainment: 2012

Source: Adapted from Ewert and Kominski (2014).

For community colleges and other sectors of higher education, a question arises: whether there is an agreement to adopt and use these definitions to establish a common set of metrics. Until this seminal work was released, these national definitions did not exist. This lack made it exceptionally difficult to examine non–college credential outcomes, and to use them in performance funding mechanisms.

Aligning Outcomes

Despite sustained efforts to streamline, consolidate, or rationalize the numerous metrics used to assess higher education (including federal and state governments and their many programs and requirements), the effort cannot be said to have been entirely successful. There remains a considerable ongoing burden on institutions for overlapping outcomes-related reporting that diverts resources that might better serve students.

However, there is real progress in aligning outcome metrics, through the promulgation of new student progress and outcomes metrics proposed by the National Center for Education Statistics (NCES) (2013b) and an inter-association-led initiative called the Student Achievement Measure. In both cases, the metrics complement the more detailed Voluntary Framework of Accountability (VFA) developed by community colleges with support from the staff of the American Association of Community Colleges (AACC) (see Table 8.1).

It may be argued—indeed, it has been—that the four primary outcomes in the SAM project encompass all possible academic outcomes at an aggregate level for all sectors of higher education. The VFA provides a more nuanced set of metrics that "fit" within the four outcome categories.

Post-College Outcomes

There is increasing interest in, and the allocation of funding is informed by, the outcomes for students after they leave college.

Labor market outcomes are associated with the workforce. Three questions are currently driving the workforce outcome conversation:

1. What is the postsecondary program's employment rate?
2. How much are completers earning?
3. At what level—student, program, or college— should earnings or other data for college completers be made available?

[Mullin, 2013d, p. 3]

The answers to the first two questions go hand in hand, because once former students can be located in a workforce dataset, the fact that they are working can be counted as well as the amount of money they are earning. At present, the first two questions

Table 8.1. The Alignment of Outcome Metrics with the AACC
Voluntary Framework of Accountability

Student Achievement Measure	Voluntary Framework of Accountability	NCES/IPEDS (proposed)
	Reported Outcome Metrics	
Graduated from original institution	Students who earn an associate's degree— without transfer	Received award
	Students who earn an associate's degree—with transfer	
	Students who earn an award of less than associate's degree (certificate)— with transfer	
	Students who earn an award of less than associate's degree (certificate)— without transfer	
Transferred to subsequent institution	Students who transfer to another post-secondary institution, with no degree or certificate	Did not receive award; subsequently enrolled at another institution (transferred)
Enrolled at original institution	Students who are still enrolled during the sixth academic year	Did not receive award; still enrolled at reporting institution
Status unknown	Students who left institution, no award, no transfer; with 30+ credits	Did not receive award; subsequent enrollment status unknown
	Students who left institution, no award, no transfer; with <30 credits	

Sources: National Center for Education Statistics (NCES) (2013b);
www.aacc.nche.edu/vfa; www.studentachievementmeasure.org.

are being answered with data from state agencies. Additional questions—how many hours they are working and whether they are working in a field related to their education—are harder to answer, because few states collect this information, and the intricacies associated with measuring the outcomes are complex; for a discussion, the reader is referred to McKeown-Moak and Mullin (2014), Mullin (2013c), and Mullin and Lebesch (2010).

The third question is still not settled. There is a desire to hold a college accountable for its outcomes while at the same time understanding program variations driven by a range of variables. With the promulgation of gainful employment regulations by the U.S. Department of Education and the availability of some finer-grained data, the answer is likely to be both the program and the college, at least for more occupationally specific programs.

The conversation regarding post-college outcomes is a tense one that pits measurable outcomes, such as earnings, and nonmeasurable outcomes against each other. It is fair to suggest that in addition to those workforce outcomes, former students use the knowledge, skills, and abilities they acquired and refined in college in their home or community (McMahon, 2009). As an example, an accountant may volunteer to assist a religious institution in handling its financial affairs. What to measure and how exactly to measure these outcomes are questions that remain open.

One difficulty with identifying post-college non–labor market outcomes is that of differentiating between an *outcome of college* that may be measured at some point in the future (that is, student satisfaction) and a measurable *post-college outcome* reflective of an activity resulting from knowledge, skills, and abilities enhanced in college and applied at some point in the future.

The requirement that someone earn a college credential, or sequence of college courses, as entry to a profession, is one criterion that may be utilized to identify a post-college outcome. In some cases the awarding of a professional license or certification is dependent, in part, upon first earning a college credential. For example, to become licensed as a registered professional nurse in Georgia, a graduate registers for the NCLEX-RN national test after an application is submitted to the state. The application must include the graduate's academic transcript inclusive of the graduation date and degree conferred (Georgia Board of Nursing, 2014).

The use of industry certifications as a post-college outcome is a possibility, but not all certifications require the completion of a college course or program. For example, to earn a Microsoft Certification, an individual is not required to attend college. Rather, Microsoft notes that

> The best way to prepare for an exam is to practice the skills listed in the "Skills measured" section of the exam details page. The exam details page also contains a list of preparation tools and resources provided by Microsoft that candidates may find helpful, and Microsoft Virtual Academy may have additional learning materials and resources to help you prepare for an exam.
>
> You may also consider reading about how tasks assessed on the exam are performed (for example, in white papers and on blogs, MSDN, TechNet, and so on), listening to others describe how tasks are performed, watching others complete them, and leveraging community resources, such as Microsoft Certification Study Groups, to learn more about the skills needed to perform those tasks.
>
> Keep in mind that training is a great first step when preparing for a Microsoft Certification exam, but it is not required and does not guarantee that you will pass the exam. Hands-on experience is required. [Microsoft, 2014]

That said, the provision of courses at a college that allow for the hands-on learning referenced in the extract is available and helpful. However, it is not required.

Another post-college outcome that may require a college degree is further educational attainment, such as a bachelor's degree, a master's degree, or a doctoral degree. In all cases, the completion of some college is a prerequisite to further growth and therefore attributable to the prior college experience.

Conclusion

This chapter focused on the issue of completion in higher education generally and community colleges specifically. It reviewed the efforts that have been under way and the data informing the broader policy discussion. Clearly both the community college mission and its contribution to society are complex but not impossible to quantify or document to a large extent.

Questions

1. What level of educational attainment, in your opinion, should be counted in international comparisons? Justify your answer.

2. How would you present the outcomes of a community college education, as captured by the Voluntary Framework of Accountability, to explain the "success" of a college?

3. Develop a post-college metric not mentioned in the chapter that you would use to discuss the outcomes of a community college and that you believe should have funding attached to it.

Chapter Nine

Costs, Efficiency, and Productivity

How colleges spend the funds they acquire extends beyond the classification of expenditures to particular categories and the development of a college budget. Community colleges are responsible for ensuring that funds are spent in educational and economically justifiable ways. In this chapter, we examine institutional costs, including unit costs studies and perspectives on college costs. The chapter closes with a consideration of efficiency and productivity in higher education.

Institutional Costs

It's helpful to examine community college expenditures within the broader context of higher education. However, due to the differences among institutional operations and the related differences in expenditure categories, comparing the total costs spent on students at public four- and two-year institutions is challenging. One way to accomplish this task is to compare the Education and General (E&G) funds cost per student to gain a preliminary understanding of how much the two sectors spend on students. In doing so, we find that community colleges spent $11,398 per student in 2011–2012, compared to $27,526 at public four-year institutions. This substantial difference highlights other differences between public sectors of higher education.

Although differences in funding based on historical precedent are a driving factor, before we complain that this is completely unfair, we must acknowledge several considerations. For one, there is the difference in the types of students accounted for (undergraduate versus graduate), the market rate price for faculty with differing credentials, and the differences in the cost of providing different levels (that is, lower division, upper division, graduate, and doctoral) of instruction. To aid in better understanding these differences, some colleges and states have undertaken elaborate unit cost studies.

Unit Cost Studies

Cost studies have been traced to the nineteenth century, and while they are a *science*—influenced by the unit of activity (such as cost per student or degree), indirect costs, and the distinction between operating and capital resources—they are also an *art* in that the resulting values provide informative yet imprecise comparisons (d'Ambrosio & Merisotis, 2000). Cost studies assist institutional leaders in optimizing their investments by serving as the basis for evaluation of efficiency, allowing for a study of alternative expenditures, and informing the development of program planning and budgets (Witmer, 1967). Further, research suggests that when costs are measured they are reduced in the future, as administrators are able to make more informed decisions (Jenkins & Crosta, 2013).

Cost study data affect state budgeting, internal budget processes, and the development of funding formulas (McKeown-Moak, 2000). Four states with substantial amounts of cost data over a number of years (Florida, Illinois, New York [SUNY system], and Ohio) participated in a study that examined their higher education costs at the program and division levels and, among other things, found that the cost per student credit hour varied by level; lower division was the least costly, upper division (junior and senior years) costs per credit hour were 1.5 times more costly than lower division, graduate I (masters level) costs were 3 times more than lower division, and graduate II (doctoral/professional level) were 4 times more costly than lower division (Conger, Bell & Stanley, 2010). These findings are consistent with other, similar studies.

Taking the analysis of unit cost differentials a step further, McKeown-Moak (2012) examined the various weights used by states in 2012 to account for differences in lower division program costs as opposed to the level of education (that is, lower or upper division). On average, the program that cost the least at the lower division of the undergraduate level was psychology (see Figure 9.1). The highest-cost program was in construction and other trades.

Benchmarking Costs

A second way to understand whether the costs of a program or service are appropriate is to benchmark against similar colleges. The notion of developing an interactive tool for institutions to compare themselves to other institutions in terms of detailed cost information was realized with the Delaware Cost Study of Instructional Costs and Productivity (Middaugh, 2000) in the early 1990s, when it was developed and refined to include information on institutional activities, cost, and productivity. Although community colleges did not participate, institutions can compare their institution to national benchmarks, and more than 600 institutions have participated since its inception.

However, with respect to community colleges, the National Higher Education Benchmarking Institute oversees three benchmarking projects for community colleges that provide tools for enhanced financial management. The first is the National Community College Benchmarking Project (https://www.nccbp.org), which includes more than 150 items in the areas of completion, retention, student performance, student satisfaction, and job market information. Second is the Workforce Training Benchmarking Project, focused on standardizing data for workforce training and continuing education (http://workforceproject.org). The third project, and most germane to the topic of cost studies,

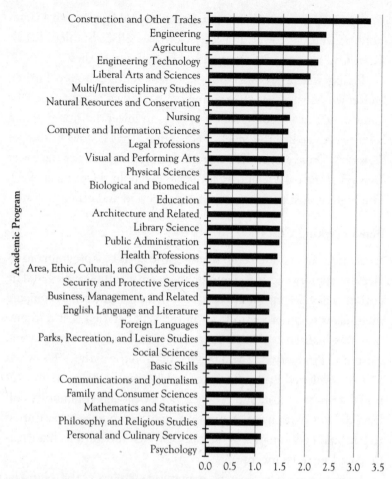

Figure 9.1   Average Credit Hour Weights for Lower Division Programs, by Academic Program: 2012

Source: Adapted from McKeown-Moak (2012).

is Maximizing Resources for Student Success. This project currently allows community colleges to benchmark costs associated with instruction, student services, and academic support. By capturing data in these areas related to key student outcomes, colleges are able to align expenditures with priorities (http://maximizingresources.org). The project completed its pilot phase in early 2014 and then opened the benchmarking tool to all colleges interested in participating in the summer of 2014, so as of this writing data are not yet available to share national trends.

Perspectives on College Costs

The various conceptions of how costs interact with institutional operations have resulted in a variety of perspectives on the cost of college, and of course, price is often confused with cost. It is helpful to understand these and more formal perspectives, as they reflect the dominant perspectives related to college costs.

Cost Disease

In 1966, Baumol and Bowen examined the finances of the performing arts. One conclusion they arrived at—which has since come to be known as "cost disease"—was that while the wages of performing artists increased, their productivity did not, because the performance is the product, and the performance itself did not fundamentally vary over time. This phenomenon contradicts those economists who believe that wages are closely associated with labor productivity—that is, one gets paid more for a greater output. Put another way, "whereas the amount of labor necessary to produce a typical product has constantly declined since the beginning of the industrial revolution, it [still] requires about as many minutes for Richard II to tell his 'sad stories of the death of kings' as it did on the stage of the Globe Theatre" (p. 164).

With some exceptions, the same may be said of education. The labor-intensive nature of education—which is largely unchanged—is at the core of policy discussions about cost. While new efforts are under way to limit the labor-intensive aspect of teaching—including online learning, credit for prior learning, and other asynchronous learning experiences—other efforts to increase the instructional output per hour of teaching, such as increasing class size, has existed for decades, without curing the basic "cost disease." In addition, technology in the classroom, not to mention other changes in related campus services, often serves to add to the cost of its delivery.

Revenue Theory of Expenditures

In 1980 Bowen introduced the revenue theory of costs. This concept suggests "an institution's educational cost per student unit is determined by the revenues available for educational purposes" (p. 17). In other words, colleges will spend whatever resources administrators can get their hands on. Bowen provides further support for this theory by reiterating a set of five laws for higher education costs—which he notes are also applicable to other non-profit organizations such as hospitals, churches, and museums:

1. The dominant goals of institutions are educational excellence, prestige, and influence.
2. In quest of excellence, prestige, and influence, there is virtually no limit to the amount of money an institution could spend for seemingly fruitful educational ends.
3. Each institution raises all the money it can.
4. Each institution spends all it raises.
5. The cumulative effect of the preceding four laws is toward ever-increasing expenditure. [pp. 19–20]

While the initial theory focused solely on the observation that institutional expenditure levels were determined by the revenues brought in, the five laws were simplified to develop the perspective that expenditures drive revenues in search of prestige. The fifth law actually notes that, in light of the accompanying laws, the focus is on increasing expenditures, not necessarily on prestige.

Given the way community colleges have embraced low-cost educational opportunity, it remains an open question, and is indeed doubtful, whether this widely regarded theory, with all its implications for institutional behavior, applies to community colleges. At the same time, the limited funding and increasing demand for numerous services suggest that community colleges would indeed find a way to spend all of the revenue they bring in to increase student completion—which has become a way to national prestige.

Costs and Subsidies

In 1995 Winston and Yen examined the connection of cost, prices, and subsidies, and in doing so differentiated higher education pricing (cost) models from those of the private sector, using two calculations. First, it is the private sector calculation that suggests that price is equal to cost plus profit. Alternatively, in higher education price equals cost minus subsidy. Further, they argue that all of higher education—public and private alike—subsidizes the cost of education through appropriations or institutional aid, to the point that nobody pays the full cost of education. In 1999 Winston noted, "Our economics and intuitions about for-profit business don't just obscure what's happening in colleges and universities, they can also seriously distort understanding and policy" (p. 34).

Efficiency and Productivity

Efficiency in higher education is defined as the cost of producing a unit, or outcome. So, for example, when teaching assistants aid the teaching of courses by faculty, enabling them to teach more courses/students, the wages increase to a lesser extent than if two regular faculty were hired. The result is a higher "return," or greater efficiency.

Productivity is a different concept in that it is a measurement of the cost of producing a unit, or outcome, when the costs of inputs *are constant*. For example, faculty are more productive when they teach more courses/students, as they are paid the same amount while the revenues from students increase, resulting in a greater return per student.

Belfield (2012) noted that while these two terms are different, they are used interchangeably in the literature. His review identified just two studies addressing productivity at the community college level. One study focused on completion rates, the other on bachelor's degree attainment. While informative, clearly these two studies do not take the range of community college outcomes into account. In this chapter we do not try to disentangle the various studies of productivity and efficiency; rather, we discuss the concept of increasing outcomes, whether the inputs hold constant or not.

Quantifying the Outcome

At its core, both efficiency and productivity rely on calculations that have a numerator, representing the amount of money expended, and a denominator, reflecting the outcome of interest. Deciding exactly how each of these values is determined may have as much of an impact on findings related to efficiency or productivity as the actions of the institution itself; productivity changes require only a change in the numerator or the denominator, not necessarily both (Bowen, 2012).

A few more prominent and recent publications on the topic of productivity in higher education are shown in Table 9.1. College leaders need to be alert of what outcomes exactly are measured in productivity studies, and determine if it helps them take appropriate action or if it inappropriately embodies the college's mission.

In the examples in the table, the outcome of interest is a degree or credential. However, this may not always be the student's intention. Our analysis of data for students beginning at a community college in 2003–04 found that 12% who had not expected to complete a degree or certificate wound up earning a college credential (Skomsvold, Radford, & Berkner, 2011). Surely the colleges these students attended are not inefficient because the students did not attain what they expected when they enrolled.

Table 9.1.   Outcome Utilized in Recent Studies of Efficiency/Productivity

Entity	Outcome	
	Measure/Variable	Components
National Research Council (2013)	Adjusted credit hours	Credit hours during 12-month academic year, credentials awarded, and the increase in earnings associated with earning a credential
State Higher Education Executive Officers (SHEEO) (2010)	Degree per FTE and Credential per FTE	Certificates, degrees, and full-time equivalent (FTE) enrollments
Kelly (2009)	Degree per FTE and Credential per FTE (weighted)	Credentials are weighted by comparing the earnings associated with the credential relative to the earnings associated with a bachelor's degree. The weights are further differentiated between STEM and non-STEM programs.

In Chapter 7, expenditure trend data from the Delta Cost Project (Hurlburt and Kirschstein, 2012) showed the decrease in funding per FTE over the first decade of the twenty-first century for community colleges. Yet, as Figure 9.2 illustrates, those decreases in support nevertheless were accompanied by increased completions. How is this possible?

The simple answer is that there was a seismic shift toward short-term credential attainment at community colleges over this time period. If we wanted to show a less favorable outcome (and

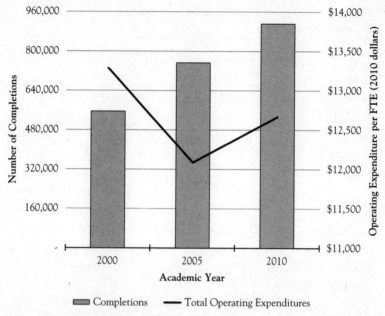

Figure 9.2   Completions and Total Operating Revenue per FTE (2010 Dollars) at Community Colleges: Select Years

Source: Adapted from Desrochers and Hurlburt (2012) and Hurlburt and Kirschstein (2012).

one using a more commonly understood measurement), we could include only associate degrees as an outcome. If transfers were included in the figure, it would show an even more pronounced increase in "efficiency."

One problem with accounting for transfer outcomes is the lack of annual data reported by either the National Student Clearinghouse, which currently has sufficient data to provide much of this critical information but does not publish it each year. No other entity is in a position to do what the Clearinghouse can. (Few are aware that community colleges do not maintain comprehensive data detailing subsequent enrollment at a public, private, or for-profit two- or four-year institution for transfer students.)

At the core of the productivity conversation is the assumption that an institution "owns" a student who initially enrolls. This perspective is a carryover from colleges that serve traditional college students and work with a well-defined cohort of students. But this mentality, and the practice it reflects, is becoming increasingly less prominent in higher education, as students engage in much more complex, irregular patterns of higher education enrollment.

Perceptions of Institutional Quality

A review of higher education finance literature shows a tension between the dual purposes of supporting access for low-income students and providing choice among institutions. Whereas access speaks to opportunity, choice has been interpreted to speak to quality, and is a term historically associated with private colleges. And quality is, or at least should be, one concern in any focus on productivity or efficiency.

The quality of an institution can be viewed in numerous ways. Most prominently, institutional quality has been defined as the academic aptitude of the student body upon entering, or the institution's selectivity. It is a measure of how influential these metrics have become that there have been reported instances of institutions falsifying these data to improve their rankings and associated prestige.

The prestige associated with college selectivity not only drives competition for students but also contributes to the acquisition of faculty of strong repute. Ironically, research accomplishments by a prestigious faculty member may well have been achieved while working at a less selective college; faculty who excel at publishing are usually hired away by "leading" institutions. The competition for faculty has been a factor in increasing costs to colleges (Archibald & Feldman, 2011) and the related prices that students pay. Irrespective of institution type, more costly and often prestigious professors are certainly not necessarily better teachers. For those who believe higher education costs need to be addressed, it may be worth reframing how we assign one major driver of cost:

prestige. This is to say, because the search for prestige drives up costs, why not acknowledge that low-cost institutions may also be prestigious? The Aspen Prize for Excellence serves as one example. More are needed.

Rather than recognizing that excellence exists in many forms, one of today's hot topics in higher education—undermatching—is a concept that warrants a critical eye, because it reinforces certain dangerous assumptions about quality. The idea behind undermatching is well intentioned. It seeks to highlight the fact that many academically advanced students (particularly low-income and minority students) attend postsecondary institutions that lag in terms of selectivity, and that highly selective institutions do a better job of serving these students, particularly in terms of graduation.

However, this perspective does tend to convey another message: that nonselective institutions are inferior to selective institutions. This assumption needs greater attention.

As stated, institutional quality in higher education has long been associated with the academic merits of the students. Part of education's role was to put the smartest people in a room and nurture their acquired knowledge, deferring to the benefit of prior knowledge and a belief in their abilities. This practice, ability grouping, is a critical part of higher education. It is a space where boundaries are pushed and advancements in thinking are made. Such classrooms, however, are not and should not be exclusive to "elite" enclaves. In fact, 10% of the community college student body is academically advanced, and institutions are meeting those students' academic needs with honors colleges (Mullin, 2012d), while also exposing them to a more diverse student body.

Surely one aspect of quality in postsecondary education is the additive aspect of learning, which clearly occurs in both selective and nonselective environments. Whether it be a greater understanding of the components of an artwork or an appreciation for the complexities of the human body, learning outcomes in all of their varieties are intrinsically valuable. They guide students in the mastery of vocabulary, skills, and abilities associated with a particular field of study. Nearly one-tenth of community college students already have a bachelor's degree and are returning to obtain the additional knowledge a course provides, although many of these students have more job-targeted goals.

It is also fair to say that many of the most selective institutions do not see older students, for example, as their target population. It is an open question whether a classroom of 19-year-olds with the same SAT score provides an opportunity for a more nuanced discussion or project development than a classroom with students aged 16 to 55 with a wider range of standardized test scores and varying purposes for attending college: it just may be that the varied life histories make conversations richer and more culturally inclusive and contribute to stronger citizenship.

Lastly, there is an assumption in the concept of undermatching that the selective institutions that did not enroll undermatched students in the first place could find the capacity to serve them. It is more likely the case that selective institutions could not dramatically increase their entering class sizes to meet demand: freshman enrollment at 31 selective liberal arts colleges increased by just over 5,000 students in two decades (see Figure 9.3), while total undergraduate freshmen enrollments increased from 2.2 to 3.1 million students. Clearly, there is a capacity problem. Alternatively, institutions could increase access for undermatched students through the transfer function (Bowen, Chingos, & McPherson, 2009). Such an initiative is laudable, though it requires additional efforts to ensure there is not a chilling effect on students new to a campus, as outlined in publications by the College Board (Handel, 2011) and The Pell Institute for the Study of Opportunity in Higher Education (Miller, Erisman, Bermeo, & Taylor-Smith, 2011).

In conclusion, there exists an unlimited number of talented people in this country from every community. Without intentional actions to value diversity in all its forms at the student and institutional level, college can become a reward rather than

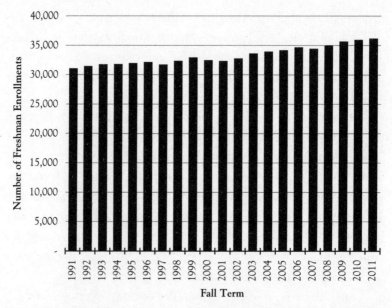

Figure 9.3 Freshman Class Enrollment Counts at 31 Private, Highly Selective Liberal Arts Colleges Constituting the Membership of the Consortium on Financing Higher Education (COFHE): 1991 to 2011

Note: Enrollment data reflect degree/certificate-seeking first-time undergraduate students. I refer to this group as "Freshman Enrollment."

Sources: Adapted from Consortium on Financing Higher Education (COFHE) (2013) and National Center for Education Statistics (NCES) (2013a).

an opportunity open to all. One must be vigilant to counter the premise, wherever it is found, that non-elite students and institutions are somehow less valuable than their more prestigious kin in higher education.

Conclusion

This chapter examined issues associated with institutional costs as well as those inherent in considerations of efficiencies and productivity. While a focus of this chapter was to increase the reader's awareness, understanding, and responsiveness to cost, efficiency, and productivity studies, there was another important motivation:

having an awareness of these important studies can allow for the development of more appropriate and ultimately more helpful studies in the future.

Questions

1. Locate and examine the costs studies from one of the four states listed in the chapter. List three things that stand out to you. Do you think the cost data should be used in funding formulas that allocate state appropriations to college? Why or why not?

2. Which outcomes do you believe should be used for a productivity study? How would you measure them?

3. Draft a response to a researcher who published a study about your institution that considered only students who transferred to four-year institutions as an outcome in a productivity calculation.

Chapter Ten

College as an Investment

All transfers of funds between parties can be viewed as either a cost or an investment. Costs are commonly perceived as transaction costs; that is, how much an item costs at a particular time. However, an investment takes into consideration not only the cost of the item when purchased but also its future value. Take, for example, the common comparison between the cost of education to the student and the price of a new vehicle. Whereas the new car depreciates the moment it leaves the dealer's parking lot, the return on educational attainment is positive for the length of one's work life and even well after that.

Given the substantial expenditures of colleges, and the increased burdens on students in the form of increased tuitions, and of competitors for students, there is an increasing need to articulate whether education is indeed a cost or an investment. Strong fiscal leadership recognizes the difference between the two and works to better document and communicate their views on this central issue.

This chapter sets out not only to help the reader better understand the indicators of an efficient investment, but also to detail actions they can take to invest strategically in an educationally and economically justifiable manner. This is accomplished by helping to frame the purpose of college. This further impacts how institutions view their students, the return on their investment in them, and approaches for investing strategically.

The Purpose of College

One way that an institution can articulate its purpose is by developing a strategic plan. The plan can lead to reports on prior performance as well as short-term tactics to meet long-term strategic objectives. In turn, this helps communicate the purpose and direction of the college to internal and external stakeholders, while providing a framework for action.

There is an enduring debate between the traditional "liberal" approach to education and a more utilitarian perspective on higher education that has grown in prominence over time. Newman's lectures on the liberal arts, published as *The Idea of a University* in 1852, set the foundation and has been revisited over time. Delbanco (2012), for example, states, "At its core, a college should be a place where young people find help for navigating the territory between adolescence and adulthood. It should provide guidance, but not coercion, for students trying to cross that treacherous terrain on their way toward self-knowledge. It should help them develop certain qualities of mind and heart requisite for reflective citizenship" (p. 3).

Extending the ideas set forth in the Morrill Act of 1862, Kerr's (1963) *Uses of the University* introduced a more practical application of college. In the twenty-first century, the perspective of Anthony Carnevale is that colleges are places where people go to get educated and trained for a job.

While these ends of the continuum push and pull conversations on educational policy, and are expressed through the allocation and use of funds, they have primarily, if not exclusively, focused on universities. One community college perspective, expressed by Edmund Gleazer, CEO of the American Association of Community Colleges from 1958 to 1972, was that community college education should be like a library, where an individual can come and check out the knowledge they want, when they want it (personal communication with the authors, 2012). His book *Values, Vision, and*

Vitality (1980) was a forceful expression of the role of the college in the community.

Education is nothing if not multifaceted in its impact on students. Therefore, it is important to first reflect and identify how the college views the student population it is serving.

Students: Consumers or Investments?

How institutions view their students influences the actions they take. Looked at through a financial lens, a college could be viewed as selling a commodity to students or as investing in students.

Hoxby (2014) suggests there is a difference in current practice at different types of institutions: nonselective educational institutions, including community colleges, sell services for payment, whereas highly selective institutions model themselves as investors. Saunders' (2014) examination of the student as customer suggests that this big difference is critical to understand. But which one is appropriate for community colleges? The answer may be "both." It is rare for all members of a college leadership to have the same perspective, resulting in a clear mandate by either a unanimous "yes" or "no" vote; rather, college leadership needs to determine where the college falls on the spectrum.

Saunders (2014) suggests that the "student as customer" model is inappropriate for higher education for three reasons. First, the acquisition of knowledge is what the student seeks from education. Second, students often do not know the path or sequence needed to meet their objective, and they may not even have an objective. This has become all too clear in the community college sector of late; witness the phrase coined by community college luminary Kay McClenney: "Students don't do optional!" By this she means that offering too many educational choices for students actually reduces their likelihood of success. Third, students at all institution types receive subsidies, which logically suggests that the consumers are not only students but in some respects the public as well.

Mullin (2013c) noted that the free market is not necessarily applicable to higher education, as students operate in a form of adaptive preference, whereby the decisions they make are informed by their circumstances and experiences. To frame the reader's understanding, Mullin asked, "As an adolescent, did someone expose you to possibilities or reinforce limitations? Did you attend a high school with a college-going culture or did your high school continually fail adequate yearly progress? If you answered yes to the latter part of these questions, or others like them, you understand the limitations of circumstance" (2013, pp. 26–27).

For those who see students not as customers but rather as investments, it will take some work to rethink how this is communicated to students and stakeholders. Hoxby (2014) suggested that the investment model, dominant in highly selective institutions, relies on a sense of connection to the college that leads to future donations from alumni who see the college as a *reason* for their present standing. For community college leaders to adopt such a stance would require them to recognize that their traits may be different from those in other sectors; that institutional aspirations to climb the status structure of higher education are a never-ending challenge, when all the while the college has the potential to be excellent in its own right.

This change would mean, in turn, that community colleges would engage with alumni in ways that few have, despite the resources provided by the Council for Resource Development (the primary community college group focused on grant procurement and fundraising) and decades of research and efforts to focus on the development of alumni/foundation offices at community colleges. But there is no doubt that progress is being made in this area, though overall the colleges have a long way to go. Private, voluntary contributions to community colleges represent a tiny minority, less than 5%, of all those made to institutions of higher education.

Whether one views students as consumers or investments, any college will be benefitted by developing a strong public identity and pricing its offerings accordingly. And the development of this identity will likely have to incorporate a balance between both perspectives described in this chapter.

Return on Investment

In 2014, the American Association of Community Colleges released a commissioned report that quantified the economic returns provided by the nation's community colleges (Economic Modeling Specialists International [EMSI], 2014). Among other findings, it noted that in 2012 community colleges contributed

1. $809 billion in income to the U.S. economy
2. An annual rate of return for students of 17.8% and an annual rate of return for taxpayers of 14.3%
3. A $19.2 billion reduction in demand for government services
4. $285.7 billion in benefits to taxpayers resulting from higher lifetime incomes and increased business outputs

Economic contribution studies have been conducted for many individual community colleges as well as at the state level. Yet there are those who think that investments are truly efficient or rational if, and only if, the returns associated with an investment are in excess of the returns from other goods and services in which it might be invested (Eckstein, 1960). To that end, research published by The Hamilton Project at the Brookings Institute (Greenstone & Looney, 2013) found that the return on investment for an associate degree is more than three times higher than for stocks or other investments, such as gold, ten-year treasury bonds, T-bills, and housing. This ability to show comparative returns, when available, is important, as it provides meaningful context.

Most commonly, the returns to education are viewed in terms of returns to the individual. To this end, Belfield and Bailey (2012) reviewed 20 studies on the earnings effects of a community college education, concluding, "[T]his review affirms that there are strong positive earnings gains from community college attendance and completion, as well as progression to a 4-year college" (p. 60). There are two other ways to examine the returns to educational attainment: academic progression and earnings overlap.

Academic Progression

One way to examine the economic contributions of community colleges to both students and the economy is to document the economic returns associated with a student's academic progression. When referring to attainment, the term "college" is commonly interpreted to mean a bachelor's degree. In fact, much of the higher education research one encounters implicitly quantifies "success" as the attainment of this one level of education—and for good reason. In 2013 only 20% of the nation's population aged 25 and over held a bachelor's degree; an additional 12% also held a higher degree (U.S. Census Bureau, 2014). Further, on average, those students who earn a bachelor's degree earn more than those that do not (Carnevale & Rose, 2011). This is the message displayed on posters hung in high schools and colleges across the country.

These data may be examined from two other perspectives. The first focuses on the gains experienced as a student reaches the next level of educational attainment, rather than an ultimate goal. Employing the perspective of the economic gains associated with educational progression, Mullin and Phillippe (2013) found positive gains for each level of attainment, with the largest percentage increase in earnings observed from students who moved from less than a high school equivalent to a high school diploma. This finding supports the heavy developmental education role that community colleges play as well as a focused effort on assisting students aspiring to earn a high school equivalency diploma, such as a GED (Long & Mullin, 2014).

A replication of Mullin and Phillippe's work with more recent data reaffirms the returns they identified (see Table 10.1). Specifically, the returns associated with a student's becoming a high school graduate are a substantial increase in earnings and a correlated increase in the taxes they pay.

Earnings Overlap

The second perspective on economic returns to educational attainment focuses on the average earnings at a particular level of education. Research published by Carnevale, Rose, and Cheah

Table 10.1. Changes in Weekly Earnings, Estimated Taxes Paid, and Unemployment Associated with Each Change in Educational Attainment: 2012

Highest Level of Attainment	Weekly Earnings (2012)		Estimated Annual Taxes Paid (2012)		Unemployment Rate (2012)
	Median	% increase from prior level	Amount	% increase from prior level	
Less than High School	$471		$4,001		12.4%
High School or Equivalent	$652	38%	$6,130	53%	8.3%
Some College	$727	12%	$7,018	14%	7.7%
Associate Degree	$785	8%	$7,836	12%	6.2%
Bachelor's Degree	$1,066	36%	$11,185	43%	4.5%

Notes: Annual taxes paid were estimated by determining taxes as a percentage of earnings for data presented in Figure 1.1 in Baum, Ma, and Payea (2013). The rates were then applied to median weekly earnings in 2012 reported by the Bureau of Labor Statistics (2014) after weekly earnings were annualized (multiplied by 52). These data present estimates; tax rates may have changed. The Some College category includes those who earned postsecondary certificates.

Sources: Baum, Ma, and Payea (2013); Bureau of Labor Statistics (2014).

(2011) found that many workers with lesser levels of educational attainment made more than those with comparatively higher levels of educational attainment (see Figure 10.1). Specifically, they estimated that 23.1% of workers with a bachelor's degree will earn less over their lifetime than a student whose level of educational attainment was some college/certificate, and further, that 28.2% of bachelor's degree earners will earn less over their lifetime than those who earn an associate's degree. Their research reinforces our understanding that although increased economic returns often stem from increased educational attainment, many other factors are at work as well. This earnings overlap is important to consider when discussing a return on investment and further reinforces the notion of investing strategically (a concept treated later in this chapter).

Not all economic returns to education are found in the labor market. These non–labor market returns, such as decreased need for social services, also have economic impacts. The returns will not be detailed here; rather, the reader is referred to Baum, Ma,

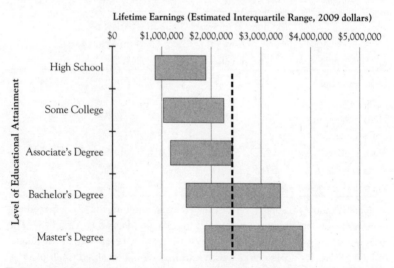

Figure 10.1 Lifetime Earnings Overlap, by Level of Educational Attainment

Source: Adapted from Carnevale, Rose, and Cheah (2011).

and Payea's (2013) publication *Education Pays: The Benefits of Higher Education for Individuals and Society*, which clearly documents the various returns to educational attainment provided by McMahon (2009) and McKeown-Moak and Mullin (2014).

A note of caution is in order when discussing any returns on education. Some suggest that there is not a causal link between educational attainment and a particular economic outcome. They would assert, rightfully, that the returns are associated with *increases* in educational attainment, not educational attainment *per se*. For example, just because someone earns a postsecondary credential does not mean that his or her health automatically improves—though it may be that those who earn a postsecondary credential engage in healthier behaviors. As such, it is prudent to use the phrase "associated with" rather than "results in" when discussing the contribution of increased levels of educational attainment.

Strategic Investments

In 2011–2012, community colleges overall spent $56.8 billion (American Association of Community Colleges [AACC], 2014), with $9.8 billion coming from local sources and $16 billion from state revenues. These funds are allocated largely on credit hour–based, enrollment-driven funding models, although that is changing. In recognition of tight fiscal times, the emphasis on completion, and the rising price that students pay for education, community college stakeholders recognize the need to make strategic investments in both the colleges and the programs they offer.

Program Growth

Community colleges need to constantly reevaluate their programs to ensure that they are meeting the needs of their community and other stakeholders. The offering of new or nontraditional programs has been called "mission creep." However, if there is a solid case to be made for demand, institutional leadership must weigh the pros and cons of history and current opportunity.

Community colleges have traditionally been flexible and responsive to community needs, even if changing program offerings is often no simple matter because of institutional constraints. But the "community" moniker applies because of a college's general willingness to build new programs when needed. There are three ways in which community colleges may respond to market potential (Kotler & Fox, 1995; Voorhees, 2005):

- Developing existing programs by finding new segments of a job market or new geographical area to introduce to the programs

- Modifying a current program to make its curriculum and content relevant to changes in the field

- Developing new programs as spin-offs of previously existing programs or as programs new to the institution

Lebesch (2012) provided examples of all three:

- Program development providing continuing education opportunities

- Program modification responding to changes in certification or licensure requirements

- New program development in hazardous materials, cyber security, and terrorism response addressing needs identified in the aftermath of the September 11, 2001 attacks

While program development is both an art and science, there are certain processes that should be followed to ensure that the endeavor is both educationally and economically justified.

Dickeson (2010) provides an A-to-Z guide for allocating resources for programs; this section augments his work by focusing on three general categories that should be of particular interest to those who must justify a new program both economically and in terms of meeting a strategic need. These categories are *identifying the need*, *clarifying the need*, and *applying filters*. (The process for program approval will vary by state. Readers should refer to governing documents for program approval purposes.)

Identifying the Need

The kernel of an idea that develops into a call for a new educational program may come from a business, industry, or external source such as a think tank or governmental agency focused on future needs to meet these demands. Determining workforce needs extends beyond a simple equation of demand minus supply. Community colleges employ both formal and informal approaches to identify workforce needs.

Formal methods include an analysis of local needs and the skills of the local labor pool. Needs are typically quantifiable measurements that originate from occupational projections from national sources like the U.S. Department of Labor, or state sources such as a department of workforce (titles vary by state). Labor market indicators also come from the U.S. Census Bureau, organizations, and commercial data providers (Lebesch, 2012).

Challenges associated with the formal determinations of demand include, but are not limited to, data lags that cannot account for rapid changes to economies, limited access to data for college personnel to analyze, and government data that do not always align with a college's service area.

Informal approaches to identifying workforce needs include direct feedback from stakeholders. These stakeholders include advisory boards, community groups engaged in economic development, business and industry, state leadership, federal agencies, and even students. Engagement with business and industry occurs at three primary levels—executive offices, human resource personnel, and line managers. Each provides a different perspective on workforce needs.

Challenges to the informal identification of demand include the fact that business and industry do not always share hiring or layoff plans in advance. This may leave the institution in the position of playing catch-up. This situation often leads to the establishment of noncredit training programs, which are in general easier to establish than credit programs. There are instances where the company does inform the college of pending layoffs. For example, a Food Lion distribution center in Clifton, Tennessee, worked with Roane Community College to ensure that laid-off employees had an opportunity to participate in a seven-week retraining program (Dembicki, 2012). There are also situations in which the employer's request for a new training program does not justify its expense.

Clarifying the Need

For fiscal leaders who will not necessarily be conducting the analysis but will be making the decision on the new program, an important first step is to thoroughly understand the data being used to justify the demand. In general, the two primary sources of data are the American Community Survey of the U.S. Department of Commerce's Census and the Bureau of Labor Statistics (BLS) of the U.S. Department of Labor. Because the ACS surveys current workers, who may have earned a degree after they started on a job or who have taken a job they are overeducated for, the result will suggest a need for a workforce with a higher level of educational attainment. The BLS data, which use multiple sources to identify the typical worker, are biased toward workers with comparatively less educational attainment. There may also be state data.

In Florida, for example, a classification scheme—BLS-Florida Education Code (BLS-FEC)—was developed to identify educational attainment needed by entry-level workers; it had the effect of suppressing estimates of higher education credential attainment needs in the state. The result was data that identified a larger number of jobs that required subbaccalaureate credentials as opposed to baccalaureate level credentials. These differences in data can have a substantial impact on the analysis and, more important, the real demand for a particular program. It is a good practice to calculate both a low and a high estimate using two data sources. The difference, if any, should be discussed as part of the third phase of the process: applying filters.

Applying Filters

After quantifying the need, the work needs to be checked to ensure that there are no contextual factors that may influence the findings. For example, if a large number of graduates from programs in a service area leave because that area includes a military installation or is on a state border, analysts may need to rerun the numbers to account for those students who stay in the area.

There may also be post-educational barriers to practice imposed by regulating bodies. For example, if you find there is a need for registered nurses in a college's service area, it is also important to know the pass rate of national exams—the National Council Licensure Examination (NCLEX), in this case—that allow the graduates from the program to actually practice as nurses. An additional consideration is an accounting for the warehousing of workers with appropriate credentials who are not currently working but may be able to fill the jobs. A scan to determine whether other colleges plan to offer similar programs should also be considered, and if doing so reveals that they do, negotiations of some sort should begin.

Each institution may undertake additional actions and have specific considerations beyond those provided here as they undertake their due diligence to ensure the sound expenditure of public, private, and institutional funds.

Focusing on Credentials

Until the recent focus on educational attainment and student progress and completion, it may be said that, to an unacceptable extent, community colleges let students go their own way. Those who engage with college presidents commonly hear anecdotes of students earning over 60 credits without a credential to speak of, leaving a college without obtaining their degree after having met the requirements for that degree, or leaving a college just short of earning a credential. This "ad hoc" nature of much of student enrollment at community colleges may have stemmed from either the criticisms of Burton Clark's "cooling-out" theory (1960), which noted that community colleges redirect student aspirations by offering a level of attainment below that which they are capable of attaining, tensions and confusion related to the purpose of a junior or community college education, or just a plain lack of interest in the fact that student enrollment was in many ways "ad hoc."

There are numerous activities under way to make sure that students have a clear, direct, and efficient path to a credential. Examples include the Completion by Design initiative of the Bill and Melinda Gates Foundation, the establishment of state student success centers, sophisticated online aids to helping students stay on path to a degree, and academic advising. In addition, there is a keen interest in ensuring that those students who will not benefit from institutional redesign efforts earn the credential they are entitled to, even after they have left the institution. Two such national efforts include Project Win-Win and Credit When It's Due.

Project Win-Win

In 2004 Adelman found that 15% of community college students earned over 60 credits and were in good academic standing (>2.5 GPA) but had yet to earn a college credential. In light of this research and the call for greater educational attainment, a project called "Win-Win" sought to award credentials to those who met the requirements and to reengage students who were just short (9 to 12 credits) of earning an associate degree (Adelman, 2013). As a result, of the 6,733 students identified to be eligible for a degree, 4,550 were awarded one. Further, of the 20,105 who were just short of earning an associate degree, 1,668 reenrolled.

Credit When It's Due

Colleges are taking action to ensure that students who leave college just short of earning an educational certificate ultimately receive the credential. Project "Credit When It's Due" focused on awarding associate degrees to students who transferred to a four-year institution prior to earning an associate degree. The project's initial 2013 report, providing baseline data, noted that of the 9,682 students from six states that were deemed eligible to participate in the program, 42% earned over 60 credit hours prior to transfer, 23% earned between 45 and 60 credits prior to transfer, and another 20% earned 30 to 45 credits prior to transfer (Taylor, Bishop, Makela, Bragg, & Ruud, 2013).

Stackable Credentials

Another approach to enhancing completion is to focus on requiring plans for student success that clearly delineate the path to a credential or goal. The key innovation in this approach is that rather than serving as alternative paths, or "soft landings" for students believed to not have the potential to meet certain levels of expectations, as theorized by Clark (1960), plans have emerged that create positive student outcomes, albeit smaller ones, in a sequential order. One term for this practice is the "stackable credential." Given the rise in performance funding and the focus on measureable outcomes, it is strategically advantageous for colleges to focus on these stackable credentials, which provides positive reinforcement to students and keeps them on a clearer path to a specific academic goal.

All three of these approaches, and others like them, create lessons to be learned for institutional operations that are beyond the scope of this book, but there is one that is germane to our investigation of community college finance: the impact of moving students who are close to a credential to the completion of a credential has fiscal implications.

Let's use a fictional college we'll call Lukila Community College to illustrate how a focus on getting students who are close to a credential to actually receiving one can make a substantial financial difference (see Table 10.2). In one year, the college has a student body of 17,500 students; 5,000 are credential-seeking, another 10,000 are focused on transferring, and 2,500 students are not seeking a credential but taking courses (nonmatriculating).

The table provides fictional data for two scenarios. First, if the college continues on its current trajectory, wherein students (a) leave the college with a certain number of credits on average (c) and generate a set revenue amount per credit (b), then the college receives $42.68 million in revenues (e). However, if it maximizes student success by getting all students to a credential, multiplying columns (a)*(b)*(d), then the result would be potential revenues from full credit hour production of $65.36 million. The difference between full potential and current practice is $22.68 million.

There are a few issues to consider with this model. Among them is whether or not nonmatriculating students—those who are not credential seeking or who do not want to transfer—may be encouraged to finish a short-term certificate. Alternatively, those students may be allowed to continue attending on a nonmatriculating basis.

Additionally, one could rightfully question the ability of a college to ensure that 100% of its students receive a credential prior to departing. However, it does point to the lost revenue for institutions when this does not occur, and it supports expenses for actions that could work to achieve a full potential model—even if it is adjusted to reflect, for example, 90% of all students earning a credential rather than 100%. Additionally, the theory that students

Table 10.2. Lukila Community College Model Focusing on Credential Attainment

Enrollment Type	(a) 12-month unduplicated headcount enrollment in one year	(b) Revenue per credit hour (6 year average)	(c) Average number of credit hours (over 6 years)	(d) Full load of credit hours to credential	(e) Current revenues from average credit hour production	(f) Potential revenues from full credit hour production	(g) Difference
Credential seeking							
Certificate	3,000	$105	18	30	$5,670,000	$9,450,000	$3,780,000
Associates Degree	2,000	$105	45	60	$9,450,000	$12,600,000	$3,150,000
Transfer students							
Certificate	7,500	$105	24	30	$18,900,000	$23,625,000	$4,725,000
Associates Degree	2,500	$105	24	60	$6,300,000	$15,750,000	$9,450,000
Nonmatriculating							
Upskilling, retraining, swirling	2,500	$105	9	15	$2,362,500	$3,937,500	$1,575,000
Impact							
TOTAL	17,500				$42,682,500	$65,362,500	$22,680,000
Per student					$2,439	$3,735	$1,296

Notes: Fictional data. (a) Reflects credit-bearing enrollment for cohort of students starting in a particular year. (b) Includes revenues from gross tuition and fees and appropriation. (c) The average number of credit hours accumulated by students in the cohort over a 6-year period. (d) The number of credits to earn a credential. (e), (f), (g) Derived values.

should complete an appropriate credential—either a certificate of less than one year (15 credits), a one-year certificate (30 credits), or an associate's degree (60 credits)—has an important basis, as research has shown that earning a credential increases labor market returns, all other things being equal. In addition, earning an associate degree prior to pursuing a bachelor's degree increases the likelihood of being successful in bachelor's programs, and the reemergence of performance-based funding models provides additional financial rewards to colleges for ensuring that students complete a credential.

Conclusion

This chapter described the indicators of what might constitute an efficient investment by institutions and provided actions and perspectives that institutional leaders may use as they invest strategically in an educationally and economically justifiable manner. This was accomplished by addressing the concepts of return on investment, approaches for investing strategically, and the framing of the purpose of college.

Questions

One community college needs to be identified before completing the following questions. Community colleges may be located by using the College Navigator tool of the National Center for Education Statistics at http://nces.ed.gov/collegenavigator/.

1. Should students be viewed as customers or as an investment? Explain why.

2. How many students completed a certificate and how many an associate degree in the community college in 2011–2012? What is the additional private and public economic return for this cohort of graduates, using the academic progression model?

Part Three

Leadership Resources

Chapter Eleven

Funding Formulas

States appropriate billions of dollars each year to operate community colleges. More often than not these funds are allocated using one or more funding formulas. The formulas can have a powerful impact on institutional behavior.

States typically use one of two types of funding formulas. The first is the traditional enrollment-based funding model, which relies heavily, if exclusively, on enrollments. The second is a performance-based funding model, which links the allocation of funds to some level of institutional accomplishment. This chapter describes the general components and prevalence of these models.

Enrollment-Based Funding Formulas

In 2010, 35 state appropriations were guided by a funding formula (McKeown-Moak & Mullin, 2014), a substantial increase from just 4 in 1950 (Mullin & Honeyman, 2007). The use of funding formulas emerged for a number of reasons, including but not limited to the desire to maintain an objective, clear, fair, and equitable distribution of funds; to enhance the ability of colleges to plan for the future by predicting revenue; and to manage the growth or reduction of programs and services offered by public colleges (MGT of America, 2001).

McKeown-Moak outlined 14 characteristics that might be considered in developing a community college funding model (see Table 11.1). These characteristics may at times conflict with each other. For example, the desirable trait of being simple to

Table 11.1. Characteristics of a Funding Formula or Guidelines

Characteristic	Summary Description
Equitable	The funding formula should provide both horizontal equity (equal treatment of equals) and vertical equity (unequal treatment of unequals) based on size, mission and growth characteristics of the institutions.
Adequacy-Driven	The funding formula should determine the funding level needed by each institution to fulfill its approved mission.
Goal-Based	The funding formula should incorporate and reinforce the broad goals of the state for its system of colleges and universities as expressed through approved missions, quality expectations and performance standards.
Mission-Sensitive	The funding formula should be based on the recognition that different institutional missions (including differences in degree levels, program offerings, student readiness for college success and geographic location) require different rates of funding.
Size-Sensitive	The funding formula should reflect the impact that relative levels of student enrollment have on funding requirements, including economies of scale.
Responsive	The funding formula should reflect changes in institutional workloads and missions as well as changing external conditions in measuring the need for resources.
Adaptable to Economic Conditions	The funding formula should have the capacity to apply under a variety of economic situations, such as when the state appropriations for higher education are increasing, stable or decreasing.

Table 11.1. *(continued)*

Characteristic	Summary Description
Concerned with Stability	The funding formula should not permit shifts in funding levels to occur more quickly than institutional managers can reasonably be expected to respond.
Simple to Understand	The funding formula should effectively communicate to key participants in the state budget process how changes in institutional characteristics and performance and modifications in budget policies will affect funding levels.
Adaptable to Special Situations	The funding formula should include provisions for supplemental state funding for unique activities that represent significant financial commitments and that are not common across the institutions.
Reliant on Valid & Reliable Data	The funding formula should rely on data that are appropriate for measuring differences in funding requirements and that can be verified by third parties when necessary.
Flexible	The funding formula should be used to estimate funding requirements in broad categories; it is not intended for use in creating budget control categories.
Incentive-Based	The funding formula should provide incentives for institutional effectiveness and efficiency and should not provide any inappropriate incentives for institutional behavior.
Balanced	The funding formula should achieve a reasonable balance among the sometimes-competing requirements of each of the criteria listed above.

Source: Reproduced with permission by McKeown-Moak (MGT of America, 2001).

understand runs counter to a formula that provides the nuance needed to ensure that the formula is sensitive to the institution's mission and activities.

Medsker in 1956, Wattenbarger and Starnes in 1976, and Mullin and Honeyman in 2007 studied the use of funding formulas for community colleges in particular. Across all three studies, funding formulas were found to have similar structural components, which can be categorized broadly.

No Formula States

The most basic type of funding is one that does not rely on a formula. Rather, appropriations to institutions are justified on precedent or through some type of negotiation that is more or less public. This generally occurs in states with fewer than eight community colleges or where the community college is part of the four-year university system.

Cost-of-Education Formulas

The next, most simple, type of funding relies on a formula that simply multiplies the number of students by an amount determined to be the "cost of education" to arrive at a total appropriation. There are variances in practice across the states that use this approach, but these unit-rate formulas were used by eight states in 2006. The challenge arises when trying to understand exactly how the cost of education value is determined. In some cases it appears that the formula is "run backward" to arrive at the cost-of-education amount. This is to say if your formula is: a (number of students) * b (cost of education) = c (appropriation), then by knowing (a) and (c) one can determine (b).

Equalization Formulas

Another type of formula incorporates an equalization component. Equalization is a carryover from K–12 funding models. The purpose of these formula components is to use state funds to offset differences in the fiscal capacity or contributions of local government/sponsors (the appropriate title for the local entity varies by state) by providing a greater amount of state resources to less-wealthy local government/sponsors and a lesser amount of state resources to wealthier local government/sponsors (see this component in Illinois, for example, in Chapter Two). Not surprisingly, this reallocation of funds can create tensions between institutions. This is particularly true when a local government/sponsor receives a large share of state resources while at the same time keeps its tax rate low. At the same time, the component integrates two disparate funding sources in a way that best meets the needs of colleges and their students.

Option Formulas

Yet another type of funding formula provides a number of options to policymakers, depending on various thresholds being met. For example, in Iowa in 2006, appropriations to community colleges were tied to the inflation rate, base funding allocations, marginal cost adjustments, and an enrollment growth component (Mullin and Honeyman, 2007).

Generalized and Tiered Formulas

The remaining two models rely extensively on data and unit cost studies to identify the costs of specific courses, programs, institutional functions, and services to arrive at an appropriation (see cost studies in Chapter Nine as an example). The distinctions in institutional mission and size may be accounted for in the formula as well as considerations of the college's context.

Although more detailed, both generalized and tiered models can be difficult to understand. This is generally not the case with formulas that rely on broad categories, such as the "cost of education," though the latter are often less precise in operation.

Changing a state's funding formula may be difficult for many reasons—politically, substantively, and bureaucratically. In 2006,

12 states outlined the funding formula in state statute; in 22 states the higher education entity in the state developed the funding model; in 5 states the community college state entity developed the funding model; and in 2 states the K–20 board developed the funding model (Mullin & Honeyman, 2008).

Performance-Based Funding Formulas

Accountability in higher education is not a new concept. Colleges have been charged with "the effective stewardship of funds, whether to the board of the institution, the church with which the institution was affiliated, or the state which chartered the institution, or all of the above, from the first days of Harvard College" (McKeown-Moak & Mullin, 2014, p. 163).

The nature of accountability as manifested in institutional funding changed in the mid-1980s when the focus was put directly on institutional performance rather than on a more straightforward accounting for expenditure use (Burke & Modarresi, 2000). For a short time, performance reporting addressed this concern. Later, the recession of the early 1990s sparked conversations focused on incentivizing greater efficiencies in higher education. These conversations, along with dissatisfaction that performance reporting lacked direct financial consequences, contributed to the implementation of performance funding and budgeting. Table 11.2 outlines the differences among performance-based accountability approaches, from reporting to funding.

The growth of performance funding in the 1990s continued into the new millennium. These funding models and the processes used to develop them were studied and published in a number of annual surveys and other publications by Joseph Burke and colleagues. Discussions for and against performance funding were at times controversial. In 1998 Burke, recognizing the tension, outlined the arguments against performance funding and potential responses (see Table 11.3).

Table 11.2.   Three Types of Performance-Based Accountability

Name	Description
Performance Reporting	The reporting out by institutions on certain common metrics. It is not tied directly to the funding of colleges, but may influence policymaker perspectives should data not portray high levels of institutional or state success.
Performance Budgeting	Common metrics gauge institutional performance. The information may, but does not have to, inform the allocation of fiscal resources.
Performance Funding	Links metrics of institutional performance directly to the funding an institution receives.

Note: Some statements in the table are direct quotes from the cited manuscript.
Source: Adapted from McLendon, Hearn, and Deaton (2006).

In 2003, an all-time high of 46 states reported having performance reporting, compared to 21 states reporting having performance budgeting and 15 states reporting having a performance funding, a decrease from highs of 28 and 19 states, respectively (Burke & Minassians, 2003). Ultimately, the use of performance funding and budgeting declined as performance reporting became "the preferred approach to accountability for higher education" (p. 1), as it was less costly and controversial.

Burke and Modarresi (2000) identified the characteristics of stable performance funding programs—or those that lasted when others failed. They found that performance funding models that lasted tended to exhibit collaboration between campus leaders, state officials, and state policymakers; shared goals of institutional improvement, external accountability, and increased funding; had policy values stressing quality over efficiency; allocated time for planning and implementation; utilized a limited number of

**Table 11.3.   Arguments Against Performance Funding and
Responses to Them**

Arguments Against	Responses
Complexity Argument: The goals of higher education are too numerous and complex for inclusion in a performance funding plan with a reasonable number of performance indicators.	Identify indicators based on their importance to stakeholders.
Diversity Argument: The campus types of two-year colleges, comprehensive institutions, and research universities are too diverse for inclusion in a performance-funding program.	Diversify funding model by allowing for a differentiation of metrics. Allow for institutional improvement as a success standard.
Quality Argument: The quality of higher education programs and services is too subjective for measurement or even assessment in any indicator system or performance program.	The goal is not to evaluate the total quality of higher education, but to assess performance on some of its important characteristics.
Funding Argument: Performance funding programs either provide too little money to produce campus changes or allocate so much that they produce budget instability.	Most performance funding programs recognize this reality by tying it to additional state funding and by making the money discretionary.
Political Argument: State budgets represent political decisions that change with current issues and frequent elections, and these political changes work against the continuity required for long-term programs such as performance funding.	Performance funding should address concerns of external stakeholders more so than politicians.

Table 11.3. *(continued)*

Arguments Against	Responses
Cost Argument: Collecting the information that performance funding requires is too costly.	Performance funding can help institutions use data in a more focused way.
Incompatibility Argument: Critics complain that the goals of external accountability and institutional improvement are inherently incompatible.	Institutional improvement and external accountability share many common goals.
Punishing-the-Poor Argument: Giving money based on performance rewards the rich and punishes poor institutions.	Withhold the performance money that a lower-funded college or university failed to earn in performance funding until the campus devises a plan for correcting the identified deficiencies.

Note: Some statements in the table are direct quotes from the cited manuscript.

Source: Adapted from Burke (1998).

metrics; provided restricted yet substantial funding; exhibited stability in state priorities; focused on budget stability; and curbed costs of implementation.

In the wake of the Great Recession, performance funding reemerged as a topic of intense focus in national and state policy (Harnish, 2011). In this version, dubbed "performance-funding 2.0," the focus shifted from institutional success to a focus on the needs of the state and its students (McKeown-Moak & Mullin, 2014). This translated into including interim measures of student success, such as retention rates, and embedding performance funding in base funding rather than as an add-on (Dougherty & Reddy, 2011).

Dougherty and Hong (2005) identified positive outcomes of community college performance funding as including an increased awareness of state priorities, an increased focus on institutional performance, and competition for status between institutions. These three findings were further refined into theories of action by Dougherty and Reddy (2011) to justify why a performance funding mechanism should be put into place. They suggested these three theories of action were in addition to the commonly held perspective that institutions will respond to financial incentives, just as businesses respond to profits.

These theories of action may in fact be the best portrayals of performance funding outcomes, as Burke and Minassians (2003) and Dougherty and Reddy (2012) did not find clear evidence of an impact from those efforts. Indeed, there are many reasons why it will be nearly impossible to link performance funding solely to particular outcomes. First, community colleges have more than one revenue stream, and although institutions will respond to performance funding incentives, they must also meet the demands stemming from other revenue generators. This leads to a second reason—the different laws, regulations, and, in general, incentive structures embedded in student financial aid programs, particularly at the federal level. A third reason has to do with the fact that there are numerous national, state, institutional, and organizational efforts already focused on college completion. For example, in April 2010, six leading community college organizations—the American Association of Community Colleges, the Association of Community College Trustees, the Center for Community College Student Engagement, the League for Innovation in the Community College, the National Institute for Staff & Organizational Development, and Phi Theta Kappa Honor Society—jointly made a commitment to increase the number of students earning a credential. Efforts like this, in combination with a myriad of student and institutional behaviors, function alongside performance funding mechanisms to ensure that more students who start college finish with a credential, and they reinforce why just one effort cannot be singled out as having an impact. Yet this does not mean that implementing performance funding does not play a role in student success.

Like their predecessors, performance funding 2.0 models raised concern. Shulock (2011), much like Burke (1998) nearly a decade earlier, provided an overview of the problems—14 in total—and possible responses or explanations for state actors. Many of the concerns mirrored prior ones, but the concerns addressed in this iteration focused heavily on the difficulties of measuring student success and the ability (or lack thereof) of institutions to control student behavior.

Toward a Typology of Performance Funding Formulas

A classification of performance-funding formulas was put forth by Friedel, Thornton, D'Amico, and Katsinas (2013). Categories include general outcome indicators, progress outcomes indicators, subgroup outcome indicators, and high-need subject outcome indicators.

These four categories largely encompass the metrics commonly applied across states. But building a funding model entails more than identifying a few metrics. It begins with the guiding principles set out in Table 11.1. These guiding principles are then operationalized with metrics. By and large, for community colleges, this focus is on students (not that this has to be the case).

The development of a student cohort, which is the general frame of reference employed for performance-based funding, requires making a number of distinctions. First is the identification of the student's academic standing (that is, first-time-in-college, transfer-in, returning student, dual enrolled, or no longer enrolled).

Then the period of observation, including both a starting and ending date, needs to be set. This may be accomplished by selecting the beginning and ending of a semester, academic year, a number of academic years, a number of years after first enrolling, or a set number of years after graduating. Graduation rates rely on applying a set number of years after a student first enrolls, whereas post-college outcomes rely on a set number of years after graduating to identify whether a student is working, for example.

The outcome that may be of interest refers to a student's current status at the end of the period of observation. For example, the number of students in the cohort after three years who either graduated, are still enrolled, or transferred may be combined. Other outcomes may include milestone events or momentum points—such as completing a GED program or 30 credit hours—as discussed in Chapter Eight.

Once the metrics are set, adjustments to the cohort need to be made for populations that may be precluded from meeting the outcome of interest by subtracting them from the denominator. Examples include students who enlist in the military or experience a significant physical or mental impairment; this is a common occurrence.

Finally, it may be of interest to weight different outcomes so that one metric is worth more than another. There are two primary ways this is achieved. One way is to give extra points for special populations (such as males or students of color) or outcomes of importance (such as graduates in science, technology, engineering, or mathematics majors). The other way is to set a benchmark that an institution has to meet or exceed in order to indicate adequate performance on a measure.

Conclusion

This chapter examined the funding formulas used to allocate funds to community colleges. Whether it is an enrollment goal, an equalization component, or a level of performance that the institution must achieve, colleges will continue to be influenced by these funding frameworks.

Questions

1. Obtain a state's community college funding model and identify which data are used to allocate funds. Which of the characteristics of a funding model provided in this chapter apply to the model you found?

2. Examine performance-based funding models used in two different states. How are they the same? How are they different?

3. Which characteristic of a funding formula (Table 11.1) do you believe is most appropriate for states to use when allocating taxpayer-oriented funds? Why?

Chapter Twelve

Setting Prices

As tuition and fees become an ever larger part of community college revenues, institutional leaders need to fully understand the approaches and logic used to set tuition and fee prices. Tuition is a flashpoint in postsecondary education, and low tuition is a calling card for community colleges. The consequences of tuition setting have tremendous implications for campuses.

There is an art to setting prices, and like all of the arts there are basic elements that pull it all together. This chapter examines the various approaches that colleges of all types have used in the setting of tuition and fees, including tuition pricing models used throughout higher education. But first, we examine the often unexamined topic of who sets tuition and fee policy.

Tuition-Setting Authority

There is a common perception that the institution's leaders fix tuitions. (Statutes tended to use the term "fixing" rather than "setting.") While that is the case at private institutions, it is less common for community colleges. An appreciation of the different governance structures and arrangements that prevail in tuition setting for community colleges helps present the options that may or may not be available in this area.

In 2006, Mullin and Honeyman reviewed every state statute related to tuition authority at public four-year and two-year institutions. They found that there are four entities primarily responsible for fixing tuition at the community college level: the state legislature, the district board, the state system, and the institution (Mullin & Honeyman, 2008). These entities may have very different perspectives on the appropriate tuition level. In many cases institutional leaders will desire greater resources, and hence higher tuitions, than those acting from a greater remove. Also, political factors will be different depending on the entity setting the tuition.

In examining the setting of tuition, the term "primary responsibility" is important to note, as in some instances institutional leadership can fix tuition within a range of a few percentage points of the amount set by an external agency. For example, in Florida standard tuition and fee rates are set in statute (48 F.S. 1009.23, 2013), but each college's board of trustees can set tuition and fees at no more than 10% below and no more than 15% above the standard tuitions. (So, for example, if the tuition and fee level was set at $1,000, an institution's board of trustees could set tuition anywhere between $900 and $1,150.)

Our understanding of the trade-offs associated with tuition deregulation—giving control to institutions to set tuition in places where it previously was vested with other parties—was studied by McBain (2010). These arguments have resonance with the sometimes differing perspectives of the tuition fixers. McBain found that the arguments for deregulation included the need to be able to respond to budget cuts, the need to generate operating revenues, and a possible desire to increase capacity and possibly reduce faculty-to-student ratios and to generate a greater amount of unrestricted revenue to use for items such as institutionally allocated student financial aid. The arguments against the deregulation of tuition-setting authority included the perspective that institutions were founded to provide low-cost access to higher education and that deregulation would likely correspond to higher prices for students, that institutions that increase prices will likely price some students out of higher education, that institutions would lose incentives to reduce costs, and that the transfer of control over tuition setting decreases state control over institutions.

Tuition Pricing Models

This section builds upon the earlier discussion and draws from practices across all sectors of higher education. It provides a list of methods and perspectives that may be used individually or in combination by institutional leadership as they set tuition and fee prices.

Differential Pricing

When student bodies did not include as many part-time students as full-time students, institutions in some cases charged part-time students a higher rate. This practice changed as student bodies began to include more part-time students (Lombardi, 1976). Challenges identified with all differential pricing strategies were the ability to accurately project enrollment and revenues as compared to uniform, or nondifferential, tuition policy (Yankowski, 1986). Another challenge (Warner, 1984), which may no longer exist due to advances in technology, was the administrative costs associated with charging differentials. Despite the challenges, colleges have employed a number of differential approaches.

Cost-Based Pricing

The costs of providing various classes and programs differ. When tuition does not differ, the revenue generated from tuition is allocated in such a way that institutional costs of low-cost programs subsidize more expensive programs. An alternative is to price programs according to their cost, as determined by a unit cost study (see Chapter Nine). So, for example, a program that is more costly to the institution (such as an associate's degree in registered nursing) should be priced higher than a program that is less costly (such as an associate's degree in history).

Strengths of this approach include the perception that it is a rational approach to pricing. Additionally, the practice is usually well received by the business and industry community. Weaknesses of this approach include eliminating cross-subsidies that equalize prices and remove the influence of price on the student's choice of program. Additionally, it may incentivize program designers to be less cost-efficient.

High-Demand Pricing

Also, higher-demand courses and programs may be assigned higher charges. High-demand courses generally are those required for a major or general education criteria and take place at the most convenient time of the day for a college's student body.

Strengths of this approach include but are not limited to maximizing institutional revenues. It may also encourage student effort if access to the required course is limited. A weakness of the model is that price increases may serve as a barrier to participation.

Off-Peak Pricing

In this model, prices are lower for courses taking place during off-peak times of the day. For example, a class at 5:00 A.M. is priced lower than the same class offered at 10:00 A.M.

Such a model increases the use of facilities and expands institutional capacity. It also provides flexible and less-costly opportunities for students. A weakness of the model is that students do not necessarily have control over their daily schedules, especially at community colleges where the majority of students work.

Level Differentiation Pricing

A practice common across and within colleges is to differentiate tuition prices by level of the course. In practice, for example, upper division courses might be set at $150 a credit compared to $100 for lower division courses.

This differentiation of tuition accounts for additional costs associated with upper division level courses. Factors include higher faculty costs and smaller classes. However, the difference in price may serve as a barrier to participation.

Clientele-Based Pricing

In the clientele-based tuition model, the price a student pays varies based on a given student characteristic. For example, alumni, employees, or additional family members may be charged a lower price than others for the same course or program.

On one hand this practice encourages loyalty to the institution; on the other, location-based populations may increase the frequency of students' applying for the discount and thereby reduce revenues.

Value-Added Pricing

In this model, tuition prices are set based on average economic returns associated with a program. In practice, programs resulting in higher average earnings would charge a higher tuition than programs whose graduates, on average, earn a lower wage. As in an earlier example, students in registered nursing programs would be charged more than students in a history program.

The strength of this approach is that the value provide by an institution is recognized. There is a weakness in that economic returns (salary) vary based on factors other than education, such as prior work experience, age, location, macroeconomic trends and, to the greatest extent, the fiscal disposition of the employer (that is, the firm effect).

Student Academic Promise Pricing

One approach to tuition pricing is to differentiate tuition prices by the student's academic promise. Students with lower academic promise, as measured by a range of academic indicators, are charged more than students with greater academic promise.

A strength of this approach is grounded in the belief that too many students go to college for its social cachet rather than the substance of the educational opportunity provided. A weakness, aside from being anathema to the core principle of educational opportunity embedded in the community college ethos, is that academic promise is difficult to measure and may be influenced by factors beyond the control of the student that might be mitigated by attending college.

Residency-Based Pricing

While basing prices on residency is a type of pricing differential, it is a unique subset, given its widespread use and, in the current environment, political implications. For community colleges with local fiscal support, there are three prices: in-district, in-state, and out-of-state. For community colleges without local fiscal support there are only in-state and out-of-state prices. Theoretically, out-of-state prices bear at least some relation to the cost of education to the institution. The price reduction for in-state students reflects the subsidy paid for by the state as a result of state tax revenue that residents have paid into. The same is true for in-district charges, where the cost of education to the institution is reduced by subsidies from both the state and local governments. That is the theory, and it is hewed to generally in most places, but its application does not usually conform tightly to actual costs of delivering education and the relevant subsidies provided by state and local government.

In-District Pricing

In practice, the states that charge in-district rates do not always charge much less than those assessed of in-state students. On average, in-district tuition in 2012–2013 was $2,573 as compared to $3,045 for in-state tuition (see Figure 12.1). Tuition for out-of-state students was $6,562. When including fees, the prices increase to $3,032, $3,526, and $7,099, respectively.

The extension of in-state tuition to populations such as veterans or undocumented students is an increasingly common practice,

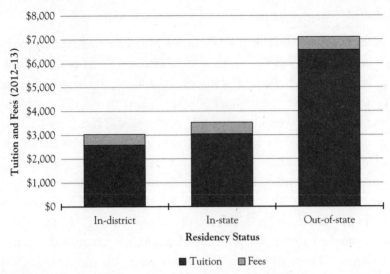

Figure 12.1   In-District, In-State, and Out-of-State Tuition and Fees: 2012–2013

Source: Authors' analysis of Integrated Postsecondary Education Data System (National Center for Education Statistics, 2014c).

or at least is up for debate, in 2015. This leaves many fewer paying an out-of-state rate and offers an opportunity to revisit in-state tuition-setting options. Two such models have been proposed: the single criterion and multiple criterion models.

Single Criterion Models

The single criterion model (Carbone, 1974) sets the tuition based on how long the student has lived in the state. For example, a student living in the state for 10 years or more pays less than a student who has lived in the state for 5 to 10 years, and this student pays less than a student who has lived in the state for just 1 year. To illustrate this concept, a student living in the state for over 10 years would pay $1,500 a year, whereas a student living in the state for 1 year would pay $3,000 (for 30 credit hours).

Multiple Criterion Model

In the multiple criterion model, tuition prices are set based on a set of criteria with weighted measures. Carbone (1974) put forth an example in which the legal status of the student, the length of residency in the state, the high school the student attended, tax status, and voter status were all measured, weighted, and considered. This was accomplished by assigning each student a score based on the number of points they earned for each criterion and then placing the total score within the tuition categories that corresponded to a range of scores.

For example, Table 12.1 presents a three-criteria model, with associated measures and points available. In the example, Student 1 earned 1.75 points across all three criteria, Student 2 earned 0.50 points, and Student 3 earned 1.25 points. As a result, Student 2 pays 100% of the tuition price, Student 3 pays 75%, and Student 1 pays 50%. The notion behind these models is that a student, such as Student 1, who has lived in the state a long time and is an active citizen should pay less than someone who is new to the state and less active, as represented by Student 2.

Institutionally Based Pricing

There are also approaches that apply institutionally based pricing. This may be accomplished by using information from entities external to the institution or by looking at institutional operations to set prices.

Externally Informed Pricing

Factors influencing tuition can also derive from sources external to the college. These include inflation indexing, peer pricing, and market-based pricing.

Under inflation indexing, tuition is set to reflect the change in a common, external price index such as the Consumer Price Index (CPI). For example, if the CPI increased by 3%, tuition would increase by 3%. This framework can help defend against

Table 12.1. Multiple Criterion Model Example

Criteria Measures	Student 1	Student 2	Student 3
Legal Status			
American Citizen (.80)	.80		.80
Non-American (.20)		.20	
Length of Residency			
10 years or more (.50)	.50		
5 to 10 years (.30)			
1 to 5 years (.15)		.15	
1 year or less (.05)			.05
Nonresident (.00)			
Voter status			
Registered in-state (.45)	.45		
Registered in another state (.40)			.40
Not registered (.15)		.15	
TOTAL	1.75	.50	1.25

Pricing Categories		
0.00 to .75 = 100%	.76 to 1.25 = 75%	1.26 to 1.75 = 50%

Note: This is a simplified presentation of Carbone's model that incorporates different measures for the criteria.

accusations of institutional "gouging" when the increases are determined. At the same time, however, the base price from the prior year, or even the increase itself, may not have been adequate to meet the institution's needs. Additionally, the link to inflation may involve time lags and so not reflect current economic conditions facing students.

Peer pricing means setting prices based on those charged by similar institutions. In practice, a college would identify a set of peer colleges and set its tuition within their range. A strength of this approach is that price is a signal of quality to some—namely, that the college is worth the same as its competitor. Further, it is a market-based approach to pricing. A weakness of this approach is that the peers selected may be aspirational rather than realistic, and mimicking them may simply drive up price in an unnecessary search for prestige that is basically anathema to community college principles.

Market-based pricing is a process whereby prices are set at the maximum level students will pay, as determined by market research. Strengths of this model are that it is a reality-tested approach and also that it attempts to maximize revenue from students. A weakness is that the price, if higher than that of other programs, may serve as a barrier to participation.

Internally Based Pricing

Internally based pricing models use information within the college to set tuition and fee prices. Examples include budget balancing, cost-recovery indexing, and proportional cost pricing.

Budget balancing is a process whereby prices are set after estimates of forthcoming expenditures are reduced by nontuition revenues to arrive at the amount of revenue needed from tuition. The amount of needed tuition revenue is then divided by estimated total credit hours to arrive at a price per credit hour. In practice, a college would estimate a need for tuition revenue ($1,750,000, for example) and credit hour production (54,000 credit hours, for example) and divide the former by the latter to determine a cost-per-credit-hour charge ($32.41 in this example). The strength of this model is that it is straightforward and justifiable. A weakness is that estimates for any of the data—expenditures, enrollments, state appropriations—may be far off and have substantial impacts on the college's financial standing.

The cost-recovery indexing model entails setting prices to reflect changes in the price of education (as measured by education and general expenditures). In practice, if an institution's expenditure decreased by 2%, the tuition price would be decreased by 2%. The strength of this model is that it is straightforward and justifiable. Weaknesses of the model include but are not limited to the observation that a reduction in revenues limits a college's ability to undertake new initiatives and serves as a disincentive to increasing efficiency.

Proportional cost pricing is a model in which the tuition price is set at a certain percentage of the cost of instruction. So, for example, if the cost of instruction per credit hour was $100, a college might set tuition at a third of the cost and charge the student $33.33 per credit. A strength of this model is that the respective responsibilities for generating revenue are clearly set across participating student and government entities. A weakness is that the partnering governmental entities may not provide sufficient funds to cover expenses.

Fixed Pricing

Another pricing strategy is to offer a set, or fixed, price for tuition and fees. Three ways in which this may be accomplished follow.

Guaranteed Tuition

A model that attempts to give potential students a clearer understanding of price is a guaranteed tuition. In this model, tuition stays the same for a set period of time, at least for a particular student. For example, a community college would hold the tuition price at a set amount for the duration of time it takes a student to earn an associate's degree. A college could set tuition per credit hour at $100 for up to 60 credit hours (an amount equal to earning the associate's degree). A strength of this model is that it is transparent and lends stability to the prospective student's financial planning. A weakness is that the guaranteed price will likely need to be higher in the first year(s) than in later years to account for any loss of revenue to

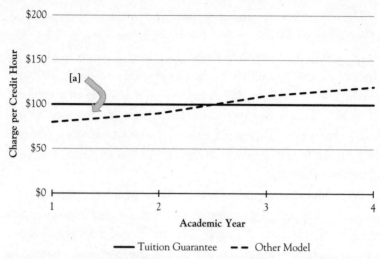

Figure 12.2   Four-Year Difference in the Charge per Credit Hour Between Guaranteed Tuition and Other Tuition Pricing Models

the institution in the years beyond the first. Students who do not complete would end up paying more for college than they would have under a different pricing plan (see Section [a] of Figure 12.2) because of the higher price paid in the first years of the tuition guarantee program.

Block Tuition

The heightened focus on college completion has drawn attention to the number of credits students were enrolling in each semester. Often, for full-time students, the answer was 12 credits. At this level of enrollment intensity, students are not able to graduate with an associate's degree in two years or a bachelor's degree in four years without also enrolling in the summer. Given this, colleges can offer a "full load" at a certain price and allow students to take additional courses, or credits, without incurring additional costs.

For example, Lorain County Community College set block tuition at $1,398.15 for summer and fall 2014 semesters and let students enroll for up to 18 credits, when this price reflected actual charges for 13 credits (Lorain County Community College, 2014). This model differs from guaranteed tuition in that the charges can change each year.

Subscription-Based Tuition

As technology becomes ever more infused into the higher education landscape, and along with it module-based learning opportunities and other competency-based models, an opportunity arises to change the way in which colleges structure their pricing. One such way is to move to a subscription-based tuition model with prices set on a time-limited basis.

The model is fairly new, so much remains to be learned from it. The University of Wisconsin Flexible Option (http://flex.wisconsin .edu/getting-started/tuition-financial-aid/) gives students two sub-scription options. The first is a three-month, all you can learn and earn model that allows students to take as many assessments as they can pass. The second model allows the learner to enroll in one suite of competencies.

This section focused on the models used to set tuition. These models continue to evolve in terms of how each metric may be conceived and calculated. Most of the literature detailing these models—including the work of Foose and Meyerson (1986), Kaysen (1960), Yankowski (1986), Litten (1984), Shaman and Zemsky (1984), and Song (2014)—was produced in the 1980s, spurred in part by a shift in higher education finance that occurred at that time, from the previous focus on setting prices, to student financing through individualizing aid packages, to enhancing enrollment management by discounting tuition. The latter prac-tice is increasing at public and private four-year colleges but not yet common at community colleges, and not likely to become so (Pullaro & Redd, 2013; Shaman & Zemsky, 1984).

Net Price

The pure act of setting prices does not take student aid into account. Any discussion of price now, in 2015, is made in a context that acknowledges the presence of student aid as a supporting revenue source for students and families. Before moving on to the following section, which examines the influence of price on students, we consider the question of how aid affects the price a student pays—the net price.

Net Price

Net price is simply the price a student pays after all student aid is deducted from the cost of attendance (see Chapter Four). The factors that influence net price are highly dependent on the circumstances of the student and to some extent the location of the institution—most particularly in the cost of living in a particular area and the availability of state aid. Nonetheless, it is a key concept that institutional leaders need to be aware of.

The Higher Education Opportunity Act of 2008 (Pub. L. 110–315, 2008) defines net price as "the average yearly price actually charged to first-time, full-time undergraduate students receiving student aid at an institution of higher education after deducting such aid." Colleges, however, have some leeway in how net price determinations are calculated, given that they must include certain input and output elements, while having flexibility in other areas. (see Table 12.2). For example, Cheng, Asher, Abernathy, Cochrane, and Thompson (2012) found that some net price calculators asked students to submit more than 70 pieces of information.

All college leaders should have a firm grasp of what types of aid—grants, loans, or tax breaks—and student budgets are used to arrive at the final net price, in order to be able to educate their audiences—particularly given the fact that the federal government is also prominently using "net cost" as a barometer of college affordability.

Table 12.2.   Required Input and Output Elements Used in Net Price Calculators

Input Elements	Output Elements
Data to approximate a student's expected family contribution (EFC), including: Income Number of people in the family Dependency status	Estimates of: Cost of attendance Tuition and fees Room and board Books and supplies Other allowable expenses Total grant aid Net price Percentage of first-time, full-time students receiving grant aid

Note: Colleges may use either the federal methodology or one of their own choosing when determining the EFC. Caveats and disclaimers must accompany outputs.

Source: National Center for Education Statistics (n.d.).

Out-of-Pocket Net Price

As if the variations in what exactly a net price reflects were not sufficiently problematic, a shift in how net price is discussed is currently under way. In 2014, the National Center for Education Statistics (NCES) released an analysis of net price, titled "Out-of-pocket net price," which they defined as the immediate amount a student and his or her family must pay to attend college. This definition is extended with a footnote stating "this measure [net price] may not reflect the actual cost to the student over the long-term because students who finance their education using loans must repay not only the principal balance but any accrued interest" (Horn & Paslov, 2014, p. 2). In other words, "net" price masks the true price students pay when they must borrow to finance their education.

Student Price Response

The financial barriers presented by tuition costs are of continual concern to all those involved in higher education. To better understand how different populations respond to price, researchers have conducted numerous studies over decades. Reviews of the research on student price response by Jackson and Weathersby (1975), Leslie and Brinkman (1987), and Heller (1997) were summarized by Heller in a single statement: "As the price of college goes up, the probability of enrollment tends to go down" (p. 649). However, subpopulations of the student body respond in different ways to price, further complicating the setting of tuition and fees. Mullin and Honeyman (2009) summarized the research, noting that (1) grants have the strongest influence on enrollment; (2) the subpopulation most sensitive to pricing differences, and therefore least likely to enroll, was that of low-income students; (3) while black students were the most sensitive to price, Hispanic students were sensitive as well; and finally, (4) community college students were more influenced by pricing differences than students at four-year public institutions. Savoca (1990) and Keeney (1960) both noted that not only does a (relatively) high price influence prospective students' decision to enroll, but it also influences whether or not they will apply to, or enroll in, college at all.

Conclusion

This chapter examined the entities charged with setting tuition and fees, along with the various approaches that have been used to accomplish this. These include tuition pricing models used by all sectors of higher education, with consideration of how students may respond to price.

Questions

One community college needs to be identified before completing question 3. Community colleges may be located by using the College Navigator tool of the National Center for Education Statistics at http://nces.ed.gov/collegenavigator/.

1. Which pricing model resonates with a college with which you are most familiar? Explain why.

2. What factors would you use if asked to develop a multiple criterion model for in-state tuition?

3. Identify the input and output elements that a community college uses when determining net price. Are they similar to or different from the required input and outputs elements provided in Table 12.2?

Chapter Thirteen

Managing a Fiscal Crisis

Economic recessions appear to be baked into the U.S. economy. Each of these fiscal downturns seems to carry with it a call for dramatic changes to the financing of higher education. The recent economic collapse, the Great Recession of 2008–2009, was no different, and the "new normal" became common nomenclature for an assumed future of significant funding constraints. However, history has shown that state economies experience continuous funding cycles, and that while higher education funding eventually—in fact, usually—rebounds following a recession, it just as inevitably will also dive once again. How, exactly, have public institutions of higher education addressed these periodic fiscal free falls?

The most common response to a fiscal crisis is to make across-the-board cuts, wherein all cost centers in the college are required to reduce their budget by a given percentage. These are simple to implement, easy to explain, and at least superficially equitable. However, they do not set priorities, and many assert that a funding crisis is a prime opportunity to make institutional changes that otherwise would be unpalatable. Drawing on the experience of governmental and institutional actors throughout periods of sharply reduced support, this chapter presents some strategies for maneuvering through a funding crisis. First governmental responses are chronicled, followed by institutional responses to managing a fiscal crisis.

Governmental Responses

When economies experience negative shocks, governments are forced to respond in a variety of ways. This section examines some of those responses.

Federal Responses

When the national economy experiences a major downturn, national leaders often use the occasion to make strategic investments, while reductions in expenditures are also contemplated (assuming that a fiscal downturn raises the budget deficit). In the case of higher education, reductions in research are often examined, in addition to expenditures on federal student aid. As community colleges are barely engaged in federally funded research activities, potential changes to federal student aid programs—primarily the federal Pell Grant program—are of primary importance (see Chapter Five) and therefore the focus of this section.

During the Great Recession of 2008–2009, the number of students relying on the Pell Grant increased dramatically—from 5.5 million to 9.5 million over the three years from 2007–08 to 2010–2011 (Baime & Mullin, 2011). This increased program costs from $12.8 billion to $34.8 billion. At the time, the U.S. Department of Education (2011) was careful to not attribute all of this growth to a faltering economy; rather, individuals identified these four contributing factors: (1) an increase in the number of eligible students (itself a byproduct of the poor economy), 40%; (2) legislative changes in the needs analysis formula, 14%; (3) the new year-round Pell Grant program, 22%; and (4) the $619 increase in the maximum Pell grant award, 25%.

Enacted Changes

For the Pell Grant program, expenditures can be difficult to reduce directly, because of the quasi-entitlement nature of the program, but they can be reduced indirectly, by limiting the number of people eligible to participate (Mullin, 2013c). During the Great Recession, with its simultaneous focus on college affordability and the purchasing power of federal student aid (as tuitions increased), student aid policies were changed. Changes made in the Consolidated Appropriations Act of 2012 included reducing lifetime Pell Grant eligibility from 18 full-time equivalent semesters to 12, eliminating eligibility for all Title IV federal student aid for students who previously demonstrated an "ability to benefit" from postsecondary education (but who lacked a high school diploma or GED), and reducing the amount of income at which a student automatically qualifies for a $0 expected family contribution (EFC) from $32,000 to $20,000.

Proposed Changes

In addition to changes enacted in 2012, other ideas for reducing costs in the Pell Grant program were proposed and continue to be debated (see Table 13.1). Most of these ideas impact nontraditional students attending community colleges, other open-access institutions, and for-profit institutions.

Amid an environment of high-profile policy discussions about the future of Title IV assistance, the Bill & Melinda Gates Foundation funded think tanks and advocacy groups to, as they put it, reimagine federal student aid. The more than 150 policy proposals contained in the Foundation's 14 Reimagining Aid Design and Delivery (RADD) papers released in 2012 and 2013 can be grouped into five strands, all potential precursors to new directions in student financial aid policy:

- The first, **Easing Entry**, includes a set of proposals that focus on the mechanics of the federal student aid programs and make recommendations to simplify the aid application process, revisit the needs analysis formulas, and encourage early financial preparation for college.

Table 13.1. A Typology of Proposed Adjustments to the Pell Grant Program: 2010–2011

Proposed Adjustments	Examples
Adjustments associated with the Pell Grant maximum award	Adopting a lower maximum award Limiting the minimum award to 10% of the maximum award
Adjustments associated with time-related aspects of the program	Changing the definition of full-time from 12 to 15 credits
Adjustments associated with the eligible student population	Eliminating eligibility for less-than-half-time students
Adjustments associated with student and parent wealth	Revisiting income protection allowance changes made since 2007–08 Expanding definitions of untaxed income to include items eliminated in the College Cost Reduction and Access Act of 2007 Capping maximum income eligibility for a Pell grant
Adjustments associated with institutional factors	Eliminating the administrative cost allowance Refining institutional eligibility requirements Tying institutional eligibility to metrics

Source: Adapted from Mullin (2013c).

• The second, **Reaffirming Investments**, includes a set of proposals focusing on reaffirming the nation's investment in postsecondary education. Recommendations focus on making the Pell Grant program an entitlement, creating a "super Pell," increasing funding for student aid, investing in research and experimental programs, reinstating year-round Pell eligibility and ability to benefit eligibility, and expanding existing programs.

- The third set of policy recommendations focuses on limiting siloed approaches to postsecondary education; it is titled **Enhancing Relationships**. This section had the largest number of policy recommendations by far, focused on reforming accreditation; strengthening funding partnerships between state and federal government; revamping national data collection; connecting college and career; incentivizing colleges, states, and systems to perform more effectively; incentivizing students to complete college programs; and providing better information to stakeholders.

- A fourth group of policy recommendations focused on making changes to current practice and **Strengthening Sticks**. These policy recommendations focused on things like implementing college cost restraints, consolidating federal grant programs, curbing abuse in federal student aid (focusing on ED oversight), and focusing on institutional eligibility and accountability.

- Finally, a set of recommendations focused on the administration of student aid is collectively referred to as **Restructuring Administration**. The recommendations support making income-based loan repayment the norm, restructuring loans, changing the higher education financing provisions in the tax code, rethinking the timing of student aid disbursements, and focusing on student progress and learning (Mullin, 2013a, pp. 1–2).

Proposals to change federal student loan programs have also been advanced in times of fiscal crisis. Many of them align with proposals put forth by St. John and Byce (1982), such as eliminating the in-school interest subsidy to federal Stafford Loans; others were already enacted, such as the creation of a government-run federal student loan program, bypassing banks and thereby reducing expenditures.

In all cases, periods of economic retrenchment allow for long-debated ideas to be rehashed and perhaps implemented. A central question guiding these and other educational debates is who, exactly, should be funded to pursue educational opportunities, with an increasing emphasis, at least currently, on graduation.

State Responses

Callan (2002) identified five general points of significance related to an economic downturn's impact on states:

1. A national recession affects each state differently.
2. Although a national recession may be short, individual states may face financial stress for much longer periods.
3. During a national recession, individual states may face financial stress for a number of other reasons [rising health care costs, for example].
4. When states face fiscal constraints, the impacts on state services vary across states, within states, and among service sectors.
5. When revenue shortfalls are allocated among state services, higher education is likely to be required to absorb proportionately larger cuts than other sectors. [p. 24–25]

In these circumstances, reductions in appropriations for community colleges and higher education generally are not so much a strategy in response to an economic downturn as they are a sheer operational reality. Hurley (2010) identified strategies states employed to increase revenues, such as increasing tax revenue on targeted items such as tobacco, park fees, vehicle registration, gambling, and other fees charged to those who use services, rather than extending taxes to all through increased property taxes or other general levies. Strategies identified to reduce expenditures included instituting furloughs and pay freezes, closing public parks, selling state assets, releasing felons early, and reducing public services such as libraries.

As for higher education, states have taken a number of actions to reduce funding that include reducing state student financial aid programs or eliminating them altogether, cutting budgets at the beginning of the year and mid-year, applying the lowest enrollment counts to allocation methodologies, and merging colleges (Johnson, Oliff, & Williams, 2009; Gaines, 2008; Verstegen, 2013). All of these make a mockery of planning.

Some approaches that increase institutional funding for community colleges include encouraging students to start at those institutions rather than four-year colleges, allowing institutions to charge differential tuition, and increasing fees (Hodel, Laffey, & Lingenfelter, 2006; Johnson, Oliff, & Williams, 2009; Verstegen, 2013). Wattenbarger and Mercer (1988) identified three actions that assisted community colleges, including deferring to the greater of, rather than the lesser of, two options when determining full-time equivalent students for funding purposes. For example, a state aid formula allowed for the greater of a three-year weighted FTE count or the most recent year's FTE count when allocating funds (Wattenbarger & Mercer, 1988). In another approach, California spread out revenue reductions over three years instead of making them in one year. A third strategy was to put a ceiling on the maximum percentage decrease in a state allocation within a given fiscal year.

Institutional Responses

Unfortunately, only a series of actions is likely to resolve the problems associated with a full-blown financial crisis, and these must align with the college's mission and be palatable to its constituencies. In reviewing decades of strategies employed by colleges to respond to financial challenges, there appear to be six broad categories of actions that a college may consider to respond to a financial crisis (see Table 13.2). These represent a comprehensive toolkit of options for the college's leadership to consider.

Table 13.2.   Institutional Actions in Response to a Fiscal Crisis

Category	Actions
Administrative Control and Management	Convert administrative positions to instructional positions.
	Defer library and equipment purchases.
	Defer maintenance.
	Delay the purchase of new equipment.
	Contract out student services, financial aid, or other academic or support services.
	Consolidate shared services across the college.
	Institute a four-day work week.
Instructional Staffing	Hire more part-time faculty.
	Reduce the number faculty and staff.
	Leave faculty and staff lines vacant.
	Freeze hiring.
	Institute furloughs.
	Freeze travel.
	Alter compensation or benefits.
	Freeze professional development.
	Reduce student work opportunities.
	Increase teacher contact hours.
	Increase faculty-student ratios.
	Share staff across colleges.
Examine Academic Offerings	Review programs to determine economic and educational viability.
	Reduce course offerings.
	Increase class size.
	Delay new program development.
	Expand programs.
	Prune and graft programs together.
	Expand alternative pathways to a credential.
	Expand dual enrollment.

Table 13.2. *(continued)*

Category	Actions
Enhance Revenues	Raise tuition.
	Issue bonds.
	Activate reserve fund accounts.
	Increase local funds.
	Increase taxes or rates.
	Sell property.
	Expand contract training.
	Diversify funding streams through increased efforts to obtain gifts and grants.
Institutional Advancement	Increase lobbying efforts.
	Engage alumni.
	Invest (buy property).
Strategic Organizational Change	Right-size the institution.
	Alter within-college allocations.
	Limit enrollments.
	Recruit new student populations.
	Enroll more students who pay the full price (that is, out-of-state and international).

Sources: Bethea (2014); Campbell (1982); Collins, Leitzel, Morgan, and Stalcup (1994); DeCosmo (1978); Keller (2009, 2013); Martorana (1978); McGuire (1978); Mumper (2001); Rivard (2013, 2014).

Administrative Control and Management

One set of actions to regain fiscal balance concerns what broadly could be termed reducing "administration." These actions would largely be designed to mitigate the impact of budget reductions on the academic mission of the college but could result in a reduction of important "wrap-around" services that ultimately are essential to students' academic success. This might include academic counseling, student support centers, summer enrichment programs, special tutoring, or other educational services.

Instructional Staffing

Obviously, instruction is at the core of college's mission. Reductions in this area are likely to be controversial on a campus. However, given the fact that, at community colleges, instructional expenditures represent a large portion of expenditures, cuts in this area can be unavoidable. Adjunct faculty are usually the first to be given reduced responsibilities. As discussed earlier, the need to make budget reductions can in fact give administrators greater leverage to make difficult decisions.

Academic Offerings

The second set of actions related to the academic mission of the college focuses on programs rather than instructional staff, though instructional staff will be impacted. This set of actions focuses on ensuring the programs being offered that cannot be justified on financial or educational grounds. In this respect, an economic crisis may provide an opportunity for institutional officials to make changes that otherwise would not be politically feasible—particularly eliminating programs that do not draw large numbers of students or have poor workforce outcomes.

Enhance Revenues

Actions to access funds and enhance revenues may help with short-term shortfalls. There are, however, long-term implications associated with some these actions, including higher prices for students, reduced reserves (which were of significant benefit to some campuses in the Great Recession), and an increase in debt service.

Institutional Advancement

Another way for colleges to cope with retrenchment is to become more engaged with constituents and other stakeholders, specifically in the area of fundraising. This emphasis is gaining momentum in many places, and it is especially compelling for colleges that are not in a position to wait for prior revenues to return to historic levels.

Strategic Organizational Change

An economic downturn may also present an occasion to overhaul major aspects of college operations and structures. Strategic actions to implement organizational change may benefit the institution in the long run but of course can be challenging for both constituents and leaders in the short term.

In sum, what is best for a college will depend on the unique circumstances of the college, its community, and its state. Examples of college actions shared in this section may be appropriate for a particular institution but must always be considered in the context of the mission and, possibly, the planning documents guiding the institution, boards of trustees, and other stakeholders.

Conclusion

This chapter provided an overview of actions by governments and colleges in response to financial crises. Although the timing of these crises are inherently unpredictable, they can, to some extent, be prepared for. Colleges can proactively identify drastic cost-cutting options that align with institutional missions and then model the impact on college budgets. Ideally, a college will have a data model built and related spending reduction options ready for use when decisions have to be made, so the information, in combination with qualitative information, can enhance decision making.

Questions

1. Why are across-the-board cuts the most common approach to coping with financial shortfalls? Do you believe this approach is wise? Why or why not?

2. Which changes would you recommend the federal government make during economically challenging times, and how would these impact community colleges and the students that attend them?

3. Which three institutional actions in response to a financial crisis would you implement in the event of a financial crisis? Explain why.

4. Which three institutional actions in response to a financial crisis would be the last actions you implement in the event of a financial crisis? Explain why.

Chapter Fourteen

Tenets of Advocacy

Other chapters of this book have focused on the nature and use of the disparate resources at community colleges. This chapter treats the essential role of the CEO in helping capture those resources. Politics is a collective undertaking, and no one individual is ever responsible for a particular outcome. But a tremendous responsibility rests on the shoulders of community college CEOs in their role of primary institutional advocate. As we detail here, this is an extremely complicated role, involving a blend of hard analysis and data gathering, political intuition and savvy, personal charm, energy, and relationship building. And, as in other aspects of life, a little luck never hurts.

The rewards of political activity, both personally and politically, can be great. Successful advocacy can bring tangible benefits to colleges in the form of resources—and less tangible but extremely valuable positive publicity.

Almost invariably, the community college CEO is unprepared for the role of chief institutional advocate. With few exceptions, none of the usual paths to the presidency require aspiring CEOs to plan and execute a political strategy for a college. Most CEOs rise through the institutional ranks, and it is rare for a government relations or external affairs individual to be named a president. Some former politicians have headed up institutions, and done so successfully. But in most cases, substantial on-the-job training is needed to create an effective advocate. Some elements of advocacy are pure common sense. Others can be learned from more seasoned colleagues, particularly through contacts and joint activity at the state level. However, no two political circumstances are ever exactly the same, and an ability to improvise as well as assess the evolving environment is critical. Experience does matter.

Still, community college CEOs have an advantage out of the gate: they are looked upon as community leaders, embodiments of the institution's fundamental public purpose and mission. They are inherently public figures and are held to extremely high ethical standards, a fact that becomes ever more challenging in a world of decreasing privacy and instantaneous communication. In that regard, community college CEOs have something of an advantage over their peers in other sectors of higher education, because, in parallel with the decline of institutional authority in general, the concept of the college president as an admired national figure or moral center has eroded, but community college CEOs still command general public respect.

But there is no doubt that the overall context for advocacy has grown more challenging. For starters, the country's overall fiscal picture has darkened over recent decades; the post-WWII era of sustained growth—and with it, steadily enhanced domestic spending—is over. As has been discussed, higher education is increasingly viewed as a private good. In addition, America's colleges and universities, as a set of institutions, have lost public support. This dynamic appears to be driven by the public's awareness that higher education is necessary to a family-sustaining livelihood, while at the same time their confidence that institutions put the interest of students first is ebbing. Much of this concern clearly stems from anxiety over the soaring increase in college tuitions. Although community college tuitions have also increased much more rapidly than inflation (College Board, 2014a), the colleges are somewhat buffered from this concern, and in recent years their stock has no doubt risen in part because of sticker shock at four-year institutions. That said, it behooves community college leaders to stay aware of shifting public views about higher education writ large. In fact, many of the "solutions" directed at problems perceived in other sectors of higher education often negatively impact community colleges.

Setting an Agenda

Identifying a political agenda for an institution is a necessary starting point for effective advocacy—what does the institution need, and what might it reasonably expect to acquire through political means? Where could the agenda be shared, and where might it be up to the institution alone to secure resources? In some ways the answer is obvious, such as maximizing state funding with other institutions. In other cases—such as whether to seek increases in local tax support, especially for dedicated projects—it is a strategic and tactical question of the highest complexity. Whatever the answer, articulation of an explicit political agenda is essential and needs to be continually reevaluated. Where applicable, this setting of priorities will be done in concert with boards of trustees, institutional leaders, and state or even national political leaders.

In addition, the time factor must always be taken into consideration. Politics is quintessentially a personal activity and therefore tremendously time-consuming. A cold-eyed triage must be conducted about how best to utilize the CEO's time in political activity. Because of these time constraints, a growing number of community colleges are creating positions largely or exclusively dedicated to external affairs or advocacy, and some colleges retain outside lobbyists.

Making the Case: General Rules and Tactics

The foundation of effective advocacy is the development of positive, trusting relationships with legislators and their staff. It is largely through these relationships that political benefits are tendered. There is no particular formula for developing ties with legislators; much of it is a matter of common sense and good manners. However, it is worth pointing out to legislators that their local community college is a particularly fruitful source of potential political support and interest. The community college can give politicians a rich opportunity to display their commitment to benefiting the local community through supporting the institution. Virtually all colleges are linked to workforce development and economic opportunity, and jobs are never far from voters' and therefore politicians' minds. Community colleges are natural spots for debates, briefings, press events, or other public gatherings. Any variety of campus convenings can provide politicians with an attractive forum for burnishing their reputation as bona fide public servants.

Trust is essential to creating lasting, mutually beneficial relationships with legislators. Reliable and timely information about the impact of proposed or enacted public policies is a valuable currency that community college leaders can provide. Legislators often cannot know how potential actions will impact institutions and students; they need and want to know this information, and institutional leaders are in a position to generate it. This pure information-providing role—being an honest broker—is one often overlooked by institutional leaders, who often assume that legislators are awash in relevant information. Even when that is the case, the policy-making environment can be abstract and lifeless, badly in need of a dash of lively human color.

Needless to say, relationships can be fatally undermined through inaccurate or misleading accounts. There are many purveyors of information and many demands on legislators' time, so misrepresentations or inaccuracies must be avoided at all costs. It is always better to simply tell a legislator that one does not know the answer to a question but will respond to them as soon as possible, rather than hazarding a guess.

In addition, it is desirable to ensure that legislators receive appropriate feedback about the impact of a given policy enactment, particularly one on which the institution has earlier made a request. This contact reminds legislators that their constituents are aware and watching. It is always important to thank legislators for positive actions taken, yet this essential and easy act is often neglected as attention focuses on the next "ask." In addition, negative feedback, stated calmly and factually, is also important to impart. "Agreeing to disagree" is a necessary aspect of political discussion.

No legislator should ever be written off. The means of success to a given objective are often unpredictable. While many votes or positions can be predicted in advance, the ability of a seemingly hostile legislator to advance an institution's interests must always be viewed as a possibility. This is particularly the case with community colleges, which have such broad public support. Interest in a given issue can be triggered despite the seeming odds against it.

Making the Case: Approaching Legislators and Effectively Imparting Information

Political decision making and the commitments that lie behind it are determined by many factors, and no general rule applies. Institutional leaders often wonder to what extent they should be anecdotal in their presentations, focusing on individual cases, primarily students, or whether they should let aggregate numbers and objective analyses carry the day. The truth is that both can be helpful, and frequently both are necessary. Policy debates generally take place in an environment dominated by numbers and the objective impact of policies, but the motivation to address a problem often is sparked by a compelling individual case.

The medium and nature of communications should also not be left to chance. A few principles apply, though they will need to be modified for individual circumstances. First, written communications should be brief. Legislators are even busier than community college CEOs. Written communications that are longer than two or three pages should be rethought. If this is absolutely necessary, to include essential information, then an upfront summary is advised.

There is no right answer as to whether a letter, phone call, e-mail, text, or face-to-face contact is the best. It will vary by issue and by legislator. If possible, ask the legislators how they would prefer to be contacted.

Meetings with legislators also must be made efficient. Naturally, it behooves the advocate to know about the legislator's background, policy priorities, and previous positions on issues, as well as the legislator's personal interests and family. Their previous efforts on behalf of the college should be highlighted. In almost all circumstances, some sort of leave-behind document should be provided, whether it relates to a specific policy issue, more generic information about the college, or both. A follow-up thank-you is *de rigueur*.

College leaders cannot fail to benefit by inviting legislators to their campuses. There is some truth to the notion that a picture is worth a thousand words, and it is on the campus that the link between legislation and opportunity comes vividly to life. College leaders also should not be afraid to share with legislators certain deficiencies, particularly concerning the physical plant, as this too can spur needed support.

Generating Allies

The CEO has many potential allies to assist in advocacy efforts. First and foremost are the institution's trustees or board of directors. Trustees are trustees because of their own political prowess, whether they be appointed or elected. Most if not all community colleges have local trustees, which gives them a natural entrée with state and local legislators. By virtue of their standing in the community they may have credibility that, at least early on, a CEO could lack. Many trustees are active with their own political parties, make campaign contributions, and generally are viewed as well-connected players. Boards can also provide essential political cover for CEOs in taking potentially controversial positions. Of course, because some trustees have political agendas that conflict with the positions traditionally taken by the institutions, severe conflict can develop.

Institutional leaders may want to enlist the help of administrators or, potentially, faculty in advancing the political agenda of the college. These individuals can add strength from their numbers as well as their own relationships. However, there is always a risk that the institution's core messages can be miscommunicated if officials beyond the CEO's influence are deployed in political activities. Administrators may also lack political savvy. But they can prove very helpful; for example, by providing substantive expertise that the CEO lacks. Examples might be the chief finance officer addressing facilities needs and costs, or the student financial aid administrator presenting information on complicated aspects of Title IV aid.

Students can add an extremely effective element to advocacy efforts. There is no substitute for their enthusiasm, immediacy, and articulation of the impact of the community college on their lives—after all, they are the reason why the institution exists. Students can also provide sheer numbers, in terms of legislative input, that can carry the day. Students do often need to be coached about making the most of their input and adequately briefed on the issues at hand.

Finally, the entire local community should be viewed as an asset in advocacy. Support for most community colleges is broad and deep. Tapping this support is not always easy, but it can pay huge dividends. As in other aspects of advocacy, using the local community has a pronounced public relations element. In this capacity alumni can also provide political clout.

Advocacy at Different Levels of Government

Because each level of government has its own unique context, how one advocates within each must vary.

Federal

First, it should be noted there is an implicit responsibility for each community college to play its part in the collective effort of all community colleges at the federal level. Community colleges must have all hands on deck when it comes to asserting their collective advocacy weight, and there is no room for what political scientists term "free riders." By dint of their particular legislators, such as a key committee member, some institutions carry particular importance and are called upon more frequently than others. Of course, this dynamic shifts with the changes that occur in the legislature.

As state and local resources have diminished, federal sources of support and the advocacy needed to maintain and enhance them have increased in importance. As outlined earlier, student financial assistance is the primary and most important means of support for community colleges, but even if student aid were not needed, federal investments would be critical. Fortunately, despite the sustained pressures on nondefense discretionary spending, virtually all of the key non–student aid programs that community colleges have come to rely on have remained in place, with only slightly reduced funding in some cases.

Members of Congress are always interested in the direct impact of federal programs—that is, simple numbers—on their districts. Whenever possible, college leaders should always take the time to compile this information before speaking to a legislator. Examples of data that would draw attention are the number of Pell Grant recipients, funds received via the Carl D. Perkins Act, or the uses of a Hispanic-Serving Institutions (HSI) grant.

The national community college associations, particularly the American Association of Community Colleges (AACC), provide detailed legislative resources for member presidents. It is AACC's responsibility to inform its members' CEOs when actions of particular import are pending. It is also desirable for institutional leaders to stay abreast of ongoing nongovernment policy developments at the national level; these not only are important in and of themselves but are increasingly influencing state level policies as well. Initiatives funded by the Bill & Melinda Gates Foundation and Complete College America are but two recent examples of private efforts that continue to have a dramatic impact on policy.

Although an undeniable cachet attaches to a visit to Washington, in truth it is usually more effective to approach legislators when they are in their home districts or states. Legislators usually will have more time and be less distracted and less likely to be thinking about the next vote, meeting, or fund-raiser. In some cases the follow-up by local staff can be even more effective than that of Washington-based aides because of their proximity to the institution.

On that note, it should be understood that aides to federal legislators are an integral part of the legislative process, and they should be cultivated as assiduously as members themselves. Most members are simply too overwhelmed with demands on their time and attention to know all the details of a given proposal or situation. As a result, they are as a rule entirely reliant on their aides to perform the bulk of the background work and information-gathering on issues, even very important ones. A community college representative should make the most of meetings with staff, rather than viewing it as reflective of their own importance in any way.

State

For most if not all community colleges, state support remains the bread and butter of their public financing. The effort to secure adequate state funding is generally organized in the state capital, by either a public or a private community college official, with periodic sharing of information and tactical updates. As at the national level, some institutions play a more critical role than others by virtue of the placement of their legislators. But perhaps even more so than at the national level, it is critical that all relevant players show up, because they are fewer players to be called upon.

In many states, "lobbying days" are planned in which CEOs advocate simultaneously, at times in concert with students and other members of the campus community. These events can bring broad public relations benefits.

Despite the general dynamic of cooperation in state-level community college advocacy, political conflict between community colleges occasionally erupts. The complex nature of community college structures and financing, with colleges in a given state differently positioned as to resources, added to the fact that legislators naturally want to target support on their local college, has given rise to a variety of heated battles between community colleges at the state level. In addition, CEOs within a state occasionally differ on strategy and policy priorities, and this obviously can complicate advocacy efforts through the delivery of different messages on the community college position.

Broader political dynamics at the state level vary widely. This is particularly the case when it comes to advocating with other public institutions. In some places community colleges and universities advocate jointly for an appropriation or at least coordinate their efforts, reflecting the belief that a rising higher education tide will lift all institutions, financially speaking. In other cases the sectors are pitted against each other. This is becoming increasingly frequent concerning to the ability of community colleges to offer four-year degrees, which senior institutions frequently oppose.

Also, private non-profit colleges also frequently complicate state advocacy efforts for community colleges. As a sector these institutions are generally well organized at the state level and have in some cases obtained direct state support and, more frequently, generous student financial aid for their students. In fact, these students receive more state aid than those attending community colleges.

Local

As described earlier, the significance of local contributions to community college budgets varies dramatically. In instances where county or municipal funding provides a significant share of institutional funding, maintaining political support is essential, even if specific changes to funding are not pending. Votes on changes to property assessment or the floating of bonds to cover institutional needs require sophisticated efforts that can take months of planning, and the outcomes are often hard to predict. Lessons in what makes for a successful campaign are ongoing.

However, even if no changes to local funding are on the table, the community college leader will always want to maintain a strong community presence that is essentially political—shoring up support for the institution in its essentially local mission. This certainly includes the business and civic communities. Many ultimately beneficial hours are logged in at Chamber of Commerce breakfasts and similar gatherings.

Further Dimensions of Advocacy: Rewards and Risks

The extent to which a community college leader should engage in partisan politics is a difficult and complex question, usually resolved on a case-by-case basis, taking into account a variety of local factors. The fundamental tensions are clear, falling into two general categories. First, the CEO often is placed in a position in which partisan politics could be perceived to be influencing their actions on behalf of their institution—this is simply the nature of their role as leader. As has been discussed, CEOs have an obligation to engage in politics as a means of generating support for their colleges. Perceived favoritism is always a risk, and, as a practical matter, certain choices may unavoidably favor an individual politician through no intention of the college's employees.

In addition, while the CEO is a public figure whose actions always reflect upon their institutions, simultaneously the CEO is a private citizen with all the implied rights and prerogatives of political participation. The line between these roles is easily blurred, but the CEO may not want to surrender potential political activity simply because of their public visibility. However, forays into this activity can create complications. Ideally, the local community and legislators acknowledge the basic right of leaders to take politician positions as they feel so compelled.

It has been said that money is the mother's milk of politics, and whether and how to make political contributions can be especially tricky for institutional leaders. CEOs are commonly solicited, indirectly or explicitly, to contribute to the campaigns of the legislators who are in a position to benefit their institution. There is no right or wrong answer as to whether presidents should make these contributions, but in an era of broad-based disclosure, it is certain that a specific philosophy or justification for actions taken is needed. In this context, it is prudent for CEOs to share their approach with their boards of trustees, where applicable. The boards can provide guidance and perhaps political cover, especially considering that they are politicians of a kind themselves.

Conclusion

The CEO has a critical role in working to secure resources for the institution through the political process. For most CEOs, the skills required largely have to be learned on the job. Advocacy is intimately linked to relationship building, but it also rests on the successful prosecution of the institution's case. The political activities of the CEO will need to be pursued somewhat differently at the federal, state, and local levels.

Questions

1. What are some of the CEO's responsibilities for advocacy on behalf of a college?

2. What are some of the skills and techniques that community college leaders need to use in advocating for their college?

3. What are some of the potential pitfalls of political activity on behalf of an institution?

Chapter Fifteen

Future Forces in Community College Finance

Looking to the future of higher education, one can perhaps be sure of only two things: there will be more of it, and it will look different than at present. All evidence points to continued increased participation in higher education. This behavior will be driven fundamentally by economic necessity; that is, the need for ever higher levels of educational attainment to enable individuals keep pace with, and generate, a more technologically sophisticated world. Simultaneously, there is a basic consensus that the current model of higher education cannot, and even should not, be sustained. At root there is just one reason: its cost.

Without doubt, new delivery modes allow higher education to be made more broadly available and less expensive than ever before. But at the same time, there is no avoiding the reality that changed delivery means a changed product, for better or worse. The debate and research on that topic, with its subtext issue (what *is* the purpose of college, and in particular, does it require an actual classroom with students participating in person?), will continue.

Given the uncertain delivery structures and program offerings that will make up undergraduate education in the future, and knowing that, of all sectors of higher education, community colleges traditionally have been the most prone to change and adaptation, what reasonable surmises can be made about the financing models and assumptions that these institutions will face? How reliable (or perhaps more accurately stated, how unreliable?)

are the current sources of support? And how altered might the basic financing structures look? As there is increased pressure to deliver more higher education less expensively and ever more flexibly, will community colleges lose the basic funding streams—however they may differ from place to place—that have characterized them so far? This final chapter provides some thoughts about possible financing models for community colleges as the twenty-first century unfolds.

Federal Support

The expenditures made by the national government in Washington, DC—that elaborate, creaky, yet ever-persevering check-writing machine—have proven notoriously difficult to significantly reduce for those who would do so. Once a program is established and a constituency develops around it, political action to eliminate that largesse is no mean feat. This reality contains some good news for community colleges. While significant increases in domestic spending, especially for programs that receive annual appropriations, have become extremely rare—and most of these programs have lost ground to inflation over the last decade—the vast majority of this enormous array of expenditures that reaches community college campuses is not likely to abate any time soon. In addition, support for student financial aid is likely to remain robust. This next section addresses the likely federal role in supporting community colleges and students in future years.

Student Financial Aid

As stated in Chapter Five, the federal government's primary financial involvement with community colleges is indirect: providing student financial assistance to millions of students each year. Despite the periodic budget-cutting proposals that the student aid programs have faced, they have proven to be politically resilient, and a substantial reduction in funding seems unlikely. All public opinion surveys show remarkably strong support for education programs in general and student aid in particular. However, over time the concept of college attendance as a social good has eroded, and with this change has come the belief (if perhaps expressed only implicitly, through ever higher tuitions) that it is appropriate to ask students and their families to bear a greater share of the cost of postsecondary education. In practice, this has taken the form of forcing students to borrow ever more, at times on less-advantageous terms. However, despite the perception that the Pell Grant program has been the target of abuse—with students allegedly enrolling in college simply to access funds, without serious educational intent—it remains something of a feel-good program that is supported strongly by both parties in both Congress and the executive branch. That seems unlikely to change.

Student Aid Policy Changes

As of this writing, the Higher Education Act (HEA) is in the process of being reauthorized. Last renewed in 2008, the next iteration of the Act is broadly expected to contain substantial changes to the Title IV programs, in terms of both student support and related institutional policies. There is a broad-based conviction in Congress that higher education needs to change in some important respects, and that the HEA, even though it primarily targets aid to students rather than institutions, is an appropriate vehicle to leverage this change. It is not useful to speculate at this point on what the outcome of the reauthorization process might be, as enactment of legislation could be a number of years away, but it is important to know that the Title IV programs described earlier could look somewhat different in the future—perhaps significantly so.

More specifically, in reauthorization, the unique mission of community colleges in serving less-prepared students could come into conflict with a Congress that is bent on encouraging completion, and reductions in support for these students, as was discussed earlier, remains a possibility. In addition, the federal government may change its policies in areas such as accreditation, online learning, program eligibility (particularly with the heated debate over "gainful employment" programs), the student aid application process, and early awareness strategies. As stated earlier, however, the essential federal role in providing student financial assistance is very like to continue.

Federal Discretionary Programs

Community colleges receive federal support from an immense array of programs across many federal agencies in addition to the more obvious Departments of Education and Labor. Some of the agencies through which community colleges receive support include the Departments of Agriculture, Defense, Commerce, Homeland Security, Housing and Urban Development, and State, as well as other seemingly unlikely corners. What these programs have in common is that, with minor exceptions, they are contained in that portion of the budget known as "nondefense discretionary." This is the approximately 16% of the budget that provides support for a broad swath of programs, primarily domestic, that receive annual appropriations, rather than being part of the automatic, statutorily guaranteed funding side of the budget known as "mandatory" or security-related spending. Despite the political popularity of many of these programs, as a group they have absorbed disproportionate cuts in the budget wars of recent years, in part because they are relatively easy to cut as a block of programs, which is generally what has been done through the budget process (leaving specific program funding decisions to the appropriations committees), in part because of the political support for the large entitlement programs such as Social Security and Medicare.

Within this fundamentally stagnant overall funding situation, there are isolated examples, which could intermittently recur, in which the political popularity and mission of community colleges translate into federal cash. More than any other sector of higher education, community colleges are still able to attract dedicated federal support from a Congress that only rarely targets resources to particular sectors of higher education. (This was particularly the case with President Barack Obama's American Graduation Initiative, proposed in 2009.) Notable examples include the Community-Based Job Training Grant program, established in the FY 2005 appropriations process at the behest of President George W. Bush, and the Community College and Career Training Program, providing $2 billion over four years through FY 2010 budget reconciliation legislation. In the early 1990s, Congress created the Advanced Technological Education Program at the National Science Foundation, and there is widespread acknowledgment that it has had a positive impact on campuses. With that has come bipartisan political support.

As can be seen, these targeted programs emphasize the workforce and technical side of the community college. Many other pieces of federal legislation that would provide support of some kind to the institutions have been introduced but not enacted.

Practices and Innovations

In community college finance, change is a constant. This section focuses on evolving practices and emerging innovations in the financing of community colleges (Mullin, 2015).

Evolving Practices

Given the incremental pace of change that characterizes higher education, it is reasonable to assume that the future of community college finance will include alterations to or the expansion of current practices to a greater number of institutions. Many of these changes are already under way.

Local Taxes

As funding decreases, more states will seek legislative action to permit community colleges to access increased levels of local property tax revenue and grant local access to a local sales tax for operations. Miami Dade College is currently attempting this. Although unsuccessful in the 2014 legislative session, should Miami Dade College succeed in its efforts, it has the potential to send ripples through other communities. Currently all but 5 states have a state sales tax, and all but 18 states allow some form of local option sales tax. These tax revenues can be used for a variety of purposes as determined by state statute (see the appendix), including community college operations and capital improvements (see Table 15.1).

A caveat must accompany the use of these local tax revenue sources. While revenues from local sales tax and local property tax earmarked for community colleges can greatly benefit an institution, these revenues will fluctuate with changes in the economy and can be difficult to predict. For example, from 2010 to 2014 community colleges in Michigan saw a 24.5% reduction in revenue generated by the local property tax. Without any increased support from the state to cover these reductions, colleges had to seek alternative funding (Jess, 2014).

Internet Taxes

If the details can be worked out, we can expect a state and possibly a local tax on the interstate Internet sales that currently go untaxed. Many states might consider an option that would dedicate these revenues to education at all levels. People would likely support this approach, seeing funds work directly in their own community rather than being dispersed by the state government.

Funding Distribution

Earlier we discussed ways in which institutional charges for education may be determined. There was also a discussion of linking student outcomes to the funding of community colleges. This shift of focus from funding opportunity to funding prescribed outcomes is not new to education. It happened in K–12 public education nearly

Table 15.1. State and Local Sales Tax Rates

State	State Rate	Average Local Rate	Combined	Rank of Combined Rate
Alabama	4.00%	2.15%	6.15%	31
Alaska	none	1.13%	1.13%	46
Arizona	5.60%	2.32%	7.92%	9
Arkansas	6.00%	1.79%	7.79%	10
California	8.25%	0.81%	9.06%	2
Colorado	2.90%	4.34%	7.24%	13
Connecticut	6.00%	none	6.00%	32
Delaware	none	none	none	47
Florida	6.00%	1.01%	7.01%	18
Georgia	4.00%	3.02%	7.02%	17
Hawaii	4.00%	0.38%	4.38%	45
Idaho	6.00%	none	6.00%	32
Illinois	6.25%	2.15%	8.40%	6
Indiana	7.00%	none	7.00%	19
Iowa	6.00%	0.94%	6.94%	24
Kansas	5.30%	1.65%	6.95%	23
Kentucky	6.00%	none	6.00%	32
Louisiana	4.00%	4.43%	8.43%	5
Maine	5.00%	none	5.00%	43
Maryland	6.00%	none	6.00%	32
Massachusetts	6.25%	none	6.25%	29
Michigan	6.00%	none	6.00%	32
Minnesota	6.88%	0.34%	7.22%	14
Mississippi	7.00%	none	7.00%	19
Missouri	4.23%	2.95%	7.18%	15
Montana	none	none	none	47
Nebraska	5.50%	1.01%	6.51%	27
Nevada	6.85%	0.74%	7.59%	11
New Hampshire	none	none	none	47
New Jersey	7.00%	none	7.00%	19
New Mexico	5.00%	1.40%	6.40%	28

(continued)

Table 15.1. *(continued)*

State	State Rate	Average Local Rate	Combined	Rank of Combined Rate
New York	4.00%	4.30%	8.30%	7
North Carolina	5.75%	2.32%	8.07%	8
North Dakota	5.00%	1.00%	6.00%	32
Ohio	5.50%	1.33%	6.83%	25
Oklahoma	4.50%	3.94%	8.44%	4
Oregon	none	none	none	47
Pennsylvania	6.00%	0.22%	6.22%	30
Rhode Island	7.00%	none	7.00%	19
South Carolina	6.00%	1.04%	7.04%	16
South Dakota	4.00%	1.52%	5.52%	40
Tennessee	7.00%	2.41%	9.41%	1
Texas	6.25%	1.14%	7.39%	12
Utah	5.95%	0.66%	6.61%	26
Vermont	6.00%	none	6.00%	32
Virginia	5.00%	none	5.00%	43
Washington	6.50%	2.28%	8.78%	3
West Virginia	6.00%	none	6.00%	32
Wisconsin	5.00%	0.42%	5.42%	41
Wyoming	4.00%	1.38%	5.38%	42
District of Columbia	6.00%	n/a%	6.00%	n/a

Source: Padgitt (2009).

30 years ago. A brief discussion of these developments might portend future financing developments.

In 1989, the fabric of K–12 finance was altered by a court case, *Rose v. Council for Better Education* (790 S.W.2d 186, 1989). Previously, the focus of K–12 finance was on money and the equitable allocation of funds across all schools in a given state. Access to local tax revenue, funded by local jurisdictions (school districts) of varying fiscal capacity was to be balanced by state funds. Poor school districts received additional state aid; wealthy districts received none. Equity analyses incorporated concepts such as the equal treatment of equals (horizontal equity) and the inequitable treatment of unequals (vertical equity). For example, it was believed that all first graders in every school district should be funded at the same rate (the equal treatment of equals) and students with special needs funded at a higher rate (the inequitable treatment of unequals). *Rose's* contribution came in the form of extending the decisions about funding from what is equitable to the amount of money needed to produce the outcomes expected of education for all children in that state. This shift heralded the expansion of new methods for determining the cost of education, a value often determined by the reverse engineering of a funding formula.

Given the current focus on student outcomes in higher education generally, and community colleges specifically, K–12 adequacy models may soon be applied to higher education, as a way to determine the expenditures necessary for a college to meet state goals.

Emerging Innovations

Technological advances open up opportunities for college to tap new sources of revenues. This section briefly presents some of those opportunities.

New Uses for Data

In contemporary society, the amount of data shared about individuals is fundamentally unlimited. Information obtained from students, faculty, staff, alumni, and administrators presents an opportunity for new insights into the people and behaviors on college campuses that could be of benefit to commercial entities of one kind or another. One way for colleges to open up a new revenue stream is to monetize (by selling) these data, while simultaneously, of course, protecting privacy. The practice of monetizing data collected by colleges is already under way, but it is a practice in which colleges have yet to significantly engage. Clearly there are delicate policy—and practical—considerations involved.

Open Online Courses

There is the chance that the extension of open online courses (OOCs)—be they massive (MOOCs) or limited (LOOCs)—aim to foster student pathways to timely completion by centralizing a set of core courses within a single institution or state system. The result could have a substantial impact on colleges, who may be able to receive a fee for certain instruction-related services, but who may at the same time lose substantial numbers of students and therefore staff. The future role of OOCs in postsecondary education remains uncertain, but the sharing of curriculum, and probably greater uniformity in it, seems quite likely. This could result in a reduction of cost for institutions, as individual faculty members are no longer responsible for developing curricula. However, this development is probably not likely in the short term, given the relative autonomy of faculty.

Public-Private Partnerships

The effectiveness of public-private partnerships (P3)—collaborative efforts between community colleges and developers—was previously discussed. These arrangements can greatly benefit the college in that buildings are constructed with little or no funding from the college. But states must allow these partnerships to exist. The potential of such relationships for the development of facilities at community colleges should be further expanded at both state and federal levels to make these partnerships even more attractive to the private sector. One mechanism to be investigated is the development of a Community College P3 Investment Tax Credit, whereby the private investor in the P3 would receive a tax credit of a specified amount for participating in the project. The amount of the tax credit would offset all or part of their tax liability in a given year. Currently the federal government and 43 states have a similar mechanism to offset federal and state tax burdens for specified public policy purposes. Renewable Energy, Historic

Preservation, and Low Income (Affordable) Housing tax credit initiatives are some of the better-known programs. A Community College P3 Tax Credit enacted at both the federal and state level would greatly enhance the appeal of these arrangements.

Conclusion

The future of community colleges is both bright and murky. It's bright because of the need that they meet in society by providing broad-based access and success to millions of student each year. But the future is also murky, because of the evolving nature of higher education and the evolving sources of support on which the institutions depend. Institutional leaders will no doubt be required to be flexible and even visionary in their efforts to secure the resources that their colleges will need in order to flourish.

Questions

1. Could private sector support for community colleges be growing? If so, indicate some trends and potential sources of revenue for your institution.

2. If there is an increasing recognition that education support needs to transcend institutional and organization boundaries, how might such recognition lend itself to new forms of support?

3. Administration (nonacademic services) has grown and may continue to grow. Is this inevitable or a crisis in leadership? What could be done to slow the growth?

4. What role might the federal government play in future years in funding for community colleges?

Appendix

Principles of Taxation

The principles of taxation raise questions concerning the equity (fairness) and benefits of the various forms of taxation. These principles were informed by the works of Smith (1776), Cannan (1904), Ricardo (1817), and countless other individuals. The actual principles were developed as part of a lecture series in Higher Education Finance offered at the College of Education, University of Florida. These principles include the *ability to pay*, *benefits received*, *neutrality*, *justice and equity*, *adequacy of yield*, *stability and flexibility of yield*, *economy of administration*, and *ease of payment*.

Ability to Pay

The *ability to pay* principle describes how the ability of the taxpayer to pay the tax is related to the tax burden imposed on the taxpayer. The tax burden should be related to the individual's income. As an individual's base (income) rises, so does the individual's ability to afford increased taxation as a result of a higher tax rate. Proposed changes in the tax base versus the tax rate are often discussed in relation to the ability to pay, categorized as progressive, regressive, and proportional tax structures. In the progressive tax structure, as the base increases, so does the tax rate. In the federal tax structure, increasing income levels are taxed at "progressively" higher tax rates. For example, the Internal Revenue Tax Code of 1954 showed 24 increasing income and associated tax brackets. Individuals with incomes up to $2,000 were taxed at 20%, individuals with higher incomes were taxed at 22% of the portion from $2,000 to $4,000, and so on, up to income over $200,000, with that top bracket of the total income taxed at 91%. For example, if an individual earned $210,000, only the excess over $200,000 ($10,000) would be taxed at 91%, or $9,100 for that bracket.

Since 1954 there have been many changes to the income and tax brackets used to calculate federal tax liability for individuals and corporations. Over time revisions of the tax code have made it less progressive in its effect on taxpayers. The 2014 brackets include seven steps, starting with incomes up to $9,075 taxed at 10%, income from $9075 to $36,900 taxed at 15%, to the highest income bracket for income equal to or greater than $406,750, with the amount over that level taxed at 39.6%. Although the brackets have been reduced from 24 in 1954 to 7 in 2014, it can be said that while the federal income tax is less progressive than previously, it is still a progressive form of taxation (Lowery, 2013).

These tax brackets are referred to as the marginal tax rates based on income, filing status (single, married filing jointly or separately, or head of household), and deductions. The tax burden is calculated for each bracket, summed, and used to calculate the total tax due and the effective tax rate for the individual/corporation.

An example of a tax calculation is given below.

Income tax for year 2013

- Single taxpayer, no children, under 65 and not blind, taking standard deduction

- $50,000 gross income—$5,950 standard deduction—$3,800 personal deduction = $40,250 taxable income

- $8,925 × 10% = $892.50 (tax amount owed for the first income bracket)

- $40,250–$8,925 = $31,325.00 (taxable amount in the second income bracket)

- $31,325.00 × 15% = $4,698.75 (tax amount owed for the second income bracket)

- Total income tax is $892.50 + $4,698.75 = $5,591.25 (total tax due, approximately an 11.18% effective tax rate on an income of $50,000)

While for a progressive tax the rate increases as the base increases, the opposite is true for a regressive tax. Here, as the base increases, the rate decreases. The property tax at the local level, sales tax at the state and local levels, and Social Security taxes by the federal government are often described as regressive. Property tax is often described as a tax with little relationship to an individual's ability to pay. Take two individuals who own property with an assessed property valuation of $100,000. They live in the same community, are taxed at 10 mills, and pay a property tax of $1,000. This looks to be a flat or proportional tax in which as the base increases the rate stays the same; that is, all residents pay the same millage rate. However, when compared to the homeowner's ability to pay, a different picture emerges. If the first homeowner earns $200,000 per year, the effective tax rate, also referred to as tax effort, is equal to 0.5% ($1,000/$200,000.) Compare this to an individual who, for example, is retired and receives $15,000 annually in Social Security benefits, and who therefore has an effective property tax rate of 6.7%. In this case, as the ability to pay goes down, the tax rate goes up. The same principle can be applied to sales taxes, especially for food and "essentials." If a family of four buys groceries, gasoline, and other essential commodities they will pay a flat sales tax rate. However, if their income should rise dramatically, and they buy the same essentials, their effective tax rate will go down as their income increases. Conversely, if they lose their job and the income associated with it and need to buy these same essentials, their effective tax rate will rise. This is the regressive nature of these taxes.

The capping of tax bases is also regressive in its effect. Social Security fund contributions currently have a maximum income cap at which payments into the trust fund stop. Up to that point contributions are proportional in nature, in that the higher income individual pays more into the fund, but at the same rate. When the income brackets stop there are no more contributions. Individuals earning above these caps have their effective tax rate for Social Security lowered. In 2013, workers were responsible for an effective tax of 4.2% on up to $113,700 of gross income (not including the equivalent employer's contribution). Individuals earning in excess of this maximum income level paid no additional taxes, reducing their effective tax rate. Again, as the income tax base—the ability to pay—increases, the effective tax rate decreases (Social Security Administration, 2013).

The 2010 state and local effective tax rates (effort) and each state's rankings are shown in Table A.1. In 2010, the national average rate was 9.9%. New York had the highest tax rate at 12.8%, while Alaska had the lowest at 7.0%.

Benefits Received

The *benefits received* principle manifests in those taxes that taxpayers pay in the course of paying for goods and services they receive. Highway tolls; national, state, and local park and museum admission fees; and state and federal gasoline taxes are often cited as examples. Individuals are willing to pay these taxes, tolls, and fees because they perceive a benefit. Shares of the federal gasoline tax and all of the gasoline tax generated within a state are used to build and maintain roads and highways within that state. In many states an additional tax is added to the price of gasoline used in boats at marinas; the revenue is used to maintain state waterways.

However, the "free rider problem" is often noted in the context of this principle. Here we must consider what happens if there are consumers who do not pay for the benefit received (the free rider)

Table A.1.   State and Local Tax Burdens by Rank: Fiscal Year 2010

State	State-Local Tax Burden	Rank
U.S. average	9.9%	
New York	12.8%	1
New Jersey	12.4%	2
Connecticut	12.3%	3
California	11.2%	4
Wisconsin	11.1%	5
Rhode Island	10.9%	6
Minnesota	10.8%	7
Massachusetts	10.4%	8
Maine	10.3%	9
Pennsylvania	10.2%	10
Illinois	10.2%	11
Maryland	10.2%	12
Vermont	10.1%	13
Hawaii	10.1%	14
Arkansas	10.0%	15
Oregon	10.0%	16
North Carolina	9.9%	17
Michigan	9.8%	18
West Virginia	9.7%	19
Ohio	9.7%	20
Nebraska	9.7%	21
Kansas	9.7%	22
Indiana	9.6%	23
Iowa	9.6%	24
Idaho	9.4%	25
Kentucky	9.4%	26
Florida	9.3%	27
Washington	9.3%	28
Utah	9.3%	29
Virginia	9.3%	30
Delaware	9.2%	31
Colorado	9.1%	32

(*continued*)

Table A.1.   (*continued*)

State	State-Local Tax Burden	Rank
Georgia	9.0%	33
Missouri	9.0%	34
North Dakota	8.9%	35
Oklahoma	8.7%	36
Mississippi	8.7%	37
Montana	8.6%	38
New Mexico	8.4%	39
Arizona	8.4%	40
South Carolina	8.4%	41
Nevada	8.2%	42
Alabama	8.2%	43
New Hampshire	8.1%	44
Texas	7.9%	45
Wyoming	7.8%	46
Louisiana	7.8%	47
Tennessee	7.7%	48
South Dakota	7.6%	49
Alaska	7.0%	50
District of Columbia	9.3%	(31)

Notes: As a unique state-local entity, D.C. is not included in the rankings, but the figure in parentheses shows where it would rank. The local portions of tax collection figures for fiscal year 2010 rely on projections of local government tax revenue.

Source: Malm (2010).

at the expense of others? This is an important public policy issue and is used in the determination of many taxation policies. For example, take 10 farmers who have farms along a river that are all of equal acreage. The river is vital to their farming operation, supplying water for irrigation. However, there have been flooding problems in the recent past. After several planning meetings and engineering studies, it is determined that the construction of a dam would benefit all the farmers by controlling flooding and reducing their flood and crop insurance rates. The dam will cost $1 million to build. Evenly distributed, this would result in a $100,000 payment by each farmer. All agree it is a good idea, and the project starts. Shortly thereafter, one farmer decides that if he does not pay his share, he will still reap the benefits of the dam, making him a free rider. The others recalculate the burden and determine that the nine remaining farms would each pay $112,000. The timing and the expected return on their shares are still good and they continue. But over time, five other farmers see the same "free rider" benefit, and they withdraw. The four remaining farmers cannot afford to underwrite the project at $250,000 each, and it is halted. Here is the public policy issue: local and state government officials monitoring the project process are aware of the benefits to be received by the state and community as a whole and then complete the project using tax revenues from the larger tax base. The government may also consider assessing a water use tax on the farmers to help pay for a part of the project.

These same principles apply to many services at the local level. Municipal water and sewer systems, trash collection, road cleaning, plowing and salting, fire protection and emergency services, public schools, and some community colleges are a few of the many services provided to the benefit of taxpayers.

Neutrality

The *neutrality* principle tells us that the effects of a tax should not change the economic position of the taxpayer. The same can be said for changes in a given tax. The local property tax is often cited as being less neutral than other forms of taxation. For example, a family recently retired is now living on Social Security. Before retirement they earned $50,000 and paid $1,000 in property tax, a 2% effective tax rate. In retirement their income dropped to $20,000. They were still required to pay their property tax at the existing rate, which resulted in an increase in their effective tax rate to 5%. As a result of this change in their economic position the property tax burden can become higher, and over the years, if the property tax rate increases significantly this burden increases further and could result in the loss of their home. The neutrality principle is the legislative rationale for deferments in the property tax in many states for the elderly and disabled taxpayers. In North Carolina the disabled or elderly can be granted an exclusion of up to $50,000 of property value if their income is below $28,000. Disabled veterans are entitled to an exclusion of up to the first $45,000 of home property value (North Carolina General Statutes 105–277.1B, 2013). California, Florida, Georgia, Louisiana, Mississippi, New York, Oklahoma, Rhode Island, Texas, Washington state, and Kentucky all have Homestead Exemptions that exclude a flat amount or a percentage of the value of property in the tax calculation. Each of these plans is designed to increase neutrality and create a tax that is more progressive and in line with the *ability to pay* principle.

As mentioned earlier, not all states allow community colleges to collect property tax revenue, but many do. For example, the Texas Association of Community Colleges projects community colleges to collect $1.652 billion from a 1.66 mils tax on property in 2014. Likewise, the Michigan legislature reported that community colleges collected more than $565 million in property tax revenue for the school year ending in 2010, and in 2013 community colleges in Mississippi exercised local property tax options ranging from 1.69 mils to 8 mils, with a statewide average for all community colleges of 3.62 mils.

Justice and Equity

This principle states that a tax must be based on a sound concept of a democratic social order (*justice*) and firm economic theory (*equity*). Further, the tax must not discriminate against any select group of taxpayers or citizens. Perhaps the most egregious violation of the justice and equity principle was the implementation of the poll tax or capitation tax in the late nineteenth century. This tax was imposed on all persons wanting to vote in a given state.

After the ratification of the Fifteenth Amendment to the U.S. Constitution in 1870, which forbade the federal and state governments from denying the right to vote based on race or color, several southern states and California enacted poll taxes in which eligible voters had to pay a fee to vote. These taxes often had provisions that grandfathered in those who had voted before and during the Civil War and allowed them to vote without paying the tax. These taxes virtually disfranchised the voting rights of African American, Native American, and poor white citizens who had moved after the war. It wasn't until 1966 that the U.S. Supreme Court ruled in *Harper v. Virginia Board of Elections* (383 U.S. 663, 1966) that the tax was illegal in all state elections. The court held that the poll tax violated the principle of justice, as it purposefully violated democratic principles of the Fifteenth Amendment and targeted select groups of taxpayers.

When discussing equity, there are generally two aspects used to identify the fairness of a tax: horizontal and vertical equity. Horizontal equity is defined as the equal treatment of equals, so the tax system should not discriminate on the basis of ability to pay. Two taxpayers with exactly the same income and the same deductions and exemptions—the same ability to pay—should pay the same income tax. Two taxpayers buying exactly the same item in a local store for the same price should pay the same sales tax. Vertical equity is defined as the unequal treatment of unequals. The tax system should expect more from those with the higher ability to pay. Vertical equity is achieved to varying degrees in the progressive federal income tax system, where higher income brackets are taxed at higher rates.

Adequacy of Yield

The *adequacy of yield* principle refers to a tax's ability to raise revenue sufficient for its purpose. When a tax is implemented for a given outcome—such as new road construction, construction of new schools, water management projects, and so on—the dollars generated by the tax should be adequate to provide the goods or services usually specified in the relevant tax code, whether it has been approved by the local government, the state legislature, or the U.S. Congress and acknowledged by the citizens affected by law.

Stability of Yield

The *stability of yield* principle holds that the revenue generated by the tax should not be adversely influenced by changes in the economy. This is a tenuous and difficult principle to maintain, as economic shifts are inevitable, and even policy changes cannot always be predicted, creating associated shifts in tax revenue. Downturns in the stock market can result in severe reductions in income tax liabilities. Similar shifts in the housing market can affect property tax revenues, while increased unemployment can affect income and sales tax revenues. In the extreme, these economic shifts have resulted in the breakup of entire communities, with the associated loss of entire tax bases designed to help the community sustain services.

Flexibility of Yield

The *flexibility of yield* principle states that a tax should be able to reflect the changing costs of delivering goods and services outlined in the creation of the tax, by allowing changes in the rate of the tax or the several indices used to determine the tax rate. For example, the U.S. Congress can change the tax brackets and/or the tax rates for any bracket to raise additional revenue. State governments can increase the sales tax rate, certain hospitality tax rates, and so on, to raise additional revenue. Local government can change the millage rate, remove any number of existing deferments or exemptions, and generate addition revenue. But there are political consequences to each of these actions. Ideally the affected taxpayers are in agreement and see the overwhelming need for an increase.

Economy of Administration

The *economy of administration* principle holds that the costs associated with the collection of the tax should not exceed the amount of tax collected. If a given level of government has to establish a costly bureaucracy to collect the tax, it will limit the money available that can be used for the original purpose of the tax. As shown in Table A.2, the IRS, often accused of being a massively inefficient organization, uses $0.46 to $0.50 per $100 collected for its costs of operation.

Sales tax at the state level presents an interesting dilemma. From the point-to-point sales perspective—for example, buying shoes at a local store—it is easy and economical for state and local governments to administer. The merchant collects the tax at the time of sale and processes tax receipts to send to the state. Costs to

Table A.2.   Internal Revenue Service Collections, Costs: Fiscal Years 2005–2009

Fiscal Year	Gross Collections (thousands of dollars)	Operating Costs (thousands of dollars)	Cost of Collecting $100
2005	2,268,895,122	10,397,837	0.46
2006	2,518,680,230	10,605,845	0.42
2007	2,691,537,557	10,764,736	0.40
2008	2,745,035,410	11,307,223	0.41
2009	2,345,337,177	11,708,604	0.50

Source: Internal Revenue Service (2009).

the state and merchant are minimal and usually done by computer. However, sales tax for online sales is creating major concerns in many states. Critics on both sides have argued that online sales tax exemptions have hurt local business, while interstate online sales companies have always indicated the difficulty in administrating sales taxes due to the calculations required by the individual states and their localities, with differing rates, exemptions like sales tax holidays, and collection and payment schedules. As early as 1967, the U.S. Supreme Court decision in *National Bellas Hess v. Illinois Department of Revenue* (386 U.S. 753, 87 S.Ct. 1389, 1967) began the debate on the future of taxing Internet sales when, in its majority (5 to 4) opinion, the court ruled that Illinois could not tax catalog sales by Hess Department Stores in other states, noting, "the many variations in rates of tax, in allowable exemptions, and in administrative and record-keeping requirements could entangle [the company's] interstate business in a virtual welter of complicated obligations to local jurisdictions."

This debate continued until 1992 when the Supreme Court ruled in *Quill Corp. v. Heitkampp*. In this case the state of North Dakota tried to collect sales tax from the Quill Corporation, an out-of-state mail order house with no offices in the state. The state wanted North Dakota residents to pay a "use tax" for items purchased from out-of-state companies for use in the state.

The court ruled: "[O]ur decision is made easier by the fact that the underlying issue is not only one that Congress may be better qualified to resolve, but also one that Congress has the ultimate power to resolve. No matter how we evaluate the burdens that use taxes impose on interstate commerce, Congress remains free to disagree with our conclusions" (*Quill*, 1992).

In 2013, the U.S. Congress tried to resolve these issues. *The Marketplace Fairness Act* was debated in Congress as S. 336, S. 743, and H.R. 684. These bills would give states the authority to collect sales tax on interstate sales via the Internet and catalogues. The Marketplace Fairness Act (2013) stipulates that states can collect sales tax on interstate sales—that is, the Internet—and catalogues sales, if they "simplify their tax codes." In essence, the simplification process must make it easier for multistate businesses to collect and pay the sale taxes to the respective states. Implementation of the Act and the details within individual states are still being resolved.

Ease of Payment

The *ease of payment* principle states that the tax payment must be convenient for the taxpayer. Income tax is paid through withholding, estimated payments, and payments filed with tax returns from the taxpayer. For taxpayers who earn their income as employees, the tax liability is withheld from each paycheck and easily collected by the governmental agency through payments made by the employer. Self-employed individuals, retirees at certain income levels, corporations, and others submit their income taxes through quarterly tax payments; electronic online options that can be scheduled in advance have streamlined the process. State income taxes are less efficient, as the taxpayer's liability in several states is not determined until the annual U.S. income taxes are calculated and filed. Sales tax is paid at the time of purchase. Collected by the merchant, these taxes are easy for the taxpayer to pay.

References

110 ILCS 805/2–16.02. *Grants.* (2013). Available from http://www.ilga.gov/ legislation/ilcs/ilcs4.asp?DocName=011008050HArt.+II&ActID=1150& ChapterID=18&SeqStart=600000&SeqEnd=4200000

United States Code § 1087ll. *Cost of attendance.* (2012).

Florida Statutes §1009.23. *Florida College System institution fees.* (2013).

Abramson, P. (2014, February). *19th Annual college construction report.* Retrieved from http://webcpm.com/research/2014/02/college-construction-report .aspx?tc=page0

Adelman, C. (2013, October). *Project Win-Win at the finish line.* Washington, DC: Institute for Higher Education Policy.

Advisory Committee on Student Financial Assistance (ACSFA). (2008, September). *Apply to succeed: Ensuring community college students benefit from need-based financial aid.* Washington, DC: Author.

Alexander, F. K., Harnish, T., Hurley, D., & Moran, R. (2010, April). *"Maintenance of effort" an evolving federal-state policy approach to ensuring college affordability.* Policy Matters: A Higher Education Policy Brief. Washington, DC: American Association of State Colleges and Universities.

American Association of Community Colleges (AACC). (2010). *Fact Sheet 2010.* Washington, DC: Author.

American Association of Community Colleges (AACC). (2012, April). *Reclaiming the American dream: Community colleges and the nation's future.* Washington, DC: Author. Available from http://www.aacc.nche.edu/21st CenturyReport/index.html

American Association of Community Colleges. (2014). *2014 Fact Sheet.* Washington, DC: Author.

American Association of Community Colleges, the Association of Community College Trustees, the Center for Community College Student

Engagement, the League for Innovation in the Community College, the National Institute for Staff & Organizational Development, and Phi Theta Kappa Honor Society. (2010, April). *Democracy's colleges: Call to action*. Washington, DC: American Association of Community Colleges.

American Recovery and Reinvestment Act, Pub. L. No. 111–5. (2009).

Archibald, R. B., & Feldman, D. H. (2011). *Why does college cost so much?* New York: Oxford University Press.

Baime, D. S., & Mullin, C. M. (2011, July). *Promoting educational opportunity: The Pell Grant program at community colleges* (Policy Brief 2011–03PBL). Washington, DC: American Association of Community Colleges.

Baker, E., & Bergeron, D. (2014, January). *Public college quality compact for students and Taxpayers: A proposal to reverse declining state investment in higher education and improve quality and accountability*. Washington, DC: Center for American Progress.

Barr, M. J., & McClellan, G. S. (2011). *Budgets and financial management in higher education*. San Francisco: Jossey-Bass.

Baum, S., Ma, J., & Payea, K. (2013). *Education pays: The benefits of higher education for individuals and society* (Trends in Higher Education Series). Washington, DC: The College Board.

Baumol, W., & Bowen, W. G. (1966). *Performing arts, The economic dilemma: A study of problems common to theater, opera, music, and dance*. New York: Twentieth Century Fund.

Belfield, C. (2012, April). *Measuring efficiency in the community college* (CCRC Working Paper No. 43). New York: Teachers College, Columbia University, Community College Research Center.

Belfield, C. R., & Bailey, T. (2012). The benefits of attending a community college: A review of the evidence. *Community College Review, 39*(1), 46–60.

Bernstein, D. I. (2014, April). Public-private partnerships: It's the right time. *Business Officer Magazine, 47*(9). http://www.nacubo.org/Business_Officer_Magazine/Business_Officer_Plus/Bonus_Material/Public-Private_Partnerships_It%E2%80%99s_the_Right_Time.html

Bethea, D. (2014, January 8). Community college explore creative approaches to counter budget cuts. *Diverse Issues in Higher Education.* http://diverse education.com/article/59943/

Bielick, S., Cronen, S., Stone, C., Montaquila, J., and Roth, S. (2013) *The Adult Training and Education Survey (ATES) pilot study: Technical report* (NCES 2013–190). U.S. Department of Education. Washington, DC: National Center for Education Statistics. Available from http://nces .ed.gov/pubs2013/2013190.pdf

Blume, H. (2008, October 19). 23 Bond issues seek new funding for schools: The voter guide. *Los Angeles Times*.

Blumenstyk, G. (2014, May 2). "Risk Adjusted" metrics for college get another look. *Chronicle of Higher Education*, A10.

Bowen, W. G. (1980). *The costs of higher education: How much do colleges and universities spend per student and how much should they spend?* San Francisco: Jossey-Bass.

Bowen, W. G. (2012, October). *The "cost disease" in higher education: Is technology the answer?* The Tanner Lectures, Stanford University. Available from http://www.ithaka.org/sites/default/files/files/ITHAKA-TheCostDiseasein HigherEducation.pdf

Bowen, W. G., Chingos, M. M., & McPherson, M. S. (2009). *Crossing the finish line: Completing college at America's public universities.* Princeton, NJ: Princeton University Press.

Breneman, D. W., & Finn, Jr., C. E. (1978). An uncertain future. In D. W. Breneman & C. E. Finn, Jr. (Eds.), Public policy and private higher education *(Studies in Higher Education)*. Washington, DC: Brookings Institution.

Breneman, D. W., & Nelson, S. C. (1981). *Financing community colleges: An economic perspective.* Washington, DC: Brookings Institution.

Brint, S., & Karabel, J. (1989). *The diverted dream: Community colleges and the promise of educational opportunity in America, 1900–1985.* Oxford: Oxford University Press.

Brothers, E. Q. (1928). *A plan for state support for public junior colleges.* Paper presented at the ninth annual meeting of the American Association of Junior Colleges, Fort Worth, TX.

Brown v. Board of Education, 347 U.S. 483. (1954).

Bullock, P. (2007, June 2). Massachusetts governor proposes free community colleges. *New York Times*.

Bureau of Labor Statistics (BLS). (2014). *Earnings and unemployment rates by educational attainment* [web page]. Washington, DC: U.S. Department of Labor. Available from http://www.bls.gov/emp/ep_chart_001.htm

Burke, J. C. (1998). Performance funding: Arguments and answers. In J. C. Burke & A. M. Serban (Eds.), *Performance funding for public higher education: Fad or trend* (New Directions for Institutional Research, No. 97, pp. 85–90). San Francisco: Jossey-Bass.

Burke, J., & Minassians, H. (2003). *Real accountability or accountability "lite": Seventh annual survey, 2003.* Albany, NY: Rockefeller Institute of Government.

Burke, J. C., & Modarresi, S. (2000). To keep or not to keep performance: Signals from stakeholders. *Journal of Higher Education, 71*(4), 432–453.

California Legislative Analyst Office. (2000). *The state appropriations limit.* Retrieved April 1, 2009 from www.lao.ca.gov

California Legislative Analyst Office. (2004). *Maintaining the master plan's commitment to college access.* Retrieved April 1, 2009 from www.lao.ca.gov/2004/college_access

California Legislative Analyst Office. (2005). *Proposition 98 primer.* Retrieved December 1, 2008 from www.lao.ca.gov

California Postsecondary Education Commission. (2010). *Fiscal profiles, 2010: The seventeenth in a periodic series of factsheets about the financing of California higher education.* Sacramento, CA: Author.

Callan, P. M. (2002, February). *Coping with recession: Public policy, economic downturns and higher education.* San Jose, CA: The National Center for Public Policy and Higher Education.

Campbell, D. F. (2002). *The leadership gap: Model strategies for developing community college leaders.* New York: Rowman & Littlefield Publishers.

Campbell, S. D. (1982). Responses to financial stress. In C. Frances (Ed.), *Successful responses to financial difficulty* (New Directions for Higher Education, No. 38, pp. 7–18). San Francisco: Jossey-Bass.

Cannan, E. (Ed.). (1904). *An inquiry into the nature and causes of the wealth of nations, by Adam Smith* (5th ed.). London: Methuen and Co.

Carbone, R. F. (1974). *Alternative tuition systems.* Iowa City, IA: The American College Testing Program.

Carmichael, O. C., Jr. (1955). *New York establishes a state university: A case study in the processes of policy formation.* Nashville, TN: Vanderbilt University Press.

Carnevale, A. P., & Rose, S. J. (2011). *The undereducated American.* Washington, DC: Georgetown University, Center on Education and the Workforce.

Carnevale, A. P., Rose, S. J., & Cheah, B. (2011). *College payoff: Education, occupations, lifetime earnings.* Washington, DC: Georgetown University, Center on Education and the Workforce.

Carnevale, A. P., Rose, S. J., & Hanson, A. R. (2012, June). *Certificates: Gateway to gainful employment and college degrees.* Washington, DC: Georgetown University, Center on Education and the Workforce.

Center for the Study of Higher Education (n.d). *The history of the California Master Plan for Higher Education (Web page).* Berkeley, CA: Author. Retrieved from http://sunsite.berkeley.edu/~ucalhist/archives_exhibits/masterplan/

Chambers, M. M. (1968). *Higher education: Who pays? Who gains?* Danville, IL: Interstate Printers & Publishers.

Cheng, D., Asher, L., Abernathy, P., Cochrane, D., & Thompson, J. (2012, October). *Adding it all up 2012: Are college net price calculators easy to find, use, and compare?* Oakland, CA: The Institute for College Access and Success.

Clark, B. R. (1960). The "cooling-out" function in higher education. *American Journal of Sociology, 65*(6), 569–576.

College Board. (2014a, October). *Trends in college pricing, 2014.* Washington, DC: Author.

College Board. (2014b, October). *Trends in student aid, 2014.* Washington, DC: Author.

College Board. (n.d.). *Trends in college pricing* [data file]. Retrieved from trends.collegeboard.org

College Cost Reduction and Access Act, Pub. L. No 110–84. (2007).

Collins, S. E., Leitzel, T. C., Morgan, S. D., & Stalcup, R. J. (1994). Declining revenues and increasing enrollments: Strategies for coping. *Community College Journal of Research and Practice, 18*(1), 33–42.

Committee on Measures of Student Success (CMSS). (2011, December). *Committee on Measures of Student Success: A report to Secretary of Education Arne Duncan.* Washington, DC: U.S. Department of Education. Available from http://www2.ed.gov/about/bdscomm/list/cmss-committee-report-final.pdf

Conger, S. B., Bell, A., & Stanley, J. (2010, September). *Four-state cost study* (updated version). Boulder, CO: State Higher Education Executive Officers.

Consortium on Financing Higher Education (COFHE). (2013). *Member institutions.* Cambridge, MA: Author. Available from http://web.mit.edu/cofhe/

Consortium on Higher Education Tax Reform. (2013, November). *Higher education tax reform: A shared agenda for increasing college affordability, access, and success.* Washington, DC: Author.

Coons, A. G. (1960). *A master plan for higher education in California: 1960–1975.* Sacramento, CA: California State Department of Education.

d'Ambrosio, M., & Merisotis, J. (2000). Foreword. In J. Wellman & C. O'Brien (Eds.), *Higher education cost measurement: Public policy issues, options, and strategies* (The New Millennium Project on Higher Education Costs, Pricing, and Productivity, p. 5). Washington, DC: The Institute for Higher Education Policy and TIAA-CREF Institute.

Dannenberg, M., & Voight, M. (2013, February). *Doing away with debt: Using existing resources to ensure college affordability for low- and middle-income families.* Washington, DC: The Education Trust.

DeCosmo, R. (1978). Reduced resources and the academic program. In R. L. Alfred (Ed.), *Coping with reduced resources* (New Directions for Community Colleges, No. 22, pp. 45–52). Jossey-Bass: San Francisco.

Delaney, J. A., & Doyle, W. R. (2011). State spending on higher education: Testing the balance wheel over time. *Journal of Education Finance, 36*(4), 343–368.

Delbanco, A. (2012). *College: What is was, is, and should be.* Princeton, NJ: Princeton University Press.

Dembicki, M. (2012, February 12). White House bus tour spotlights top-notch partnerships. *Community College Times.*

Department of the Interior (DOI). (2008). *Policy on deferred maintenance, current replacement value and facility condition index in life-cycle cost management policy.* Washington, DC: Author.

Desrochers, D. M., & Hurlburt, S. (2012). *Spending and results: What does the money buy?* (A Delta Data Update 2000–2010). Washington, DC: American Institutes for Research.

Dickeson, R. C. (2010). *Prioritizing academic programs and services: Reallocating resources to achieve strategic balance* (2nd ed.): San Francisco: Jossey-Bass.

Dixon, D. (2005). *Never come to peace again: Pontiac's uprising and the fate of the British empire in North America.* Norman, OK: University of Oklahoma Press.

Dougherty, K. J., & Hong, E. (2005, July). *State systems of performance accountability for community colleges: Impacts and lessons for community colleges* (Achieving the Dream Policy Brief). Boston: Jobs for the Future.

Dougherty, K. J., & Reddy, V. (2011, December). *The impacts of state performance funding systems on higher education institutions: Research literature review and policy recommendations.* (CCRC Working Paper No. 37). New York: Teachers College, Columbia University.

Eby, F. (1927). The junior college movement in Texas. *Texas Outlook, 2*(2), 9–12.

Eckstein, O. (1960). The problem of higher college tuition. In S. E. Harris (Ed.), *Higher education in the United States: The economic problems* (pp. 61–72). Cambridge, MA: Harvard University Press.

Economic Modeling Specialists International (EMSI). (2004, February). *Where value meets values: The economic impact of community colleges.* Moscow, ID: Author and American Association of Community Colleges.

Eells, W. C. (1931). *The junior college.* Boston: Houghton Mifflin.

El-Khawas, E. (1976). Clarifying roles and purposes. In J. Stark (Ed.), *Promoting consumer protection for students* (New Directions for Higher Education, No. 13, 35–48). San Francisco: Jossey-Bass.

Erickson, C. G. (1969). "Rebirth in Illinois." In R. Yarrington (Ed.), *Junior Colleges: 50 States/50 Years*. Washington, DC: American Association of Junior Colleges Press.

Evenden, E. S., Strayer, G. D., & Engelhart, N. L. (1938). *Standards for college buildings*. New York: Teachers College, Columbia University.

Ewell, P. (2007). *Community college bridges to opportunity initiative: Joint state data toolkit*. Austin, TX: Bridges to Opportunity Initiative and Community College Leadership Program, University of Texas at Austin.

Ewert, S., & Kominski, R.(2014, January). *Measuring alternative educational credentials: 2012* (P70–138). Washington, DC: U.S. Department of Commerce, Economic and Statistics Administration, U.S. Census Bureau.

Fain, P. (2014, April 1). Back in business. *Inside Higher Ed*. Available from www.insidehighered.com

Foose, R. A., & Meyerson, J. W. (1986). *Alternative approaches to tuition financing: Making tuition more affordable*. Washington, DC: National Association of College and University Business Officers.

Friedel, J. N., Thornton, Z. M., D'Amico, M. M., & Katsinas, S. G. (2013, September). *Performance-based funding: The national landscape*. Tuscaloosa, AL: The University of Alabama, Education Policy Center.

Gaines, G. (2008, December 1). *Focus on SREB states' responses to the economic slowdown: Budget actions affecting education in 2008–2009*. Atlanta: Southern Regional Education Board.

Garms, W. I. (1977). *Financing community colleges*. New York: Teachers College Press.

Garrett, R. L. (1999). Degrees of centralization of governance structures in state community college systems. In T. A. Tollefson, R. L. Garrett, & W. G. Ingram (Eds.), *Fifty state systems of community colleges: Mission, governance, funding and accountability*. Johnson City, TN: The Overmountain Press.

Georgia Board of Nursing (2014). *Information sheet for licensure by examination as a Registered Professional Nurse for graduates of Georgia Board of Nursing approved nursing programs and traditional nursing education programs*. Macon, GA: Author. Available from http://sos.ga.gov/PLB/acrobat/Forms/38%20Application%20-%20Licensure%20by%20Exam%20for%20Graduates%20of%20Approved%20and%20Traditional%20Nursing%20Programs%23.pdf

Gladieux, L. E., & Wolanin, T. R. (1976). *Congress and the colleges: The national politics of higher education*. Lexington, MA: Lexington Books.

Gleazer, E. J. (1980). *The community college: Values, vision, and vitality*. Washington, DC: American Association of Community and Junior Colleges.

Government Accountability Office (GAO). (2012, May). *Improved tax information could help families pay for college* (GAO-12-560). Washington, DC: Author.

Government Accountability Office (GAO). (2013). *VA education benefits: Student characteristics and outcomes vary across states* (GAO-13-567). Washington, DC: Author.

Government Finance Officers Association (GFOA). (2014). *GFOA Best Practices in Budgeting for Community Colleges: Budgeting framework*. Chicago, IL: Author.

Governmental Accounting Standards Board (GASB). (2006). *The General Accounting Standards Board's fixed assets building component depreciation policy*.

Grant, W. V., & Lind, C. G. (1973). *Digest of educational statistics: 1973* (OE 74-11103). Washington, DC: U.S. Department of Health, Education, and Welfare, Office of Education, National Center for Education Statistics.

Greenstone, M., & Looney, A. (2013, June). *Is starting college and not finishing really that bad?* Washington, DC: Brookings Institution, The Hamilton Project. Available from http://www.hamiltonproject.org/papers/what_happens_to_students_who_fail_to_complete_a_college_degree_is_some/

Hammil, P. (2011, November 23). Legislature advances plan to resolve community college squabble. (Scottsbluff, NE) *Star-Herald*.

Handel, S. J. (2011). *Improving student transfer from community colleges to four-year institutions: The perspective of leaders from baccalaureate-granting institutions*. Washington, DC: College Board.

Hardin, T. L. (1975). *A history of the community junior college in Illinois: 1901–1972*. Unpublished doctoral dissertation, University of Illinois, Urbana-Champaign.

Harnish, T. L. (2011, June). *Performance-based funding: A re-emerging strategy in public higher education financing* (A Higher Education Brief). Washington, DC: American Associations of State Colleges and Universities.

Harper v. Virginia Board of Elections, 383 U.S. 663. (1966).

Harris, S. E. (1960). *Higher education in the United States: The economic problems*. Cambridge, MA: Harvard University Press.

Hauptman, A. M. (2013, June 20). Challenging 10 claims about higher education's decline (essay). *Inside Higher Education.*

HCM Strategists. (2012). *Accounting for differences in college outcomes* (Context for Success Issue Brief). Washington, DC: Author. Available from http://www.hcmstrategists.com/contextforsuccess/briefs/2%20Accounting %20for%20Differences%20in%20College%20Outcomes.pdf

Health and Education Reconciliation Act, Pub. L. No. 111–152. (2010).

Heller, D. E. (1997). Student price response in higher education: An update to Leslie and Brinkman. *Journal of Higher Education, 68*(6), 624–659.

Hentschke, G. C. (2010). Evolving markets of for-profit higher education. In G. C. Hentschke, V. M., Lechuga, & W. G. Tierney (Eds.), *For-profit colleges and universities: Their markets, regulation, performance, and place in higher education* (pp. 23–46). Sterling, VA: Stylus.

Higher Education Act of 1965 (HEA), Pub. L. No. 89–329 (1965).

Higher Education Opportunity Act of 2008 (HEOA), Pub. L. No. 110–315. (2008).

Hodel, R., Laffey, M., & Lingenfelter, P. (2006, October). *Recession, retrenchment, and recovery: State higher education funding & student financial aid.* Normal, IL: Center for the Study of Education Policy, Illinois State University, National Association of State Student Grant Aid Programs, State Higher Education Executive Officers.

Honeyman, D. S., Wood, R. C., Thompson, D. L., & Stewart, G. K. (1988). The fiscal support of school facilities in rural and small schools, *Journal of Education Finance, 13*(3), 227–239.

Horn, L., & Li, X. (2009, November). *Changes in postsecondary awards below the bachelor's degree: 1997 to 2007* (NCES 2010–167). Washington, DC: National Center for Education Statistics.

Horn, L., & Paslov, J. (2014, April). *Out-of-pocket net price for college* (NCES Data Point. NCES 2014–902). Washington, DC: National Center for Education Statistics, Institute for Education Sciences, U.S. Department of Education.

Hoxby, C. M. (2014). *The economics of online postsecondary education: MOOCs, nonselective education, and highly selective education* (NBER Working Paper No. 19816). Cambridge, MA: National Bureau of Economic Research.

Hurlburt S., & Kirschstein, R. J. (2012). *Spending: Where does the money go?* Washington, DC: Delta Cost Project at American Institutes for Research. Available from http://www.deltacostproject.org/sites/default/ files/products/Delta-Spending-Trends-Production.pdf

Hurley, D. J. (2010, March 11). *State outlook: Fiscal and state policy issues affecting higher education in 2010*. Presentation to the ACCT/AACC National Legislative Summit, Washington, DC.

Hurley, D., & Harnish, T. (2014). *Top 10 higher education state policy issues for 2014*. (Policy Matters: A Higher Education Policy Brief). Washington, DC: American Association of State Colleges and Universities.

Illinois Community College Board. (1967 to 2013). *Data and characteristics of the Illinois public community college system* (Annual Reports). Springfield, IL: Author.

Internal Revenue Service (IRS). (2009). *Internal Revenue Service collections, costs, fiscal years 2005–2009*. Washington, DC: IRS Publications.

Jackson, G. A., & Weathersby, G. B. (1975). Individual demand for higher education. *Journal of Higher Education, 46*(6): 623–52.

Jackson, N. M. (2013). *New York school district will build and renovate 40 schools thanks to "P3 partnership."* Norwalk, CT: District Administration.

Jenkins, D., & Crosta, P. (2013, April 20). *An economic model for the community college completion agenda*. Presentation to the Community College Research Center Board, San Francisco.

Jess, D. (2014, March 12). Michigan community colleges beset by cuts in aid, loss of tax revenues. *Detroit Free Press*.

Johnson, E. L. (1960). Is the low-tuition principle outmoded? In S. E. Harris (Ed.), *Higher education in the United States: The economic problems* (pp. 44–47). Cambridge, MA: Harvard University Press.

Johnson, N., Oliff, P., & Williams, E. (2009, January 28). *An update on state budget cuts: Governors proposing new round of cuts for 2011; At least 43 states have already imposed cuts that hurt vulnerable residents*. Washington, DC: Center of Budget and Policy Priorities.

Junior College Act of 1965. 110 Illinois Compiled Statutes (ILCS) 805. (1965).

Kadamus, J. (2013). *The state of facilities in higher education: 2013 benchmarks, best practices and trends*. Guilford, CT: Sightlines.

Kadamus, J. (2014). *The state of facilities in higher education: 2014 benchmarks, best practices and trends*. Guilford, CT: Sightlines.

Katsinas, S. G., D'Amico, M. M., & Friedel, J. N. (2011, December). *Jobs, jobs, jobs: Challenges community colleges face to reach the unemployed*. Tuscaloosa: The University of Alabama, Education Policy Center.

Katsinas, S. G., Lacey, V. A., Adair, J. L., Koh, J. P., D'Amico, M. M., & Friedel, J. N. (2013, November). *Halfway out of recession, but a long way to go*. Tuscaloosa: The University of Alabama, Education Policy Center.

Katsinas, S. G., Tollefson, T. A., & Reamey, B. A. (2008). *Funding issues in U.S. community colleges: Findings from a 2007 survey of national state directors of community colleges*. Washington, DC: American Association of Community Colleges.

Kaysen, C. (1960). Some general observations on the pricing of higher education. In S. E. Harris (Ed.), *Higher education in the United States: The economic problems* (pp. 55–60). Cambridge, MA: Harvard University Press

Keeney, B. C. (1960). A college administrator views the tuition problem. In S. E. Harris (Ed.), *Higher education in the United States: The economic problems* (pp. 40–43). Cambridge, MA: Harvard University Press.

Keller, C. K. (2009, November). *Coping strategies of public universities during the economic recession of 2009: Results of a survey on the impact of the financial crisis on university campuses*. Washington, DC: Association of Public Land-grant Universities.

Keller, C. K. (2013, November 11). *Survey on sequestration effects: Selected results from private and public research universities*. Washington, DC: Association of American Universities, Association of Public and Land-grant Universities, and The Science Coalition.

Kelly, P. J. (2009). *The dreaded "P" word. An examination of productivity in public postsecondary education* (Delta Cost Project white paper series). Washington, DC: Delta Cost Project.

Kerr, C. (1963). *Uses of the university*. Cambridge, MA: Harvard University Press.

Kerr, C. (1968). Financing higher education: The policy dilemmas. *Public Interest, 11*, 99–136.

Koos, L. V. (1924). *The junior college*. Minneapolis: University of Minnesota.

Kotler, P., & Fox, K. (1995). *Strategic marketing for educational institutions*. Upper Saddle River, NJ: Prentice Hall.

Laitenen, A. (2012, September). *Cracking the credit hour*. Washington, DC: New America Foundation.

Lebesch, A. (2012, Spring). Using labor market information in program development and evaluation. In C. M. Mullin, T. Bers, & L. S. Hagedorn (Eds.), *Data use in community colleges* (New Directions for Institutional Research, No. 153, pp. 3–12. San Francisco: Jossey-Bass.

Leinbach, D., & Jenkins, D. (2008, January). *Using longitudinal data to increase community college student success: A guide to measuring milestone and momentum point attainment* (CCRC Research Tools No. 2). New York: Community College Research Center, Teachers College, Columbia University.

Leslie, L. L., & Brinkman, P. T. (1987). Student price response in higher education: The student demand studies. *Journal of Higher Education, 58*(2), 181–204.

Lichtenberger, E. J., & Dietrich, C. (2013). *The community college penalty and bachelor's degree completion: Fact or fiction?* (IERC 2013–1). Edwardsville, IL: Illinois Education Research Council at Southern Illinois University Edwardsville.

Litten, L. H. (1984). Advancing a research agenda on undergraduate pricing. In L. H. Litten (Ed.), *Issues in pricing undergraduate education* (New Directions for Institutional Research, No. 42, pp. 91–98). San Francisco: Jossey-Bass.

Lombardi, J. (1973). *Managing finances in community colleges.* San Francisco: Jossey-Bass.

Lombardi, J. (1976, October). *No or low-tuition: A lost cause* (Topical Paper No. 58). Los Angeles, CA: University of California Los Angeles, ERIC Clearinghouse for Junior Colleges.

Long, A., & Mullin, C. M. (Eds.). (2014), *America's forgotten student population: Creating a path to college success for GED completers.* Sterling, VA: Stylus Press.

Lorain County Community College. (2014). *Tuition and fees.* Retrieved from www.loraincc.edu/Tuition+and+Fees/

Lowery, A. (2013, January 4). The tax code may be the most progressive since 1979. *New York Times.*

Lu, A. (2014, March 12). States explore free community colleges. *Stateline: The Daily News Service of The Pew Charitable Trusts.*

MacAllum, K., & Glover, D. (2012, May). *Student and guidance counselor feedback on the College Navigator website.* Washington, DC: U.S. Department of Education, National Postsecondary Education Cooperative.

Malm, L. (2010). *Annual state and local tax burden rankings for 2010.* Washington, DC: The Tax Foundation.

Marketplace Fairness Act, S 336, S 743, and HR 684, the U.S. Congress. (2013).

Martorana, S. V. (1978). Shifting patterns of financial support. In R. L. Alfred (Ed.), *Coping with reduced resources* (New Directions for Community Colleges, No. 22, pp. 1–14). San Francisco: Jossey-Bass.

McBain, L. (2010, May). *Tuition setting authority and deregulation at state colleges and universities* (Policy Matters: A Higher Education Policy Brief). Washington, DC: American Association of State Colleges and Universities.

McGuire, W. G., (1978). Emerging trends in state support. In R. L. Alfred (Ed.), *Coping with reduced resources* (New Directions for Community Colleges, No. 22, pp. 15–26). San Francisco: Jossey-Bass.

McKeown-Moak, M. (2000). A view from the states: A survey of the collection and use of cost data by states. In J. Wellman & C. O'Brien (Eds.), *Higher education cost measurement: Public policy issues, options, and strategies* (The New Millennium Project on Higher Education Costs, Pricing, and Productivity, pp. 10–27). Washington, DC: The Institute for Higher Education Policy and TIAA-CREF Institute.

McKeown-Moak, M. (2012). *The "new" performance funding in higher education.* Paper presented at the National Education Finance Conference, San Antonio, TX.

McKeown-Moak, M., & Mullin, C. M. (2014). *Higher education finance research: Policy, politics, and practice.* Charlotte, NC: Information Age Publishing.

McLendon, M. K., Hearn, J. C., & Deaton, R. (2006, Spring). Called to account: Analyzing the origins and spread of state performance-accountability policies for higher education. *Educational Evaluation and Policy Analysis, 28*(1), 1–24.

McMahon, W. L. (2009). *Higher learning, greater good: The private and social benefits of higher education.* Baltimore, MD: Johns Hopkins University Press.

Medsker, L. L. (1956). Financing public junior college operation. In N. B. Henry (Ed.), *The public junior college: The fifty-fifth yearbook of the National Society for the Study of Education, Part 1* (pp. 247–266). Chicago: University of Chicago Press.

Mensel, F. (2013, June). Birth of the Pell Grant: The community college role. In *Reflections on Pell: Championing social justice through 40 years of educational opportunity* (pp. 50–55). Washington, DC: The Pell Institution for the Study of Opportunity in Higher Education.

MGT of America. (2001, March). *Funding formula use in higher education.* Discussion paper prepared for the Commonwealth of Pennsylvania State System of Higher Education.

Microsoft. (2014). *Exam policies and FAQ.* Redmond, WA. Available from http://www.microsoft.com/learning/en-us/certification-exam-policies.aspx

Middaugh, M. F. (2000). The Delaware study of instructional costs and productivity: A consortial approach to assessing instructional expenditures. In J. Wellman & C. O'Brien (Eds.), *Higher education cost measurement: Public policy issues, options, and strategies* (The New Millennium Project on Higher Education Costs, Pricing, and Productivity, pp. 28–73). Washington, DC: The Institute for Higher Education Policy and TIAA-CREF Institute. http://www.udel.edu/IR/cost/

282 REFERENCES

Miller, A., Erisman, W., Bermeo, A., & Taylor-Smith, C. (2011). *Sealing the gaps: Supporting low-income, first generation students at four-year institutions in Texas post-transfer*. Washington, DC: The Pell Institute for the Study of Opportunity in Higher Education.

Morgan, J. M., & Dechter, G. (2012, November). *Improving the college scorecard: Using student feedback to create an effective disclosure*. Washington, DC: The Center for American Progress.

Morrill Act of 1862, Pub. L. No. 37–108. (1862).

Morrill, J. S. (1887). *Commemorative addresses 1862–1887*. Amherst, MA: J.E. Williams, Books and Job Printer.

Mullin, C. M. (2010a, September). *Doing more with less: The inequitable funding of community colleges (Policy Brief 2010–03PBL)*. Washington, DC: American Association of Community Colleges.

Mullin, C. M. (2010b, November). *Just how similar? Community colleges and the for-profit sector* (Policy Brief 2010-04PBL). Washington, DC: American Association of Community Colleges.

Mullin, C. M. (2011, October). *The road ahead: A look at trends in educational attainment by community college students* (Policy Brief 2011–04PBL). Washington, DC: American Association of Community Colleges.

Mullin, C. M. (2012a, April). *It's a matter of time: Low-income students and community colleges* (Policy Brief 2012–02PBL). Washington, DC: American Association of Community Colleges.

Mullin, C. M. (2012b). Student success: Institutional and individual perspectives. *Community College Review*, 40(2), 126–144.

Mullin, C. M. (2012c, September). *Transfer: An indispensable part of the community college mission* (Policy Brief 2012–03PBL). Washington, DC: American Association of Community Colleges.

Mullin, C. M. (2012d, February). *Why access matters: The community college student body* (Policy Brief 2012–01PBL). Washington, DC: American Association of Community Colleges.

Mullin, C. M. (2013c, March 13). *An analysis of the Reimagining Aid Design and Delivery (RADD) white papers*. Washington, DC: American Association of Community Colleges.

Mullin, C. M. (2013b, Summer). Past, present, and possibilities of the future of the Pell Grant program. *Journal of Education Finance*, 39(1), 3–14.

Mullin, C. M. (2013c, June). The Pell Grant: A signal of value. In *Reflections on Pell: Championing social justice through 40 years of educational opportunity* (pp. 26–27). Washington, DC: The Pell Institute for the Study of Opportunity in Higher Education.

Mullin. C. M. (2013d, June). *Post-college workforce measures: Issues facing policymakers, analysts, and researchers.* Washington, DC: American Association of Community Colleges.

Mullin, C. M. (2015, Spring). Evolving practices and emerging innovations in community college finance. In T. W. Bers, R. B. Head, & J. Palmer (Eds.), *Budget and finance in the American community college* (New Directions for Community Colleges, No. 168, pp. 115–125). San Francisco: Jossey-Bass.

Mullin, C. M., & Frost, R. (2011). Maintaining an agreement: The one-third philosophy in Illinois and New York. In S. E. Sutin, D. Derrico, E. J. Valeau, & R. L. Raby (Eds.), *Increasing effectiveness of the community college financial model: A global perspective for the global economy* (pp. 207–224). New York: Palgrave Macmillan.

Mullin, C. M., & Honeyman, D. S. (2007). The funding of community colleges: A typology of state funding formulas. *Community College Review, 35*(2), 113–127.

Mullin, C. M., & Honeyman, D. S. (2008). Statutory responsibility for fixing tuition and fees: The relationship between community colleges and undergraduate institutions. *Community College Journal of Research and Practice, 32*(4–6), 284–304.

Mullin, C. M., & Honeyman, D. S. (2009, Summer). An examination of stratified price structures and state resources on public postsecondary education participation between 1960 and 2000. *Enrollment Management Journal: Student Access, Finance, and Success in Higher Education, 3*(2), 26–53.

Mullin, C. M., & Lebesch, A. (2010, March). *Moving success from the shadows: Data systems that link education and workforce outcomes* (Policy Brief 2010–01PBL). Washington, DC: American Association of Community Colleges.

Mullin, C. M., & Phillippe, K. (2013, October). A national economic case statement for community colleges. *Planning for Higher Education, 41*(4), 44–54.

Mumper, M. (2001). State efforts to keep public colleges affordable in the face of fiscal stress. In M. B. Paulsen and J. C. Smart (Eds.), *The finance of higher education: Theory, research, policy, and practice* (pp. 321–349). New York: Agathon Press.

National Association of State Student Grant and Aid Programs (NASSGAP). (2013, November). *43rd annual survey report on state-sponsored student financial aid: 2011–2012.* Washington, DC: Author.

National Association of Student Financial Aid Administrators & JBL Associates. (2013). *No clear winner: Consumer testing of financial aid award letters.* Washington, DC: National Association of Student Financial Aid Administrators.

National Bellas Hess v. Illinois Department of Revenue 386 U.S. 753, 87 S.Ct. 1389. (1967).

National Center for Education Statistics (NCES). (n.d.). *Net price calculator information center.* Retrieved from http://nces.ed.gov/ipeds/resource/net_price_calculator.asp#NPCRequirement

National Center for Education Statistics (NCES). (2013a, February 19). *Finance for degree granting public institutions using GASB reporting standards* (IPEDS 2012–2013 Survey Materials). Washington, DC: U.S. Department of Education, Institute of Education Sciences.

National Center for Education Statistics (NCES). (2013b, March 6). *Integrated Postsecondary Education Data System (IPEDS) 2014–2016: Proposed changes to the IPEDS data collection instruments for 2014–15 and 2015–16* (OMB No. 1850–0582 v. 13). Washington, DC: Institute for Education Sciences, U.S. Department of Education.

National Center for Education Statistics (NCES). (2014a). *College Affordability and Transparency Center* (web tool). Retrieved from http://collegecost.ed.gov/catc/#

National Center for Education Statistics (NCES). (2014b). *College Navigator* (web tool). Retrieved from http://nces.ed.gov/collegenavigator/

National Center for Education Statistics (NCES). (2014c). *Integrated postsecondary education data system* [data file]. Retrieved from http://www.nces.ed.gov/ipeds

National Center for Education Statistics (NCES). (2014d). *Powerstats* [data file]. Retrieved from http://nces.ed.gov/datalab/

National Council for Public-Private Partnerships. (2012a). *The seven keys to success.* Retrieved from http://www.ncppp.org/ppp-basics/7-keys

National Council for Public-Private Partnerships (2012b). *Top ten facts about PPPs.* Retrieved from www.ncppp.org/ppp-basics/top-ten-facts-about-ppps

National Defense Education Act (NDEA) of 1958 (Pub. L. No. 85–864). (1958).

National Research Council. (2013). *Improving measurement of productivity in higher education.* Panel on Measuring Higher Education Productivity: Conceptual Framework and Data Needs. T. A. Sullivan, C. Mackie, W. F. Massy, and E. Sinha. Committee on National Statistics and Board on Testing and Assessment, Division of Behavioral and Social Sciences Education. Washington, DC: The National Academies Press.

North Carolina General Statutes § 105–277.1B. *Property tax homestead circuit breaker*. (2013).

Organisation for Economic Co-Operation and Development (OECD). (2004). *Education at a Glance 2004: OECD indicators*, OECD Publishing.

Organisation for Economic Co-Operation and Development (OECD). (2012). *Education at a Glance 2012: OECD indicators*, OECD Publishing.

Padgitt, K. (2009). *Fiscal fact No. 196*. Washington, DC: The Tax Foundation. Retrieved from http://taxfoundation.org/article/updated-state-and-local-option-sales-tax

Palmer, J. (2008, June). *Grapevine compilation of state higher education tax appropriations data for fiscal year 2008*. Normal, IL: Illinois State University, Center for the Study of Education Policy. Available from http://grapevine.illinoisstate.edu

Pffefer, J., & Salanick, G. (1978). *The external control of organizations*. New York: Harper Row.

Phillippe, K., & González Sullivan, L. (2005). *National profile of community colleges: Trends & statistics* (4th ed.). Washington, DC: American Association of Community Colleges.

Phillippe, K., & Tekle, R. (2013a, September). *Pending CEO retirements* [AACC DataPoints]. Washington, DC: American Association of Community Colleges.

Phillippe, K., & Tekle, R. (2013b, December). *Community college loan volume* [AACC DataPoints]. Washington, DC: American Association of Community Colleges.

President's Commission on Higher Education (1947). *Higher education for democracy: A report of the President's Commission on Higher Education* (Vols. 1–6). New York: Harper & Brothers.

Preston, V., Damsbaek, N., Kelly, P., Lemione, M., Lo, L., Shields, J., & Tufts, S. (2010, March). *What are the labor market outcomes for university-educated immigrants?* (TIEDI Analytical Report 8). York University, Toronto Immigrant Employment Data Initiative. Available from http://www.yorku.ca/tiedi/doc/AnalyticalReport8.pdf

Public Policy Institute of California. (2008, June). *Proposition 13: 30 years later*. San Francisco: Author. Retrieved from http://www.ppic.org/content/pubs/jtf/JTF_Prop13JTF.pdf

Pullaro, N., & Redd, K. E. (2013). Tracking the discount: Tuition discount rates, net tuition revenue, and efforts to inform institutional practices. *AIR Professional Files, 133*, 17–32.

Quill Corp. v. Heitkampp, 504U.S. 298. (1992).

Ricardo, D. (1817). Principles of political economy and taxation (vol. i, p. 6). In P. Sraffa (Ed.), *The works and correspondence of David Ricardo*, 10 vol. (1951–55). Cambridge, MA: Cambridge University Press.

Rivard, R. (2013, November 21). U. of Michigan tries to save money on staff costs, but meets faculty opposition. *Inside Higher Ed.*

Rivard, R. (2014, April 9). Shrinking as a strategy. *Inside Higher Ed.*

Rose v. Council for Better Education, 790 S.W.2d 186. (1989).

Rouse, C. E. (1995). Democratization or diversion? The effect of community college education on educational attainment. *Journal of Business & Economic Statistics*, 13(2), 217–224.

Ruppert, S. S. (2001). *Where we go from here: State legislative views on higher education in the new millennium*. Littleton, CO: National Education Association.

Saunders, D. B. (2014). Exploring a consumer orientation: Free-market logic and college students. *Review of Higher Education*, 37(2), 197–219.

Savoca, E. (1990). Another look at the demand for higher education: Measuring the price sensitivity of the decision to apply to college. *Economics of Education Review*, 9(2), 123–134.

Securities Industry and Financial Markets Association (SIFMA). (2013). *About municipal Bonds: The tax-exempt municipal bond market: How big and who buys?* Retrieved from http://www.investinginbonds.com/learnmore.asp?catid=8&subcatid=53&id=243

Servicemen's Readjustment Act of 1944, Pub. L. No. 78–346. (1944).

Shaman, S., & Zemsky, R. M. (1984). Perspectives on pricing. In L. H. Litten (Ed.), *Issues in pricing undergraduate education* (New Directions for Institutional Research, No. 42, pp. 7–18). San Francisco: Jossey-Bass.

Shulock, N. (2011, May). *Concerns about performance-based funding and ways states are addressing the concerns* (IHELP Brief). Sacramento, CA: CSU-Sacramento.

Skomsvold, P., Radford, A. W., & Berkner, L. (2011, July). *Six-year attainment, persistence, transfer, retention, and withdrawal rates of students who began postsecondary education in 2003–04* (web tables; NCES 2011–152). Washington, DC: U.S. Department of Education, Institute for Education Sciences, National Center for Education Statistics (NCES).

Smith, A. (1776). *An inquiry into the nature and causes of the wealth of nations* (1st ed.). London: W. Strahan.

Smith, E., & Mullin, C. M. (2014, May 21). *Off-target and off-focus: Examining the myth of on-time graduation at 4-year institutions.* (NASPA Blog). Washington, DC: NASPA Student Affairs Administrators in Higher Education. Available from www.naspa.org/rpi/posts/off-target-and-off-focus-examining-the-myth-of-on-time-graduation-at-4-year

Snyder, T. D. (1992, November). *Digest of education statistics: 1992* (NCES 1992-097). Washington, DC: U.S. Department of Education, Institute of Education Sciences, National Center for Education Statistics (NCES).

Snyder, T. D., & Dillow, S. A. (2009, March). *Digest of education statistics: 2008* (NCES 2009-020). Washington, DC: U.S. Department of Education, Institute of Education Sciences, National Center for Education Statistics (NCES).

Snyder, T. D., & Dillow, S. A. (2010, April). *Digest of education statistics: 2009* (NCES 2010-013). Washington, DC: U.S. Department of Education, Institute of Education Sciences, National Center for Education Statistics (NCES).

Snyder, T. D., & Dillow, S. A. (2012, June). *Digest of education statistics: 2011* (NCES 2012-001). Washington, DC: U.S. Department of Education, Institute of Education Sciences, National Center for Education Statistics (NCES).

Snyder, T. D., & Dillow, S. A. (2013). *Digest of education statistics 2012* (NCES 2014-015). Washington, DC: U.S. Department of Education, Institute of Education Sciences, National Center for Education Statistics.

Snyder, T. D., & Dillow, S. A. (2014). *Digest of education statistics 2014.* Washington, DC: National Center for Education Statistics, Institute of Education Sciences, U.S. Department of Education.

Snyder, T. D., & Hoffman, C. M. (1995). *Digest of education statistics 1995* (NCES 95–029). Washington, DC: U.S. Department of Education, Office of Educational Research and Improvement, National Center for Education Statistics.

Snyder, T. D., & Hoffman, C. M. (2000). *Digest of education statistics 1999* (NCES 200–031). Washington, DC: U.S. Department of Education, Office of Educational Research and Improvement, National Center for Education Statistics.

Social Security Administration (SSA). (2013). *2013 Social Security changes.* Washington, DC: Author.

Solomon, M. (2011). *Annual survey query tool* [data file]. Washington, DC: National Association of State Grant and Aid Programs.

Song, J. (2014, February 3). Long Beach City College experiments with tiered pricing. *Los Angeles Times.*

St. John, E. P., & Byce, C. (1982). The changing federal role in student financial aid. In M. Kramer (Ed.), *Meeting student aid needs in a period of retrenchment* (New Directions for Higher Education, No. 40, pp. 57–68). San Francisco: Jossey-Bass.

State Higher Education Executive Officers (SHEEO). (2010). *Degree production and cost trends.* Boulder, CO: Author.

State Higher Education Executive Officers (SHEEO). (2014). *State higher education finance*. Boulder CO: Author.

Taylor, J. L., Bishop, C., Makela, J. P., Bragg, D. D., & Ruud, C. M. (2013, October). *Credit when it's due: Results from the baseline study*. Champaign, IL: Office of Community College Research and Leadership, University of Illinois at Urbana-Champaign.

Tekle, R. (2013, August). On campus housing (AACC DataPoints). Washington, DC: American Association of Community Colleges. Available from http://www.aacc.nche.edu/Publications/datapoints/Documents/Campus House_8.28.13_final.pdf

Tillery, D., & Wattenbarger, J. L. (1985). State power in a new era: Threats to local authority. In W. L. Deegan & J. F. Gollattscheck (Eds.), *Ensuring effective governance* (New Directions for Community Colleges, 49, pp. 5–23). San Francisco: Jossey-Bass.

Tollefson, T. A., Garrett, R. L., Ingram, W. G., & Associates. (1999). *Fifty state systems of community colleges: Mission, governance, funding and accountability*. Johnson City, TN: The Overmountain Press.

U.S. Census Bureau. (2013). Years of school completed by people 25 years and over, by age and sex: Selected years 1940 to 2012 [data file]. Washington, DC: Author.

U.S. Census Bureau. (2014). *Educational attainment in the United States: 2013 – Detailed tables* [data file]. Washington, DC: U.S. Department of Commerce.

U.S. Department of Commerce. (n.d.). *National Accounts and Product Information* [data file]. Washington, DC: Bureau of Economic Analysis. Retrieved from http://www.bea.gov/iTable/index_nipa.cfm

U.S. Department of Education. (2011). *Fiscal year 2012 budget request: Student financial assistance*. Washington, DC: Author.

U.S. Department of Education. (2014a). *Fiscal year 2015 budget request: Student financial assistance*. Washington, DC: Author.

U.S. Department of Education. (2014b). *Fiscal year 2015 Department of Education justifications of appropriation estimates to the Congress (Vol. II: Student financial assistance)*. Washington, DC: Author.

U.S. Department of Labor (2014). *Employment status of the civilian noninstitutional population, 1943 to date* [data file]. Washington, DC: Bureau of Labor Statistics. Retrieved from http://www.bls.gov/cps/cpsaat01.htm

Vaughn, G. B. (1987). *Pursuing the American dream: A history of the development of the Virginia community college system*. Richmond, VA: Virginia State Department of Community Colleges.

Verstegen, D. A. (2013). Nevada, the Great Recession, and education. *Educational Considerations*, XXXX(2), 34–44.

Virginia Community College System. (n.d.). *Educating Virginia since 1966* (web page). Richmond, VA: Author. Retrieved from http://www.vccs .edu/about/

Voorhees, R. A. (2005). Institutional research and new program development. In R. A. Voorhees and L. Harvey (Eds.), *Workforce development and higher education: A strategic role for institutional research* (New Directions for Institutional Research, No. 128, pp. 5–12). San Francisco: Jossey-Bass.

Warner, T. (1984). Priorities, planning, and prices. In L. H. Litten (Ed.), *Issues in pricing undergraduate education* (New Directions for Institutional Research, No. 42, pp. 35–45). San Francisco: Jossey-Bass.

Wattenbarger, J. L. (1978). The dilemma of reduced resources: Action or reaction. In Richard L. Alfred (Ed.), Coping with reduced resources (New Directions for Community Colleges, No. 22, 61–66). San Francisco: Jossey-Bass.

Wattenbarger, J. L., & Mercer, S. L. (1988). *Financing community colleges, 1988.* Washington, DC: American Association of Community Colleges.

Wattenbarger, J. L., & Starnes, P. M. (1976). *Financial support patterns for community colleges.* Gainesville, FL: Institute of Higher Education.

Wellman, J., & Ehrlich, T. (2003). *How the student credit hour shapes higher education: The tie that binds* (New Directions for Higher Education, No. 122). San Francisco: Jossey-Bass.

Witmer, D. R. (1967). Unit cost studies. Madison, WI: Wisconsin Board of Regents of the State Universities. (ERIC No. ED 013492)

Winston, G. C. (1999). Subsidies, hierarchy and peers: The awkward economics of higher education. *Journal of Economic Perspectives, 13*(1), 13–36.

Winston, G. C., & Yen, I. C. (1995, July). *Costs, prices, subsidies, and aid in U.S. higher education* (Discussion Paper No. 32). Williamstown, MA: Williams Project on the Economics of Higher Education.

Yankowski, R. A. (1986). Tuition and fees: Pricing strategies. In M. P. McKeown & K. Alexander (Eds.), *Values in conflict: Funding priorities for higher education* (Seventh Annual Yearbook of the American Education Finance Association). Cambridge, MA: Ballinger Publishing Company.

Yarrington, R. (1966). *Junior colleges: 20 states.* Washington, DC: American Association of Junior Colleges.

Zumeta, W. (1995). State policy and budget developments: Small gains on the fiscal front but clouds continue to build. In H. Wechsler (Ed.), *The NEA 1995 almanac of higher education* (pp. 73–96). Washington, DC: National Education Association.

Index

If you enjoyed this book, you may also like these:

The American Community College, 6th Edition
by Arthur M. Cohen, Florence B. Brawer,
Carrie B. Kisker
ISBN: 9781118449813

Confessions of a Community College
Administrator
by Matthew Reed
ISBN: 9781118004739

Want to connect?

Like us on Facebook
http://www.facebook.com/JBHigherEd

Subscribe to our newsletter
www.josseybass.com/go/higheredemail

Follow us on Twitter
http://twitter.com/JBHigherEd

Go to our Website
www.josseybass.com/highereducation